# We Remember Lest the World Forget

Produced by

Memories of the Minsk Ghetto

## Minsk Charitable Public Organisation - GILF

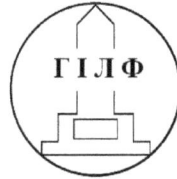

Translated By

Michael Hornsby Ph.D., D.Litt.

Rostyslav Kanibolotskyi M.Sc.

Iuliia Kuznetsova B.A.

Edited

by

Hilda Bronstein Ph.D.

Bett Demby

**The original book in Russian was published by**

**MINSK I.P. LOGVINOV PUBLISHERS   2012**

Editors of the Russian version were: Maya Krapina, Tamara Kurdadze, Yakov Murakhovskiy, Frieda Reizman and Vladimir Trachtenberg.

**This translation from the original Russian to English is a project that was initiated, facilitated and managed by UK Charity The Together Plan (1154167).**

### Published by JewishGen

**An Affiliate of the Museum of Jewish Heritage - A Living Memorial to the Holocaust**

**New York**

We Remember Lest the World Forget
Memories of the Minsk Ghetto

First Printing: July 2018, Tammuz 5778
Second Printing: March 2019, Adar II 5779

Translation Project Coordinator UK: Debra Brunner, Director of the Together Plan
Translation Project Coordinator Belarus: Artur Livshyts, Director of the Together Plan
Editors: Hilda Bronstein Ph.D. and Bett Demby
Translators: Michael Hornsby Ph.D., D.Litt., Rostyslav Kanibolotskyi M.Sc.
    and Iuliia Kuznetsova B.A.
Layout: Joel Alpert
Cover Design: Olga Volcheck

Published by JewishGen, Inc.
An Affiliate of the Museum of Jewish Heritage
A Living Memorial to the Holocaust
36 Battery Place, New York, NY 10280

"JewishGen, Inc. is not responsible for inaccuracies or omissions in the original work and makes no representations regarding the accuracy of this translation. Digital images of the original book's contents can be seen online at the New York Public Library Web site."

The mission of the JewishGen organisation is to produce a translation of the original work and we cannot verify the accuracy of statements or alter facts cited.

Printed in the United States of America by Lightning Source, Inc.
    Library of Congress Control Number (LCCN):  2018948407

ISBN: 978-1-939561-67-1 (hard cover: 268 pages, alk. paper)

Front cover photograph of the Minsk Ghetto, attribution: archival signature and source archive copyright of "Yad Vashem Photo Archive, Jerusalem 10470/5"

Back cover photograph: The Yama (Pit) Memorial, Minsk. Bronze sculpture 'The Last Way,' by architect Leonid Levin and sculptors Elsa Pollak and Alexander Finski, courtesy of the Republic of Belarus. Photo by Olga Volcheck, courtesy of the photographer.

# Credits from the Original Book

### Compilers:

M.I. Krapina, T.S. Kurdadze, Y.M. Murakhovsky, F.V. Reizman, V.L. Trachtenberg.

### Editorial Council:

Reizman Frida Vulfovna is the Chairman of the Executive Board of GILF; Trachtenberg Vladimir Lazarevich is the Deputy Chairman of the Executive Board of GILF.

### Members of the Executive Board of GILF:

Aslezov Elfrida Davydovna, Banah Eleonora Suleymanovna, Golubeva Irina Davydovna, Krapina Maya Isaakovna, Galperina Rimma Abramovna (the chairman of the revision committee of GILF), member of the Project Coordination Council.

The testimony of former ghetto prisoners, many of whom were afraid not only to write, but also to recall the experience of more than seventy years, became the basis for this collection. Every life story is a reflection of the tragedy not only of the Jewish population of Belarus, but of all Europe. The book is designed for a wide audience, and in the first place is intended for the young reader, as well as for everyone who cares about the history of their Motherland. In fact, this collection is a testament from the outgoing generation, which was a living witness to military events.

# Table of Contents

**Page    Title**

# Acknowledgements

Michael Hornsby Ph.D., D.Litt., Rostyslav Kanibolotskyi M.Sc. and Iuliia Kuznetsova B.A. for translating the original Russian text to the first draft English version.

Hilda Bronstein Ph.D. and Bett Demby for their tireless and diligent commitment to the editing of the stories and Hilda Bronstein for the creation of the glossary and assistance with the Yiddish.

Arkadiy Dobkin for his invaluable support of the project and for providing access to his family archives.

Jonathan Clingman for being available at all times for cross checks to the original Russian text and for setting up and managing the IT platform.

Paul Ginsburg for his invaluable support and assistance in helping to creating the IT platform for The Together Plan and providing ongoing training which assisted this project and enabled the Minsk and London team to work in close virtual proximity.

Anna Parijskaia for her consultancy on the book, assisting with translation and for giving contextual reference to the language and cultural idioms.

Sonia Richardson for translating the Leonid Ruderman story which was an addition to the original book, and for her commitment to the project.

Arkadiy Shulman, Vitebsk, for work on the original texts and for providing additional photographic material.

Jake Goldman for support with PR throughout the development of the project.

Jeanette Josse for the introduction, and to Anna Josse for leading us to Ilana Salem.

Ilana Salem for her diligent reading of the text and for her valued feedback.

Tamara Kurdadze in Minsk for facilitating access to material from the original book and providing information from the ghetto survivors and their families.

Vladislav Zaiko in Minsk for his language skills, and help with setting of the photographs into the texts.

Arina Levina in Minsk for assistance with communication with the ghetto survivors.

Michael Bronstein and Paul Demby for reading the edited texts, for the helpful comments and their support.

Frida Reizman, Chair of the Ghetto Survivors Association GILF.

Tamara Vershitskaya, Novogroduk, for helping to verify historical data.

Lisa Bittles for help with regards to the Belarusian language.

David Meltser, New York, author of The Black Book with Red Pages – Tragedy and Heroism of Belorussian Jews, for permission to reprint the story of Polina Dobkina.

Valery Price of VIA Press, Vestnik Publications for permission to reprint the story of Polina Dobkina from 'The Black Book with Red Pages – Tragedy and Heroism of Belorussian Jews'.

Polina Dobkina for speaking to us on conference call from the USA and telling us her story.

Sofia Dobkina for her help with the Skype interview with Polina Dobkina.

Daniel Shekhtman for insight to his family story and for his help with the interview with Polina Dobkina.

Michael Brunner for assistance at the outset of the project.

Her Britannic Majesty's Ambassador to Belarus HE Fionna Gibb OBE, for her support of The Together Plan's work with the Minsk Ghetto survivors.

Joel Alpert and Lance Ackerfield of the Jewish Gen Yizkor Book Project for their guidance and partnership in the publication of the book.

Nina Schwartz / Impulse Graphics: Design Consultant.

The USC Shoah Foundation, Los Angeles for giving the survivors the courage to speak out in 2000, giving them the confidence to write their stories for this book.

Staff and volunteers of The Together Plan in the UK and Belarus for their general assistance throughout.

To all donors to The Together Plan, specifically those who have given material and financial aid to support the work that we do with, and for, the Minsk Ghetto survivors and their families, and to those who donated towards this project and enabled it to become a reality.


Special thanks to Samantha, Jacob and Abigail Brunner for their belief, encouragement, love and unwavering continuous support.

# Preface

It was in 2014 that I first attended a gathering of former ghetto prisoners at the Holocaust Research Studio in Minsk. It was a bitterly cold evening; there was snow all around and the pavements were hellishly slippery as we made our way into the wooden building on Sukhaya Street. It was my trusted colleague, co-founder and director of The Together Plan UK, Artur Livshyts who had orchestrated the liaison that night. For some time, he had been introducing me to Jewish groups, isolated communities, vulnerable families and individuals. Together we had covered the length and breadth of Belarus, and I was developing a deep understanding of its traumatic history and its impact on the country as a whole. On that night, I met a brave and resilient group of people who had survived the most unthinkable tragedies, and yet here they were, still living on or close to the territory of the ghetto. I left deeply affected by these extraordinary men and women, who had never moved away from where they had lost so much. I had entered the building empty handed but came away clutching a recently published book in Russian. I am not a Russian speaker but was told that it contained a collection of the memories of survivors who had been children in the Minsk Ghetto (1941-43), many of them present in the room that very evening. I later discovered that only 300 copies of the book had been printed. I was intrigued.

I soon came to understand that this book had been produced only for private circulation due to a lack of funds, and thus it was prevented from ever reaching a wider audience. With the help of Artur Livshyts, I was able to ascertain that the texts offered clear, raw and personal insight into the tragic stories of loss and survival forged from the horrors of the Minsk Ghetto. In keeping with The Together Plan's ethos to empower people and give them a voice, it became an imperative that we seek to translate these narratives, in a quest to amplify the voices of the survivors, thus ensuring that their stories could be shared with the English-speaking world. And so began the project which has led to the publication in English of this extraordinary book, a four-year journey which far surpassed the expectations that we had at the outset.

On returning from Belarus in 2014, I established a connection to the Jewish Gen Yizkor Book Project who agreed to publish the book once a translated version could be achieved. The Together Plan team gratefully acknowledged the potential partnership and turned its attention to the task of bringing this extraordinary project to fruition. It would be a formidable undertaking. Our first challenge was to find a translator for the Russian text. As a small charity with limited resources, we reached out to our network in the hope of support and we finally reached the ear of Professor Michael Hornsby at the Adam Mickiewicz University in Poznań who asked us to send him the book. He quickly responded in the affirmative and so it all began. Professor Hornsby enlisted support from Rostyslav Kanibolotskyi and Iuliia Kuznetsova, and eventually, an English version in loose translation landed, as promised, in Debra Brunner's email in-box in January 2017. It was an exciting day.

We had already enlisted two volunteer editors in London, Hilda Bronstein and Bett Demby, who now divided the book between them, each taking half of the stories with the remit of shaping and editing for an English readership. We had expected that this phase would entail smoothing some rough edges in preparation for the production of a first draft. However, we now began to comprehend the complexities with which we were faced. We had not anticipated the challenges of working with a text in translation, especially as we all had agreed at the outset that we must at all times remain true to the original narratives. We found ourselves confounded by anomalies such as code words (why was a hiding place referred to as a 'raspberry'?), words and phrases in foreign languages (including German, Russian and Yiddish), not to mention specific terms associated with ghetto life and the world of the partisans. This was unfamiliar territory. There were references to significant historical dates in each of the stories which we had to cross-check to ensure accuracy. For example, research was required to check and verify the dates of events as quoted across the stories. A glossary was created to provide the English reader with information concerning places of significance, offer explanations for the Russian and Yiddish terms, list the dates of the pogroms that took place in the ghetto, and introduce the English reader to significant characters. Since neither of our editors are Russian speakers, we recruited a team (Anna Parijskaia and Jonathan Clingman in London and Arina Levina and Artur Livshyts in Minsk) to whom we were able to turn when we needed to call on their language skills. Regular editorial meetings took place in London, while a project team was also established in The Together Plan's office in Minsk. There was constant liaison between the editorial teams and the remaining ghetto survivors. The IBB Holocaust Research Centre in Minsk was on hand for historical verification and Frieda Reizman, Chair of the Ghetto Survivors Association GILF (herself a survivor) was available at all times to answer questions and connect us to survivors, or families of survivors, to clarify details.

In order to have an IT platform that enabled the two offices in Minsk and London to work on the book, our IT specialist and member of The Together Plan team, Jonathan Clingman, worked tirelessly to ensure that we had a system in place. With support from our volunteer professional IT specialist Paul Ginsberg in the Netherlands, we knew that we were in good hands.

During the development of the book, two stories came to light which were not in the original Russian version and these were added. The first was the story of survivor Polina Dobkina, now 93 and residing in Philadelphia. The London editorial team were able to interview Polina on a conference call which proved to be an extraordinarily meaningful and deeply moving meeting. Polina's recollection and memories of the ghetto were clear and lucid as she gave a detailed description of her escape to join the partisans. The second story tells of the survival of Leonid Ruderman which unfolds through a series of original letters including one by his mother Liza, from within the ghetto. It is a heart-wrenching story and one which is particularly chilling as we actually experience the immediacy of hearing the voice of someone who, only weeks later, tragically perished in the ghetto. That the letters survived and have been given new life in the book is somehow poignant.

On completion of the editing process, photographs were added in Minsk by Together Plan team member Vlad Zaiko, following which Artur and I edited and expanded the wording of the captions from the versions in the original book to provide more detail and context. Each story was meticulously proof-read by Ilana Salem in London, before finally going back to Minsk, where Artur read each text in English alongside the original Russian to cross-check for any anomalies or missed details. The stories were then returned to the London office.

This task took on an extremely personal significance for Artur, whose wife Tatyana, as a young woman, fought and lost a year-long battle with cancer while the book was in development. For Artur, his understanding of the trauma of loss was suddenly deepened by his own experience. He now had a new relationship with the project and with the ghetto survivors who, as children, had also come to appreciate the inestimable value and fragility of human life. Each story resonated profoundly with Artur and bears the results of his emotional labour. Artur dedicates his contribution to the book to his late wife Tatyana.

In early 2018, we finally reached a point where our contacts at Jewish Gen Yizkor Book Project were brought back into the frame, and the stories were slowly transferred to them for formatting. They sharpened the images from the original book and hours of dialogue ensued regarding the style, font, the length, line spacing, book size, page layout, and all the technicalities of creating a finished product ready for publication. This phase of the project involved communication across three time-zones, connecting Belarus, the UK and the USA. At every step, Artur coordinated the project in Minsk and I coordinated in London. The lines of communication were always open and the liaison between the two sides was close with continuous, ongoing collaboration.

So what of the ghetto survivors, the protagonists of these powerful and hitherto untold stories? Let us go back to that cold, snowy night in Minsk 2014, when I was first handed the book. This incredible community of survivors was assembled in the IBB Holocaust Research Centre and, although they were acquainted with Artur, I was at that point unknown to them. The room was dark, the snow was evident through the windows, and the group, seated in a semi-circle around the room, remained guarded and suspicious. Who was this English woman and what did she want? Coats remained on as if to say, 'we are not planning to stay long'. The body language was clearly demonstrating that they were not at all sure that I could be trusted. However, the guard was slowly lowered and my words of friendship seemed to give them the reassurances they needed. We ended our meeting on that cold evening with hugs and hand-shakes and the book was entrusted into our care. Since that first meeting our friendship has grown considerably.

Over the past four years, The Together Plan has built a programme of support for this wonderful community of survivors and their families. We plan and deliver events, often on

Sabbath evenings, as a vehicle to bring people together offering some sense of the Jewish life they lost. We have witnessed the engagement of young Jewish adults in our training sessions in communities throughout Belarus. Many of them now spend time with the survivors and they often take the lead in Sabbath services in Minsk, ensuring that there is a growing sense of Jewish community.

Her Excellency British Ambassador Fionna Gibb has been a great supporter and friend to the Ghetto Survivors. She has become an invested participant in the home visits project that we run, which brings people together in friendship, and the survivors themselves are regular and welcome guests at The British Embassy.

Throughout the last four years, The Together Plan team has worked together with the ghetto survivors and our associates to bring this vitally important book to fruition. In our journey over that time, the survivors have become energized, valued and empowered. They have been a part of a dedicated team in a project that will now ensure that the English-speaking world has access to their stories.

The Together Plan Charity has a passionate belief in community, identity and connections. We strive to seek out those Jewish people who have no voice, are cut off and isolated from their own Jewish identity and from the rest of the Jewish world. It is our mission to address this need and find solutions to repair and revive communities coming out of collective trauma. So many books about the Holocaust focus on loss, eradicated communities, destruction and hopelessness, the vacant spaces, the ghosts of history. It is an inevitable reality of the biggest genocide that history has ever known. Yet here, in this book 'We Remember, Lest the World Forget' we hear from twenty-seven survivors, people who endured. These are the narratives of the living. Remarkably not one of their stories expresses bitterness. Each one carries a sense of dignity and humanity in spite of the unthinkable suffering and loss. Some of the writers even find moments to acknowledge enemy soldiers who, in some instances, turned a blind eye or aided escape. Each story, although deeply tragic is a study in bravery, friendships, hope and salvation. It is not just a book about what is written on the pages, but what is unspoken. There is so much in-between the lines for us to talk about and consider. It is our hope that this book will be used to educate and inspire for many future generations, as we pray for a world of tolerance, acceptance and understanding.

So many of us have been profoundly moved throughout this project. We feel humbled and privileged to have worked together with these brave and stalwart heroes, enabling them to have the voices they so deeply deserve.

**Debra Brunner**

UK Director and Co-Founder of UK Charity The Together Plan (1154167)

The Together Plan is a UK Charity, whose mission is to rebuild and revive Jewish communities coming out of collective trauma in the former Soviet Union.

# Editors' Introduction

In 2000 the USC Shoah Foundation carried out a series of interviews with elderly survivors of the Minsk Ghetto. Most of the interviewees were members of the Ghetto Survivors' Centre in Minsk, now called the Historical Workshop on Holocaust Research named after Leonid Levin. Some of them were initially reluctant to speak about the traumatic events of their early lives but, with the encouragement of the Foundation interviewers, they were finally able to share their tragic stories. The accounts were then gathered together and published in Russian through a project created by the Minsk Ghetto Survivors' Association GILF, and funded by the German Foundation: Memory, Responsibility, Future.

In 2017 Bett Demby and I were approached by The Together Plan Charity (TTP) and asked if we were interested in editing a translation of those stories with a view to publication in English. Initially, the task seemed to be straightforward. We knew that the accounts had already been published in the original Russian and that TTP had subsequently arranged for them to be translated 'roughly' into English. We agreed to read the translations, and edit them where necessary to make them accessible to an English-speaking readership. How unprepared we were for what we found!! The task was overwhelming in so many ways. When we met again a few weeks later for a preliminary 'review of progress' we were only just coming to terms with the mountain which confronted us.

These were the most extraordinary human stories, told by aging survivors after a gap of several decades. They were personal accounts of separation, loss, deprivation and fear, as well as extraordinary fortitude and bravery. For many of the writers, the task of recalling and recording their experiences must indeed have been an onerous one. Some of these memories had been suppressed for decades. Even during the early years after the war, for most victims in the Soviet Union, speaking of their experiences had simply been too 'difficult' and painful. What is more, when it came to identity, the expectations of the State in 1944 were clear: Jews, like everyone else, were expected to re-integrate into society as loyal Soviet citizens. Not to do so could seriously damage educational and career prospects. This kind of state anti-Semitism meant that many children born to Jewish parents during the war and after 1944 were not even aware that their families were Jewish.

Were these survivors emotionally able or prepared for the task in 2000 of summoning and recording their recollections? For the most part, these narratives were factual accounts of unthinkable suffering and tragic experiences, devoid of descriptive adjectives or expressions of emotion. How were we going to remain faithful to the writers' intentions while finding acceptable words in which to express the spirit of their texts.  Neither of us was a Russian speaker and so we had no access to the unique expressive spirit of that language. To complicate matters, we had been warned that the translations, carried out by generous volunteers, were just 'rough' drafts. Furthermore, there were some references in the writing to places, characters, historical events with which Belarusian and Russian readers would be familiar, but which were strange to us - as they would be to most English-speaking readers. The need for some research and the provision of a glossary became quickly apparent. Finally, as we worked through the texts, we gradually began to realise that this small band of writers consisted of the members of a tragically unique elite – *they* had miraculously survived the Minsk Ghetto, a place where thousands of others had died. In one account, that of Mikhail Treister, this is poignantly and memorably acknowledged.

The intention of the Nazis had been to excise the Jewish race from the region…to murder all Jews, and remove every trace of their existence. Indeed, the Minsk Ghetto is estimated in 1941/2 to have held between 80,000 and 100,000 people. The residents were under constant threat of death. Random raids and night-time killings were punctuated by major pogroms. Apart from those desperate, foolhardy and courageous enough to reach the partisans in the forests, and a few hundred who had escaped in other ways, (some of them revealed in this book), estimates of survivors of the Minsk Ghetto after the final pogrom range from 20 to just 1.

I have now come to understand that, in the history of the Holocaust, the story of the Minsk Ghetto was unusual, if not unique. For one thing, the area was secured by a barbed wire fence rather than by solid walls (as actually specified by the Germans in their initial edict). Furthermore, security was regularly breached, in spite of the threat of instant death upon discovery. Most relevant of all, there was almost no place to which escapees could run. Some brave families living outside the ghetto in the 'Russian District' are known to have sheltered Jewish children, but this was rare because the penalty was simply too high. Similarly, some of these accounts tell of the personnel at certain orphanages and children's homes in Minsk who risked their lives by sheltering and protecting Jewish children. In these stories, amid the barbarity there are even moments of unexpected kindness by German soldiers. However, for most, escape seemed impossible: the forests were far off, and partisan groups, especially in the early years, were reluctant to accept Jews. What is more, new recruits were only accepted by the partisan authorities if they were young, fit and owned a weapon. Nevertheless, the underground movement inside the ghetto did succeed in organising the escape of many Jews to partisan groups in the forest. The survival rate for those who escaped in this way was much higher than for those desperate enough to attempt such a perilous journey on their own. Finally, in 1943, the formation of Zorin's Jewish partisan group, known as the 106th, made possible the rescue of hundreds of Jews from the ghetto, including children, the elderly and the infirm.

Most of us living in the West are familiar with the history of the Warsaw and Vilna Ghettoes, the statistics of which are by now well documented by academics and institutions worldwide. Monuments have been constructed in their memory, they have been featured in film and TV documentaries, TV dramas and series, and in Hollywood movies. However, how many of us are familiar with the events surrounding the tragic history of the Minsk Ghetto? How many people even know where Minsk is located geographically? How many realise the extent to which victims of the Holocaust in the countries of the Former Soviet Union had been repressed for several years as communists, even before their traumatic experiences under the Nazis. Indeed, as I stated earlier, even after the appalling events of 1939-1943 which are recounted here, the survivors of the Minsk Ghetto were simply unable to tell their stories while they were still living in the USSR, and only felt 'free' to do so after the fall of the Soviet Union and Belarusian independence in 1991. Historical evidence concerning the Jews of Belarus has been sparse. It was not until 2008 that the scholarly record compiled by Barbara Epstein was published under the title *The Minsk Ghetto 1941-1943*, while in 2009, Yitchak Arad's monumental tome *The Holocaust in the Soviet Union* was published with a number of pages devoted to events in Minsk. Several of the writers of the stories recorded in this book are also mentioned in those publications. To both Epstein and Arad, we offer our deepest thanks.

And so the process began of editing the texts in English in order to give as authentic and accurate a voice as possible to the narrators, remaining true to their own words and reflecting the spirit of their texts and their experiences.  We have also tried to provide some simple explanatory information where necessary. This is by no means an academic publication, but we hope that the result is a work which informs and educates, and may even provide a starting point for those seeking links to their own heritage in Belarus today.

**Hilda Bronstein**

It is simple to answer the question of why I became involved this project: keeping the stories alive. Each year fewer Holocaust survivors remain with us. Relating their stories to the world, particularly, those that are lesser known, such as these from the Minsk Ghetto becomes ever more imperative.

As an avid reader, I have always been drawn to stories on the subject of the Second World War and the Holocaust. Whether fact or fiction, they have always held a fascination, borne from a deep-rooted sense of empathy and disquiet. When reading book reviews of stories based on actual Holocaust events, I am often surprised and sometimes a little shocked to learn that many readers are discovering, for the first time, the harrowing incidents described.

My extended family originated and fled from the Pale of Settlement during the closing years of the 19th century. As a Jewish child, born in the relative security of 1960's Britain, I grew up with the knowledge of the dark deeds that had foreshadowed my parents' generation. Through the benefit of a Jewish community and education, my children have also understood and carried with them, the knowledge of those lost generations. Families who, but for a quirk of geographical misfortune and timing, ended their days in the most dire and unthinkable circumstances. So, often, individual faces that look out at us from photographs of the lost, are always poignant and strangely familiar. They look so similar to our relations that they could have been taken from our own family albums.

I first met some of the survivors of the Minsk Ghetto on an educational Jewish journey to Belarus in March 2012. Still living in and around the vicinity of the original ghetto territory, they accompanied us as we toured the streets and monuments of the city, culminating with solemnity and some trepidation at Yama, 'The Pit'. This memorial commemorates the place, where in 1942, over 5,000 individuals were executed. An obelisk, stands in the pit and on the descent, an unbearably moving sculpture by artists Leonid Levin and Elsa Pollak. Named 'The Last Way' it symbolises a group of men, women and children, walking down the steps into the pit, towards their death (seen on the back cover of the book). Almost abstract and conceptual in style, the sculpture is extraordinarily haunting, once seen, the featureless figures are impossible to forget. One female is turned away from the inevitable, head buried in the shoulder of a loved one. Children hide behind the adults, clinging to their legs for protection. An unborn baby, is shielded within its pregnant mother's stomach by caressing hands. Some heads appear to be bowed in submission, but the last figure is not empty handed. He carries a violin, a refusal perhaps to relinquish all possessions and all identity.

Editing the stories of the Minsk Ghetto survivors, has proved to be a deeply emotional and memorable experience.  These storytellers have related the ordeals of people, trapped within an extraordinary and desperate environment, describing a time when they were little more than children. The memories unfold often with brutal candour. Time after time, the children in these narratives experience complete abandonment, the disappearance of parents and grandparents at a moment's notice. The words, 'I never saw her again' and 'he never came back' punctuate the narrative with heart-breaking frequency. Family members vanishing without a trace in the daily cycles of random violence, round-ups and executions. Often the accounts offer no explanation for the missing loved ones. Yet despite their traumatic nature, between the lines of these stories, there is so much more than fear and sadness. In the sections that describe their lives as partisans, tragedy and heroism have in some way merged, entwined amid the everyday rituals of simply trying to stay alive.

It has been harrowing and painstaking work to put these exceptional memories in order. However, the strength of the storytellers' characters and personalities, always present behind their words, has helped bring them to life. It has been a privilege to participate in this project and knowing that these stories will be shared with a wider audience is a fitting tribute to each of the brave survivors.

**Bett Demby**

With grateful thanks to Arkadiy Dobkin for partnering with The Together Plan in bringing this book to life, and ensuring that the story of the Minsk Ghetto will be told to the English speaking world for generations to come.

# The Yellow Patch

Yellow patch on display in the
Jewish Museum, Minsk 2018

Photo attribution: Olga Volcheck

**Minsk 1941**

**Group of Jewish women and children, wearing yellow patches**

Photo attribution: Bundesarchiv, N 1576 Bild-006 / Herrmann, Ernst /   CC-BY.
Source: German Federal Archives. Photographer: Ernst Hermann

The photograph above (left) is one of the original circular pieces of yellow fabric, which Jews in the Minsk Ghetto were ordered to wear (as seen on the right). The order applied to everyone over the age of ten (see the order below). The patches were to be 10cm in diameter and attached to the outer garments, on both the left side of the chest, and on the back. The prisoners referred to the patches in Yiddish as *late*, pronounced: *lata* or *laty* (see glossary).

### From Communiqué №31 of the Security Police and the SD on the creation of the Jewish Council (Judenrat)

Minsk 23<sup>rd</sup> July 1941

"As the German soldier cannot always unfailingly distinguish Jewish people from non-Jewish local population, in some cases misunderstandings have occurred. A regulation has therefore been issued requiring that with immediate effect, Jewish men and women aged 10 and older wear yellow sewn-on patches on their breasts and backs at all times."

# Prologue in the Original Book

As time passes, we inevitably become distanced from the dark events of the apocalyptic forties. Seven decades have intervened. Alas, the last survivors and chroniclers of that terrible period are now dying. However, their words, as recorded in this volume, will stand us in good stead as new tides of xenophobia and hatred continue to shake our restless world.

The Holocaust in Belarus remained a closed book for too long. It is only in recent years that the vibrant Yiddish-speaking world that once existed, and then sank from view like the lost city of Atlantis, has finally been officially recognised by the government of Belarus. The publication of this collection of written testimonies signals a new and momentous moment in our world outlook.

The magazine publication of *War and Peace* in the 20th century, and the appearance of Vasily Grossman's immortal novel *Life and Destiny* remain unforgettable moments for all readers of the post-*perestroika* press. My grandfather, a veteran combatant, used to say that the plain truth about war had not yet been written. In Grossman's book, the genocide of European Jewry is mercilessly described for the first time in its naked truth. Responsibility for it was laid at the door of Hitler's Nazi totalitarianism and, indirectly, of Stalin's totalitarian socialism which left Russia's citizens to their fate. Readers were finally becoming aware of the depths of hell suffered by those inside the concentration camps and the ghettos. A medieval darkness was revealed that removed the veneer of cultured civilization from modern Europe. Most terrible is the banality of evil of which Primo Levi wrote in his Auschwitz diaries entitled *Is this a Man* (1947), and Hannah Arendt in *Eichmann in Jerusalem: A Report on the Banality of Evil* (1963). It is that very banality that strikes us as we start to read this book of memories written by the survivors of the Minsk Ghetto.

As a fourth generation Minsk native, I am certainly not an unbiased critic. It is impossible for me to read without a shudder the description of the pre-war city, cosy and patriarchal, which was almost levelled to the ground during the merciless tempest of war. By comparison, life until then had seemed relatively settled and untroubled, despite the repression and fear suffered during the expansion of USSR territory during the thirties. What is most astonishing for the reader is the sudden transition from a peaceful mundane existence in the summer of 1941 – including graduate proms of tenth-graders and the opening of Minsk Lake – to the devastating fires, the landing of German troops, and the rounding up of refugees like cattle back into the city which now became a deadly trap for its inhabitants.

Soviet and Communist Party bureaucrats displayed criminal irresponsibility when they took to their heels as early as four days before the Nazi arrival in the city, without announcing any organised evacuation. On the contrary, they cynically discouraged displays of 'alarmism', thus ultimately leading to the tragic deaths of dozens of thousands of Jewish Soviet citizens. In the memories which are described in this book, we see the world of fascism through the eyes of children who would be forced to grow up too fast during this period of infernal horror.

The Soviet Union of pre-war years had lacked any sense of civil society. This, together with the existence of 'hyper violence' by the state against the individual, led to an appalling subservience in a repressed population. Instructions issued by the occupying authorities were carried out almost unquestioningly. It was thus that new orders involving an endless chain of humiliation and horror were imposed on formerly 'ordinary' people. That the inhabitants of the ghetto continued to survive and fight for their very existence, and for the lives of their nearest and dearest, inspires a feeling of true reverence. Indeed, it is thanks to that profound will to live, that the 'Final Solution', as planned by heartless Fascist beasts, was ultimately not achieved. It is hard to imagine what daily tasks had to be carried out by prisoners against their will, in order just to survive for just one more day in a hell that was worse than Dante's inferno!

In these stories, even the brief sketches of everyday life, still manage to shock: the mother warns little Volik that in the case of extreme need, he will have to pee on his clothes and use the fabric as a filter in order to have any chance of surviving in a gas chamber. And one wonders about the effect on children of witnessing scenes in the ghetto following a pogrom when bleeding people were 'falling asleep in the middle of the road', while the SS camp at Shirokaya Street seems to offer us the perfect example of Dante's final circle of hell.

Descriptions of children going under the barbed wire to reach the 'Russian' part of Minsk, in order to find a morsel of food for their families, strike the reader with their everyday tone, their matter-of-fact simplicity. There are descriptions of 'selections' taking place inside an orphanage on the territory of the ghetto, when a child conceals herself in an oven, and you start to realise how very slender was the line between life and death. We watch as children grow old before their time as they face the unrelenting fortunes dealt out to them by cruel fate. Even the happy chance of finding yourself among partisans, and maybe become one of them, did not guarantee your chances of staying alive. Sometimes, in order to achieve that goal, young teenagers were exposed to actual trials of survival, such as gathering or finding weapons or munitions, or taking much-needed specialists out of the ghetto and through dangerous terrain to the partisan zones. Such tasks were not easy even for mature adults, let alone for tortured young prisoners. Yet it is incredible how successful those young avengers and guides often turned out to be.

Particularly memorable is the laconic story by Lev Kravets who tells of his experience taking prisoners from the hell of the ghetto to join the partisans. Lev is an ordinary teenager entrusted by the partisan command with the sacred mission of saving a large group who were, otherwise, doomed to annihilation. These youngsters were forced to orientate themselves to situations where they must accept adult responsibilities and make life-changing decisions instantaneously. Such decisions sometimes turned out to be defining moments between life and death for the dozens of people who were placing their trust in him. Stories like these can only inspire awe and give an optimistic message for future generations. Despite their extraordinary trials and tribulations, the young survivors never lost their strong will to live. Maybe their sufferings even provided them with the capacity to overcome the endless difficulties of life after the war. It is impossible to overestimate the value of these testimonies. They illustrate the many ways by which the victims coped with the events of a time when it seemed that everything had become impossible, a time when all human qualities and failings were starkly exposed. We see here the extraordinary capabilities of the human spirit when it is pushed to the extreme in seemingly hopeless circumstances.

These simple accounts by ordinary people are essential reading for anyone seeking to understand the times in which we live now, since the past was won with so much pain and suffering by our fast disappearing older generation.

*Lecturer at the Department of Culturology of Belarus State University*

A.G. Birger

# Dedication

*The Minsk Ghetto survivors dedicate this book*

*to their children and*

*grandchildren*

# From the Bible

Only be careful, and watch yourselves closely so that you do not forget the things your eyes have seen or let them fade from your heart as long as you live. Teach them to your children and to their children after them.

Deuteronomy 4:9

# Geopolitical Information

Minsk is located at 53°54' N, 27°34' E

Alternate names: Minsk [Bel, Rus, Yid], Mińsk [Pol], Minskas [Lith], Mensk, Miensk

| Period | Town | District | Province | Country |
|---|---|---|---|---|
| Before WWI (c. 1900): | Minsk | Minsk | Minsk | Russian Empire |
| Between the wars (c. 1930): | Minsk | Minsk | Belarus SSR | Soviet Union |
| After WWII (c. 1950): | Minsk | | | Soviet Union |
| Today (c. 2000): | Minsk | | | Belarus |

Jewish Population in 1900: 48,000

## Nearby Jewish Communities

Samokhvalovichi 12 miles SSW

Astrashytski Haradok 13 miles NNE

Zaslawye 13 miles WNW

Uzlyany 21 miles SSE

Smilavichy 21 miles ESE

Rakov 22 miles WNW

Radashkovichy 22 miles NW

Dukora 22 miles SE

Dzyarzhynsk 23 miles SW

Smalyavichy 23 miles ENE

Lahoysk 24 miles NNE

Hajna 24 miles NNE

Rudensk 24 miles SSE

**BELARUS**

| | 2012 Border |
| --- | --- |
| | 1940 Border |

**BELARUS**

0  25  50   75   km

0   25   50    75 miles

ESTONIA

LATVIA

RUSSIA

LITHUANIA

RUSSIA

VILNIUS •

**BELARUS**

• MINSK

1940 Border

• SLONIM

• RUZHANY

POLAND

UKRAINE

Map of Belarus showing Minsk

# Saved Thanks to the Courage of Good People
## Elena Antonova

**Elena Antonova**

My name was Lena Shofman. I was sent to the Minsk Ghetto in July 1941 with my mother Bertha and Grandma Genya. I was only six years old when I had to face the brutality of the Nazis and, as such a young child, it traumatized my soul. Being trapped by wire fences, trying to exchange things for food, attempting to escape into the 'Russian district', facing pogroms and mass shootings, these are all things that I will never forget.

My grandmother was killed during the first pogrom on 7 November 1941. The Jews were given red flags to hold and driven to pre-dug pits, where they were shot.

The Germans did not spare adults or children. There was one particular orphanage in the ghetto that was home to more than three hundred children and babies between the ages of two months and thirteen years, whose parents had been killed. The Nazis killed all of the children, including sixty-eight who were sick, and the staff. They just threw open the windows and doors and the sickest children froze to death in the icy winter weather. The others were brutally murdered.

My mother was taken every day to Dolgobrodskaya Street as part of a labour group which had to dig ditches for tanks. My mother was afraid to leave me alone and would always take me with her.

My mother died in 1943 and, after that, I managed to escape from the ghetto. I wandered around the city a stray, homeless child until, eventually, I was picked up and taken to Children's Home Number 7. The director of this children's home, Vera Leonardovna Sparning, wrote my name down in the record as Elena Antonova, a Byelorussian name. She did this to save my life, and I have used the name Elena Antonova ever since. She worked with Vasiliy Orlov who was the Inspector of Orphanages. He worked in the Department of Children's Homes for the Minsk City Commissariat and saved many Jewish children. They risked their own lives many times, saving over thirty-five children in our home, as well as others in orphanages across the city. Many years later Vasiliy Orlov was awarded the title, 'Righteous Among Nations'.

The Nazis were constantly searching and trying to identify which were the Jewish children in the orphanages and Children's Homes across the city. They issued a strict order, which was presented to all the directors. This had to be signed and Jewish children had to be declared.

On the doors of my Children's Home, however, there was a sign with the words 'Spotted Typhus' written in both German and Byelorussian. It hung there more or less permanently. Because of this, we rarely had visits from the Germans. If we did happen to have a visit, the director would make sure that all the children who were Jewish, or who looked Jewish, were put to bed, and the Germans were told that they were ill with Typhus.

When the Germans completely prohibited food supplies being delivered to orphanages, Vasiliy Orlov would drive around the surrounding villages and try to barter with them for rye. He would take the rye to one of the collective farms, where there was a mill, and he would beg the millers to grind it so that he could then distribute it to the orphanages.

The Christian community also tried to provide assistance. Anton Mitrofanovich Ketsko, the priest, worked together with Vasiliy Orlov to collect shoes, clothes and food from members of the community to distribute to the orphans.

When the Red Army finally liberated Minsk from the Fascists, we wrote a letter of gratitude to Vasiliy Orlov. This letter is still on display in the Museum of the Great Patriotic War. Here are some excerpts from it:

'We thank Comrade Orlov. We are free. We are saved! There is heartfelt delight in our eyes full of dark, joyful tears! No more *SD* [see glossary], and no more ghetto!'… 'Some former friends were afraid to acknowledge us, and we ourselves were pleased when they didn't do so. But there was a man who did not turn away from us, who saved us from the horrors of the ghetto and hunger.'… 'We have been saved by the courage of good people and will remember them for all our lives and we thank them.'… 'We must do everything in our power to make sure fascism never happens again.'

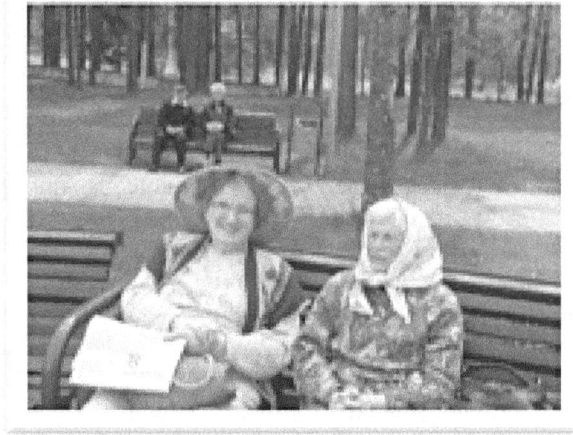

On vacation at the 'Alesya' resort, Belarus.

Elena Antonova with former ghetto prisoner Nella Gerbovitskaya in 2011.

# My Wartime Childhood
## Elfrida Aslezova (Frida Kissel)

**Elfrida Aslezova (Frida Kissel)**

I was born in November 1935 in Minsk. When the war began I was five years old and can remember many things from that time. I lived in the Komarovka area at 26 Pushkin Street, with my parents and grandparents in the house of my uncle's family. My uncle, Sani Kissel, worked in the 'Yanka Kupala', The Artists' Theatre. My Aunt Birute was an actress also from the theatre. She had a daughter called Rutochka from a previous marriage and, before the war, when the theatre company went on tour, Rutochka also came to live with us.

Nowadays, this street is called Independence Avenue and where our house once stood, there is a Department Store called 'Minsk'. However, back then, single storey wooden houses stood there, which were built before the revolution, and there was a tramline running along the street. Today, in this area, there is a factory named after Lenin, but before the war, it had been the Radiozavad engineering plant, and even earlier, it had been a woodworking factory where my grandfather Reuben Kissel had worked during the 1920's as a *stolyar* [Russian: a highly skilled cabinet maker]. My grandfather had already retired before the war, but my mother and father were still working. As children, we would play and have fun with our friends in the leafy courtyard and garden of our house. In the centre was a large cherry tree and a lilac bush, as well as many flowers. However, on 22 June 1941, a clear and sunny day, our carefree childhoods came to an end, and the war began.

Minsk was bombed heavily in those early days. It was terrible to walk past the ruins of collapsed and smoldering houses. On the third day of bombing, my parents and I tried to leave Minsk on foot, hoping to escape to the east, but it was already too late. We were quickly overtaken by fascist troops. Despite managing to avoid being killed by the bombing, or executed by the Germans, we had no choice but to return to our pre-war house on Pushkin Street. My grandparents had stayed in the house, as neither of them was well enough to walk, so they had not even attempted to leave.

**My paternal grandfather, Ruvim Kissel, prisoner of the Minsk Ghetto**

**Killed during the pogrom on 20 November 1941 at the age of 67**

After the 'Order of Settlement of Jews' in July 1941, all Jews had to live in the ghetto. We were forced to leave Pushkin Street and moved into Zamkovaya Street, where we were able to find housing. Here, we all lived in one room of a single storey wooden house. There were eight of us: me, my parents, grandfather, two grandmothers, my aunt Sonya and her daughter Riva. My cousin was older than me and had recently graduated from high school. She and her friends would spend hours writing, putting up, and distributing leaflets around the ghetto. Like many other underground workers, they risked their lives by trying to listen to news on illegal radio sets. Afterwards, they would report the actual situation in the form of leaflets. This was how we discovered that Moscow had been captured, and that we had to hide during the pogroms that followed. Under the floor of the room where we lived, my father built a *malina* [Russian: hiding place for sheltering during pogroms].

The first big pogrom swept through the ghetto on 7 November 1941. Rumours that something was going to happen had been gathering for days, so, on the 6 November, my family insisted that my mother and I try to hide in the Russian area where we may be safer. Once it was dark, we crept out of the ghetto to the house of our family friends the Lepeshkos, who lived on Tsnyanskaya Street. 'Uncle' Arkadiy was away at the front, but my 'Aunt' Maroussia and her daughter Galya, who was my age, were at home. I can remember my mother knocking gently to be let in at their kitchen window, and how scared my aunt was. She kept asking who we were because she couldn't see us properly in the dark. We stayed with them for three days, hidden in the basement, so that the neighbours wouldn't see us. Aunt Maroussia managed to feed us well, even with her limited food supply.

We did have to return to the ghetto eventually. Staying there meant that we had all been at risk of being arrested, and even possibly executed. When we got back we were thankful to see that the right side of Zamkovaya Street, where we lived, had not really been affected by the pogrom, and all of our relatives had survived. However, the residents on the left side of the street had been targeted and murdered. The left-hand side of the street was now separated from the right by a barbed wire fence. A few days later new people began to appear on the left-hand side; they were beautifully dressed and spoke German. They were Jews arriving to live in the newly created section of the ghetto, established for German Jews deported from the West.

**My maternal Grandmother Osipovna Revekka Movchenzon**

**Killed during the pogrom 28 – July 1942**

**David Ruvimovich Kissell, my father**

**Born 1908 – Died 1996**

**Prisoner of the Minsk Ghetto from July 1941 to November 1942**

On the 20 November another pogrom engulfed the ghetto. It began before dawn, and we barely had time to get down to the *malina.* Grandpa refused to come down there and hide with us, so he covered over the entrance to the hideout and went back to bed. This time our side of the street was not spared. Two Germans came into the house and dragged my grandfather out of bed. They tried to force him to go out of the house but he flatly refused, so they shot and killed him there and then, in the bedroom. After his brutal murder, the executioners left the house. We were still alive. At the cost of his own life, my grandfather had saved the family.

The Jewish survivors of this pogrom were once again ordered to immediately vacate their homes. We were forced to find somewhere else to live, in one of the ever-decreasing number of streets in which Jews were still permitted to reside. We were lucky to be offered shelter by friends of my parents who took us all in. They lived on the corner of Krimskaya and Flaksa Streets, so we all lived there together in even more cramped conditions than before.

The Jews in our new area came mostly from Western Germany, and we referred to them all as the Hamburg Jews. Other parts of the ghetto were also divided and named after cities in Germany.

On the 2 March, there was yet another pogrom throughout the whole of the ghetto. Once again, our immediate family managed to survive by hiding in a new *malina* built below an outhouse. Tragically, this time we lost many of our relatives.

During my years in the ghetto I was frequently sick. Food was scarce and nutrition poor, so, consequently, I had dysentery and had to drink Castor Oil. After I had swallowed the hated medication, I can remember my grandmother sprinkling black bread with salt and giving it to me to take away the taste! When we were in Flaksa Street, I became more seriously ill, with a high fever and bouts of unconsciousness. I was now diagnosed with paratyphoid. Eventually, I recovered. It seems that it was my destiny to survive!

Both my parents were allowed out of the ghetto to work, my father in a furniture shop and my mother looking after the German Shepherd dog belonging to an officer in the General Commissariat. She was able to get hold of cigarettes and would sometimes bring home a canteen of left over soup that had been prepared for the dog. Along with my father's bread rations that soup helped us to survive. Occasionally, in the summer, my mother took me with her to work. In the mornings we'd walk along the lines of soldiers, and we would take the same journey back in the evening. On one occasion, we were ordered by the soldiers not to return to the ghetto. We hid in the attic of friends for four days. During this time, on the 28 July, there was a pogrom that lasted for those four days. Although my father and Riva were safe, both my grandmothers died.

**Esther Yulevna Kissel-Movshenzon, my mother**

**Born 1919 – Died 2005**

**Prisoner of the Minsk ghetto from July 1941 – November 1942**

After this, my parents felt that it was no longer safe for me to be in the ghetto, and that I was certain to die if I remained there. My appearance was not very different from that of other Byelorussian children, with my blond hair, snub nose, and grey blue eyes, so they made a plan to smuggle me into the Russian district.

My life in the Russian region outside the ghetto began in the autumn of 1942, when I was almost seven years old. Even though I wasn't a baby it was terrible to be left with a stranger. I buried my nose in my mother's skirt and hugged her legs tightly, not wanting to let go, but she had to leave. My parents had taken me to live with Olga Nikolaevna George. She was a Muscovite and a military doctor, and also fluent in German and English. She lived with two sisters Elsa and Irma Leiser, whom my mother had known before the war. They had introduced my parents to Olga. All three were active members of an underground group run by Ivan Kovalyov. His underground name was 'Jean' but I simply knew him as uncle Sacha. We all lived in the same house, Olga and I on the first floor, and Elsa and Irma above us. We often spent our evenings together. During the day, when she went to work, Olga usually locked me in the house for safety, but sometimes she gave me jobs to do, such as putting medicines in bags and then covering them over with biscuits.

In early 1943, Irma had joined a partisan unit, but she was captured by the Gestapo in an ambush. Tortured and unable to withstand the suffering, she betrayed 'Jean' to the enemy. He was arrested along with Elsa and they were later both murdered. After their arrest, Olga was terrified that she would be next. She was extremely frightened that, if that happened, I would also be taken away and severely punished. She thought it best to say nothing to me about this. Concerned once again for my safety, she asked her friends if they would be willing to take me in, but they refused. Unlike Olga and the Leiser sisters, they had no connection to me, and didn't want to take responsibility for me.

After a pogrom, in March 1943, Olga was finally arrested. An elderly German officer took her away, and they talked in German before they left the house. It was possibly because of that conversation, or because I was a *klein kind* [Yiddish: small child] that I was saved and allowed to be sent to a neighbour. The apartment was searched and sealed, but I never found out what they were looking for, or if they found anything. Olga died, but despite all our enquiries after the war in both Minsk and Moscow, we were never able to find out exactly what happened to her.

The neighbour to whom I'd been sent, put me in an orphanage after only a couple of weeks, under the name of Frida George. The Orphanage was on Storozhovskaya Street, near to the Opera House. On the night of the 2 May 1943, Soviet planes bombed Minsk and one wing of the Opera House was hit. The explosion blew out all of the Orphanage windows and, as we didn't have a bomb shelter, we all sat huddled together, terrified, on the floor of the hallway, and waited for the air raid to end.

Life in the Orphanage was horrible. We were always cold and hungry and often had to gather nettles and quinoa to eat. My braids had been cut off, but even my short hair had lice! We were all expected to help out in the Orthodox Church and were all baptized. My baptismal name was 'Helen' and for a long time I wore a cross as protection. I stayed in the Orphanage until the end of August 1943, when things in my life changed yet again.

Stefa Vavilova was a dwarf, and a neighbour of Olga Nikolaevna. She was poor but saw a way to remedy this by taking over the property left by Olga following her arrest. As I was seen as Olga's beneficiary, the only way for her to do this was by adopting me. I didn't want to become Stefa's daughter, but I was eight years old, and nobody asked my opinion!

So now my name changed once again. I was now Lena Vavilova, and Stefa enrolled me in school. I found all of the school work difficult. I had been able to read from the age of five, but here the language taught was Byelorussian with Latin script. Things progressively became worse, and when the first frosts of the winter arrived, I had to walk to school barefoot, as I had no shoes.

At the end of September 1943, the Germans forced us out of Olga's house. A family that Stefa knew took us in for a while and, in return, she did their laundry and helped out with the housework. However, this was only temporary, and we soon had to look for somewhere else. We finally moved into a derelict house near Komarovsky Market, on Belomorskaya Street. I would sometimes bump into our pre-war neighbours, but we would keep our heads down and pretend not to know each other. We were starving, sometimes managing for a whole day on a couple of boiled potatoes. All of Olga's remaining belongings had long ago been sold for food and drink for Stefa. Despite our desperate hunger, Stefa loved to drink and acquired alcohol whenever she could.

Despite all of this hardship, we managed to survive and hold on, waiting for our troops.

On the 3 July 1944, the Soviet tanks entered the Logoisky Tract, and our fear disappeared to be replaced with hope. Maybe my parents would still be alive and could find me? From the day of our separation, when my mother had left me with Olga, we had heard nothing from each other.

I found out that my parents had joined the partisan brigade at the end of November 1942 and had fought in the Dzerzhinsky Baranovichi partisan unit. They joined forces with the Red Army on the 23rd July near the village of Lyubcha. During a partisan parade on the 16th of July 1944, they had still been fighting the retreating Germans. Thank heavens they survived and that, after joining the Red Army, they arrived in Minsk and found me!

I went with my mother to Ljubco and once I was back in her care, she cleaned me up and deloused me. Food was not so scarce there and the whole community helped to fatten me up! Eventually we returned to Minsk, back to our pre-war apartment at 26, Pushkin Street, which was still standing. My parents went back to work, and I went back to school into the second grade, even though I had missed the first. I was a good student and caught up quickly. For a little while, my parents invited Stefa to live with us, but she didn't like the 'sober' life of a family, so she left.

Like my grandparents, my father's sister Sonya had died. Fortunately, Riva was still alive, but she had not returned to Minsk as she worked in Grodno. She only returned, along with my aunt and uncle, after the Yanka Kupala Theatre was re-opened. Once again, our family was gathered under one roof. We were reduced in number, but at last our life began to improve.

**Frida Kissel, Spring 1945**

# My Childhood, A War of Fire
## Georgiy Birger

**Georgiy Birger**

Time inexorably rushes forward. I recently celebrated my 77th birthday. It has been over 67 years since the liberation of Minsk from the German Occupation. Over those years I have come to realise how little is known about the lives of ordinary people in an occupied city, or how they survived. From the depths of my memory, a bright picture has gradually emerged of those distant times, once conjured in the stories of mothers and grandmothers.

My father's name was Nikolai Yefimovich Birger and my mother was Sofya Josephovna Chepelyanis. She was a bright, attractive young woman and the romance between my parents began in Minsk. Everyone who knew them, admired this beautiful couple. My father was Jewish and a well-known athlete in the city. He had won the Championship of the Republic, for javelin, discus and lifting weights.

My father was arrested in 1940, and I recall that, before being led away by the security officers, he leaned over my bed to say goodbye. The next time I saw him was in the autumn of 1944. Meanwhile, my wartime childhood, and the years of ever increasing suffering for my mother, began on 22 June 1941. During those years my mother succeeded in saving the lives of her two sons, enduring with courage the difficult years of deprivation and misery.

Sunday 22 June 1941 was warm and sunny, the longest day of the summer. Komsomol Lake in Minsk had been opened up to the general public. We lived in a little house on Engels Street, and on that day everyone in the house looked excitedly up at the sky, where aeroplanes flew high overhead. Very quickly realisation struck that we were under attack, and panic broke out among the population of the city. I went with my mother and grandmother to the house of my father's relatives on Kollektornaya Street, but when we arrived no-one was there. A stranger took us to Chelyuskintsev Park where we spent the night in the woods with numerous other civilians and soldiers. I had an aunt and great aunt in Moscow and so, in the morning, along with other evacuees, we took the highway east. The locals in one village stopped us and asked where we were heading.  They informed us that the Germans had deployed troops a short distance ahead, and advised us to 'stay and wait it out'. We stayed with these kind people for a few days, after which my grandmother decided that she wanted to return to Minsk. She was a brave, strong willed, enterprising woman and she wanted to see if it would be possible to save our home.

The BSSR (Byelorussian Soviet Socialist Republic) government had shamefully fled from the city of Minsk hastily on 24 June 1941. They had done this without announcing their departure. So, whilst Minsk was in flames following heavy bombing raids, the city had no government for four days. One building that stands out in my memory, was the five-storey apartment block number 3 Maxim Bogdanovich Street. It had been built in 1936 and was called 'The 3rd House of the Soviets'. There was an air raid shelter under the building. It was used by the tenants, who were mostly women and children. The German bombs had demolished the building and blocked the entrance to the shelter. Following the destruction that rained down from the skies onto Minsk, the building came to be seen as a symbol of hell.

**Georgiy Birger 1938**

It still astounds me when I think about my father's cousin, Kolya Gurvich. He succeeded in driving his car through the streets of a burning and bombed-out Minsk, in order to rescue all eight of his relatives. They told me later that he had also made the journey to Engels Street, in the hope of rescuing us, but we had not been there.

Despite the bombing in Minsk, our grandmother returned to us, bearing the news that our home had been spared. The memories of our return journey to Minsk are still clear, as if frozen in my mind. The Minsk-Moscow highway was jammed with columns of German tanks. I remember the tank drivers laughing and pointing at my mother who, at that time, was a strikingly beautiful thirty-two-year-old.

During those first months in occupied Minsk there was no work and no food stamps. People would carry any food that they could lay their hands on back to their houses, filling sacks with whatever goods they could find. I remember how my grandmother once managed to bring home some sugar syrup. Eventually, in Autumn 1941, agencies of the occupation authorities were formed, and women were now forced to work in the canteens as dishwashers, cleaners and waitresses.

It's a surprising aspect of memory, that I can't often recall what I did three days ago, but yet that some episodes of my childhood in German occupied Minsk remain fresh and bright. I can clearly remember when Sofia Samoilovna, a neighbour, and a friend of my grandmother, went into the Jewish ghetto. My mother and grandmother had asked her to stay with us, and we had been making preparations, but then it became too late to hide her.

On Engels Street, there was a German military base. One day a German soldier forced his way into our house. At the head of the bed in the main bedroom, there hung a picture of my father in profile. It had been taken by his friend who was a professional photographer. The soldier pointed at the portrait and declared: 'Jude!' [German: Jew]. He then left, taking no further action. Later that autumn our house was raided by the police. There were four or five of them. The head of this motley crew was a former prisoner, who had known my father, having been imprisoned with him in the same cell following his arrest. They returned to the house on a number of occasions over a period of several days. During this time, my grandmother hid in the attic.

In October 1941, punitive measures which had been introduced by the Nazis resulted in public executions. Close to Engels Street, in front of the yeast producing factory, they hanged three people: a man, a girl and a teenage boy. Footage of the punishment was later used at the Nuremberg Trials, recorded in history books and used in the documentary film, 'Ordinary Fascism' by Mikhail Rom. Photographs were also displayed in the Minsk Museum of the Great Patriotic War. Following the war, it became known that those executed, had been members of an underground anti-fascist group. They assisted Soviet Red Army commanders, to escape from the hospital prison camp, by providing them with documents, civilian clothes and places to hide in the city. The man, Kiril Trus and the teenager, Volodia Shcherbatsevich who were hanged were recognised and posthumously awarded the Order of the Patriotic War. However, the girl fell into the 'unknown' category because she was Jewish. Her name was Masha Bruskina [see glossary] and she was seventeen years old. As a seven-year-old child, I witnessed the executions of these patriots. I was taken to watch by a young man who had come to town, bringing food from his village which he hoped to exchange. I can clearly remember how the Germans stood watching the executions from the windows of the 'Minsk Kristall' Factory. The building is still there.

Because my father was Jewish, my mother was constantly afraid that I might get taken into the ghetto. She tried to hide me with friends, but I stubbornly kept returning to my old street. Once, my mother sent me to stay with a friend of hers who lived in the village of Lysovschina. The winter of 1942 was harsh, with severe frosts, and I remember returning to Minsk one ice-cold night, underneath a bright moon and starry sky.

Back home in Minsk, the children would tease me and call me 'Jew', and my grandmother would chase them around the yard. I was friends with some older boys, and I remember sitting with them on the curb of Engels Street. Once when a German boy passed by, my friend Sergey said loudly: 'I would have killed that German by now!' The German boy responded in Russian, replying: 'Really, so you want to kill me?' Provocations such as these were commonplace. Teenagers made tools from scraps of board, hollow metal dowels, nails, rope and match heads. When the stretched-out rope and nail hit the wall, it made a loud bang, which sounded like a gunshot. Some of the older boys would risk trying this out by 'shooting' at passing Germans. The Germans, thinking the shots were real, would chase after them. Fortunately, the boys were able to out-run them and hide in the ruins of buildings with which we children were familiar. Once, as I was walking down the street, I passed two female German soldiers with sheepdogs. One dog suddenly slipped off its leash and bit my leg badly. I wept from the severe pain.

There was very little food. Although my mother always tried her best to feed the family, it was very difficult. In order for me to be eligible for bread on my ration card, my mother was forced to enrol me in school. However, I did not go to classes for fear of being identified as Jewish and being sent to the ghetto. On one occasion, I accompanied my mother to Baranovichi, where she had a friend who could provide us with supplies. Her friend was a beautiful, young Polish woman called Wanda. Wanda's parents were prosperous villagers who lived on a farm. They were later shot and killed by partisans. We returned to Minsk that night by passenger train. All the civilian passengers crowded into the vestibules, as the Germans soldiers occupied the carriages. Suddenly the train braked sharply and all the lights went out. Everybody hurriedly lay down on the floor and partisans opened fire on the carriages. There was a collective sigh of relief when the lights came back on and we slowly began moving again.

One evening, shortly afterwards, I saw my mother and grandmother looking anxiously out of the window. Two German soldiers in SS uniforms appeared to be intently scrutinising the house. 'I think that they are looking for us', said my mother, in trepidation. Sure enough, she was right. The soldiers knocked on the door, and then surprised us by delivering food parcels that had been sent to us from Wanda.

My mother secured a job in the bakery on Myasnikov Street, where bread ration cards were issued to the populace of the city. Nearby was the Town Council, where many Polish people worked. The head of the trade department was Boleslaw Bierut, who later became the leader of the Polish People's Republic. My mother regularly withdrew permits from the council that could be used for travelling to Minsk. She would pass them to her friends who were associated with the partisans. Later, following the liberation of Minsk from German occupation, our neighbours denounced us. They pointed at us and accused us of being Jews. The KGB arrested my mother but evidence of her having obtained the permits during the occupation, assisted her case. She was not put on trial and was released from prison.

We lived in a wooden house and, in order to avoid the worst of the bombing, my mother arranged with friends to rent a room at a farm located about two to three kilometres outside the city. My grandmother and brother spent their days at the farm and in the evenings after she finished work, my mother returned there to sleep. I was supposed to live outside of the city as well, but I didn't want to be in the country. I always preferred the city, because that was where my friends were.

It is important that I try to preserve the random memories that come to me from that time. For example, I remember seeing processions of Soviet military prisoners of war, and recall a time when my grandmother saw two elderly, and hungry-looking prisoners passing by, she tried to help them by giving them something to eat. I also remember seeing blood on the pavement in front of the Palace of the Pioneers on Engels Street. People would pass by and say: 'This is where the Nazis shot and killed a young man.'

One episode in particular stands out. It occurred whilst I was in the company of several older boys. We were walking along the street by the barbed wire fence of Number 1 Minsk City Power Plant, on the bank of the River Svisloch, opposite Gorky Park. The policemen on guard duty at the power plant, came out and arrested all of us. We were taken to the police station and locked in a small dark room. After being held for what felt like a long time, we were finally escorted to the German commander-in-chief. We were shoved into a brightly lit room, where we were confronted by the sight of the commander holding a belt in his hand. Looking back, I realise that he was probably just in the process of getting dressed, but I was terrified that we were about to get a beating and I started to cry. The German commander stared at each one of us in turn, very slowly, and then spoke to the policeman who had escorted us. On his orders, we were marched into another office with different policemen and made to stand in a row. The one in charge, said: 'Now you are going to be hanged!' Then, without further explanation, they released us. The police may have been trying to frighten us but, in reality, the horror was unquestionable.

In the city, Soviet citizens were hanged from trees in the Central Square at the entrance to the Dynamo Stadium. At home, everybody was discussing the pogroms taking place in the ghetto. A number of my mother's friends, with Jewish husbands, had had their children seized, during raids. Dr. Vladysik, one of Minsk's most well-respected doctors, lost his mind after the

Nazis had taken away his Jewish wife and twelve-year-old son. We heard that the boy had cried out in terror to his father, shouting: 'Daddy, daddy, help me, do something!'

Despite this, daily life in the city continued. Three cinemas were still operational for the civilian population. The Minsk City Theatre (Theatre J. Kupala) was situated on Engels Street, (renamed Teaterstrasse by the Nazis). On one occasion, the underground resistance had discovered that Reichskomissar Wilhelm Kube (the senior official of the occupying government) would be in the audience, during a particular matinee performance. The resistance planted and detonated a mine in the theatre. It backfired, however, and civilians were killed instead of Germans. I actually saw how the stalls of the cinema had been destroyed. The Nazis staged a funeral for those who had been killed and the coffins of the victims of the Kupala Theatre, were exhibited in the Lenin Library on Krasnoarmeyskaya Street.

In June 2007, the newspaper *Trud*, published a photograph showing a bird's eye view of Engels Street taken in 1944. Our house, with its woodshed at the back, can clearly be seen. You can also make out the house at Number 27, where Reichskomissar Wilhelm Kube lived with his family. This was the same house in which he was later assassinated in September 1943. On one occasion, I had walked past Kube's house with my friends, and saw that his children were playing outside in the garden. They looked at us over the fence and smiled at us. They were just children, the same as we were.

When the news of Kube's assassination reached the inhabitants of our house at Number 41 Engels Street, we were all paralysed with fear. Everybody knew that reprisals would follow, and we feared the taking of hostages. Everyone hid. Some people refused to leave their houses and would fearfully observe the German police from behind their curtains. We would watch them, walking with Alsatian dogs, up and down the desolate and deserted Engels Street.

Anxiety and fear were constantly present in our home. My mother became like someone haunted. She told my grandmother how the Gestapo had taken away a German friend of hers, who had turned out to be Jewish. She hid me from her friends, and tried to prevent me going out into our yard or onto the street where the neighbours would see me. To keep me off the street, my mother would take me to the Red Church. Earlier, In the autumn of 1941, my brother and I had been baptized in the Marinsky Cathedral in Liberty Square. I was accepted into a group of boys for whom the priests held classes and he prepared us for confirmation. I became a member of the Red Church, and I remember going to confession. Sometimes I dressed in a white outfit and participated in the service at the Marinsky Cathedral.

The winters were cold with frost and snow, and the streets of the city were covered with ice. The children would go out sledding and skating and I would use my mother's old 'snow maiden' skates, which I attached to my own shoes. Sometimes we would cling to the hooks that hung from wires over the sides of German trucks. I recall that, a German truck driver once spotted us clinging to the side of his vehicle, so he turned the wheel sharply and we all fell off, ending up in a deep snowdrift.

When 1943 came, after the defeat of the Germans at Stalingrad, they would wear mourning armbands on their uniforms. Our planes now bombed the city often. First, I heard the explosion of bombs and then sirens. I remember the night when Minsk was bombed and we were hiding in a bomb shelter, the entrance of which was from the City Hospital Number 3. Throughout the night, the earth trembled from bomb explosions, and the bright, white light of flares illuminated the sky. Spotlights crisscrossed the heavens and highlighted the planes firing strings of tracing bullets. Anti-aircraft guns returned fire and all around there were falling splinters from shells. After a night of bombing, the outer wall and left wing of the hospital-building collapsed and blocked Marx Avenue with bricks and rubble. The Germans carried away the many dead and wounded on stretchers.

After the Liberation, there was much talk about the Smolenski SD [see SD in glossary]. It was located on Ostrovsky Street and had been established in the city after the liberation and following the fascist occupation of Smolensk. It was allegedly run by former police officers and members of the Red Army. With their slavish desire to serve the fascists, this Nazi organisation spread fear among the civilian population of the city.

Earlier during the occupation, a policeman appeared at our house. I recall that my mother had given him all of our few remaining valuables and he went away. In the Spring of 1944 however, he came back. This time he was wearing a German officer's uniform and was accompanied by other officers in similar uniforms. They kicked us out of our house. We found accommodation, again on Engels Street, in a single room in an apartment block. It seems that the former policeman had now become a Nazi officer. He had a conversation with my mother which made her cry and she made me leave the room. Following the officer's visit, I no longer lived with my mother. I was sent to the City of Vilna and cared for by a woman named Maria. Now I didn't know where my mother and father were, or whether I would ever see them again. All I can remember is riding in the back of a German truck on the way to Vilna and being shot at by partisans along the way.

My life in Vilna with Maria began. She was a kind and sincere woman. She lived in a small one storey house with an attic, located on a narrow, quiet street lined with small private houses. The area was in the central part of the city close to the green metal bridge that spanned the River Vilija. In the long distant pre-revolutionary years, Maria's mother had been a friend of my grandmother. However, I think that she must have forgotten about this, as Maria's mother was old, sick and confined to her bed in the attic. She was hostile towards me and would have preferred to kick me out of the house. I tried not to go into her room and kept well out of her sight. Maria rented out the rooms in her house to tenants. They were all Polish nationals and included the family of Mr. Baranowski. I remember them well: he had a beautiful grown up daughter and a son called Jerzy. Renting another room, was a tall, handsome man, who we later discovered, was a commander who led an underground group of resistance fighters that was affiliated with the Polish National Army.

When the German heavy artillery intensified its bombardment, the residents of the house sensed that the Red Army was close. Small groups of men now began to gather in the courtyard of the house. They were soldiers of the National Army resistance who started to prepare for defence of the area. Some of them would disappear on missions, while others would sit playing cards, waiting for an order. One day, a rumour began to circulate that German soldiers with Alsatian dogs were coming to search all the houses on the street. The soldiers of the National Army resistance ordered everyone to hide in the basement and be ready to do battle with whatever weapons came to hand. To our joy, no one came to our house.

The resistance fighters, headed by the commander, eventually left and never returned. Shortly afterwards we were frequently targeted by an unknown sniper. From a two-story brick building close to our house, someone regularly fired shots in our direction. The occupants of our house avoided venturing into the courtyard, afraid of becoming victims of this unidentified gunman. The random shootings continued for a few days and then grenade explosions could also be heard. During this time, the residents and their children would gather in the apartment of Mr. Baranowski. They sat quietly, reciting prayers, hoping that the tightly closed and shuttered windows would protect them from stray bullets and shrapnel grenades. Then, as suddenly as it had begun, the shooting and grenade eruptions ceased, and silence descended. Out of the blue, two Soviet tanks rattled into the yard, driven by uniformed soldiers. They climbed down, looked around and stood for a while, observing us gathered in the yard. One brave tenant addressed them hopefully: 'Help us' he said, 'we are being shot at, from that brick building!'. The Soviet tank drivers replied: 'You have a lot of your own men here, deal with it yourself!'

A few days later, the German garrison attacked the city centre. The Soviet defence line held the River Vilija and the railroad tracks. German planes flew overhead and dropped containers of supplies by parachute. We watched our planes fly in and attack aircrafts with twin engine bombers. The day after the shelling and bombing of the city centre, Vilna was liberated from Nazi occupation. On the day after the cessation of fighting in the city, one of the tenants came to see Maria. He was wearing the uniform of a Polish officer and wore a *konfederatka* [Polish: National Cap] on his head. He said goodbye to everyone in the house, and left for Warsaw. He was not alone; we saw whole columns of Polish partisans leaving. Some were dressed in Polish uniforms, some in German uniforms and others in civilian clothes. Some partisans even wore German helmets on their heads.

Peace gradually descended on the city, but civilians from the suburbs could not go into the city centre. The Nazis had blown up the metal bridge over the River Vilija. Wooden boards had been laid over the remains of it, and the pavements were exposed to flooding. Dreadful sights were still in evidence, people would cross back and forth across the boards, passing by the decaying corpse of a man wedged in the structure of the destroyed bridge.

Refugees who had been hiding in the surrounding villages and farms, began returning. Officers of the Red Army came to the house and we could hear them laughing and singing in the courtyard. One time, a truck with several soldiers in the back appeared in the courtyard. They invited some of the children from our house, including me, to climb up into the back of the truck. The soldiers sang a very famous war song called 'The girl was following the fighter to his position.' The melody still remains with me to this day.

Maria's mother finally died and after the funeral I stopped hiding. Starvation had affected us all, and I would accompany Maria out into the country, to visit the villages where she had friends who were farmers. She took needlework commissions in exchange for whatever food she could procure. One sunny summer's day, we passed by an enormous field sown with peas. Later at the home of a villager, I was told a story of a dogfight, and how the battling aeroplanes had crashed into that field of peas.

I think that I was something of a burden to the kindly Maria. She was unable to exercise much control over me, and I spent most of my time with my older friends. I continued to spend much of my time with older children and teenagers. Out in the streets we came across old guns and bullets that had been discarded, including an old German carbine rifle. We would often fire these guns behind the barns, although the adults tried to forbid us from playing these dangerous games. To discourage us, they told us horror stories about children who came across guns and shells and tried to take them apart. They would be blown up, badly injured or killed in the process. Undeterred however, we travelled to the former military warehouses at the foot of the hills on the outskirts of town, to shoot the weapons that we found, riding there in a trolley cart on the narrow-gauge railway.

On 22 July 1944 I turned ten years old. The two elderly and very cultured ladies who lived on the ground floor of Maria's house, discovered that it was my birthday and gave me a present. I can still recall now how grateful I felt. I received two bars of chocolate, two postcards showing European cities and a box made out of colourful shining paper. It was handmade without glue, and, when I opened it, there was another box within it, that had a tiny elephant inside it. I kept it as a special memento of my time in Vilna. It reminded me of the kind, unselfish and compassionate people there and Maria in particular.

My father later told me, that, on the very same day, a fierce battle had taken place near to Lviv. During the battle, my father, Nikolai Yefimovich Birger, had commanded a rifle platoon and had been seriously wounded by an explosive bullet. He lay on the ground bleeding, unable to be rescued due to heavy enemy fire. He later recalled that he thought about me as he lay there and regretted that he may be about to die on my birthday.

It was around that time that I also sustained an injury, and my right arm was in a sling. The adults' dire warnings had finally come to pass: a boy of my own age, had shot me at close range. I had been with a group of boys in an outbuilding, shooting German cartridges at photographs of Molotov and Ribbentrop, ripped from pre-war Polish and German magazines. After the accident, my arm and face were bleeding and I was covered in grains of gunpowder. I was taken to the military hospital, but the doctors there refused to help, and I had to go to the

City Hospital. The city was without electricity at that time, because the Germans had blown up the power plant. I was operated on under general anaesthetic, but illuminated by kerosene lamps. Three years later, after an x-ray in school, I became the classroom hero because of the metal shards from a German bullet still visibly lodged in my shoulder.

On a cloudy autumn day, a Soviet soldier arrived at Maria's house. He was wearing an overcoat and a forage cap. His left arm was bandaged and hung in a sling across his chest. He asked the tenants: 'Does a boy from Minsk live here?' I was duly summoned to Maria's room, where I found the soldier standing in the middle of the room waiting for me. He said: 'Boy, do who know who I am?' Of course, I knew immediately and said: 'Yes, you're my father!' He told me the story of his return to Vilna. He had been a prisoner of war. When the bombing of Minsk began, the prisoners assumed it was a drill. Nevertheless, they were released from their cells and made to march along the Mogilev highway. My father walked with great difficulty as he had badly blistered feet, but his fellow inmates helped him along. In the column were many Polish officers, but also many sick and wounded, who had difficulty keeping up. The security officers shot the weakest ones. At night, the column of prisoners stopped at the village of Cherven. In the morning, upon waking, they discovered that the guards and the dogs had disappeared. The prisoners divided themselves up into two groups, one returned to Minsk, and the other travelled to the east. My father, was part of the crowd of refugees, and with an unbelievable stroke of luck, met up with my grandfather during one of the rest periods. Together, they were able to reach my uncle Max. From there, my father made his way to Vilna, and then to me.

One evening, my father and I left the city of Vilna on a freight train, jumping from one car to another. A young officer and his girlfriend, also bound for Minsk, helped us carry our modest belongings. After twenty-four hours of travelling on different carriages, we finally returned to our hometown. In December 1944, my father enrolled me in the second class of school number 42, located in the former governor's house on Svoboda Square. This building is now the College of Music.

Time puts everything into perspective. In 1964, I went back to Vilna, for the first time since the war. I immediately returned to the street, and the house in which I had lived with Maria. To my deep regret, everyone who had lived with me in that house during the war, had gone. They had all relocated to permanent homes in Poland.

**The Birger Family**

**Parents Nikolai Yefimovich and Sofya Josephovna**

**Georgiy on the right, 1956**

# There Were Thirty-Six of Us - Only One Remained
## Polina Dobkina

**Polina Dobkina in a photograph taken in Minsk**

**just after the war had ended - around 1945-46**

How sunny and bright it was on that Sunday, 22 June 1941. All of the children in our courtyard went to the opening of Komsomol Lake. However, the terrible word *war* was echoing from loud speakers, and erased our carefree life. Turmoil began: everyone was running about. The radio constantly transmitted the same words, 'Take cover in the air-raid shelters and listen to the radio.' Boys were rushing to the military registration and enlistment offices, but they were not operating. In some places, people were already looting stores. On the second day, the entire centre of the city was in flames. Some said that the fire was not so much a result of the bombardment, but had been caused by arsonist saboteurs. Disguised in Red Army uniforms, enemy scouts were setting houses on fire. Our whole family descended into the air-raid shelter in the big house on the corner of Respublikanskaya and Myasnikov Streets. My grandmother and my father's brother lived there with his family. We could not leave the city. Grandmother was old and sick, and twins had just been born in my uncle's family. Father said that the Germans would be crushed and that they would not get to Minsk. He added that the Germans were civilized people with a long cultural tradition. In the First World War, he had been captured by the Germans, and he spoke German very well. Therefore, father considered that we should not leave.

In our courtyard, there were many fellows of enlistment age and they decided to find a functioning military registration and enlistment office, wherever it might be. They thought that there would be one in Borisov, and so my brother Grisha, Izya Belsky, Lyonya Kantorovich, and the Idelson and Tsikhanovsky brothers set off there on foot. I went with them. It was 68 kilometres to Borisov, so we decided to stop at night and rest. It was dark and horrible, and I started to cry. Grisha put me on his bicycle and took me home to Minsk. He went back to catch up with the others and they made it…

During the night of 23 June, our house burnt down as a result of the bombing. We stood and watched everything burning – the home nest, the school and the stores. We went to Belomorskaya Street, where mother's brother lived. However, when the Nazis entered the city, we discovered that they were not those Germans that father had talked about. He was among the first to get caught in the round-up on 26 August. We never saw him again.

During the pogrom on 7 November, some of us hid in a *malina*. It was a shed with double walls. Through a crack, I could see Lithuanians entering the house. Mother's cousin said, 'Yasha is gone, and there is no point for me to live.' With these words she moved the logs to one side and left the hideout with her son, and I went after her. They took us out into the street, which was already full of Jews, and I lost my relatives in the crowd. By chance, I ended up near Grisha Kaplan. He was trying to prove to a German that he worked at the felt factory, and he was showing him some kind of pass. 'And this is my sister,' he said, pointing at me. They let us go to Tankovaya Street, where I found my mother with my little brother Vovochka. That was how I got lucky during the first pogrom. But now the ghetto was reduced. That is when we began to live with my father's sister at Krymskaya Street.

My father, his brothers, and brother-in-law were craftsman at moulding plaster. To this day many buildings in Minsk bear the fruits of their labours. They decorated the Central Committee building, the Officers' House, the Academy of Sciences, and the Opera Theatre. Uncle Symon, who worked, took us on as his dependents. But nothing could keep us from the daily robberies. Policemen often came into the house to grab something; sometimes they even brought their girls along and let them choose anything they wanted. Sometimes, one of them felt the need for blood, and then they would select a house and shoot everyone in it, one by one. In reality, the pogroms in the ghetto didn't actually stop for a single day.

By that time, we had nothing left to exchange for food. That was when I met girls from our courtyard who took me with them to the Russian area, where they went to trade things. We crawled through the wire and went to Chervensky Tract. We would get back home by joining a work column returning to the ghetto from Sverdlov Street.

**Shifra Bederson - Polina's mother at the age of 18. This is the only photograph remaining to Polina of her mother. Shifra was killed in the ghetto at the age of 41, together with her husband Sholom As and her younger brother Vova (Velvur). An older brother Grisha survived and went with his family to the USA in 1995. He died in 2002.**

Once I was attacked by a group of our own Jewish boys, who were younger than I was. They were after anything that I was carrying. They said that if I didn't give everything to them, they would tell a policeman that I had crawled through the wire. At the time, I was carrying a leather sole which, with luck, I was hoping to trade for a loaf of bread. Even that sole had belonged to someone else. I refused to give it up, so the boys followed me and, just at that moment, a policeman came towards us. The boys ran up to him and calmly betrayed me. There was just one likely punishment for me: being shot on the spot! I just stood there, not raising my head. The policeman said, 'Let's go!' When we were passing the prison, I became weak at the knees. However, the policeman just led me straight past the prison and then suddenly asked, 'Where's Grisha?' It was only now that I raised my head and looked at him. I now recognised the same fellow who used to come to our courtyard to play soccer with my brothers. I said that I thought that Grisha was in the army. 'Where would you like me to take you?' he asked.

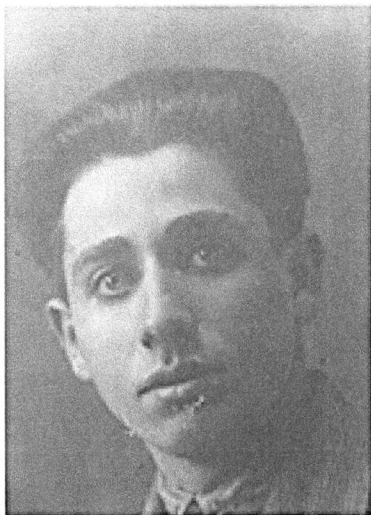

Gershel Bederson- Polina's uncle. He was killed in the ghetto along with two of his six brothers.

Zoya and Tolik Bederson, Polina's cousins. They were the children of her uncle Gershel Bederson (left). They were also killed in the ghetto.

Once I had removed my patches [see *lata* in glossary], I was able to walk around the Russian area for a long time, before finally rejoining the column. I was able to walk around in the Russian zone relatively easily, since I did not look like a Jewess. The main thing was to avoid meeting acquaintances. However, inside the ghetto, there was danger at every step. Aunt Asya was a very smart woman. She was my youngest and as a result my favourite aunt. She often said that I should leave the ghetto. I would reply, 'Let's go together!' But she said that it wouldn't work out with the children, and she would not leave without them.

However, we were always uneasy in the ghetto; you could feel the next pogrom coming. When we were outside with a workforce, we could tell that a pogrom had begun when the Germans driving the columns didn't let the work column return into the Ghetto. This was not because the Germans were such kind people, but because they were saving their work force. This happened in the summer of 1942. I remembered that, the day before, I had brought some blueberries home from work for mother and Vovochka. At work, they still gave us some food such as soup or oatmeal, and I tried not to eat it, but would bring it home instead. Now, when they finally led our column back into the ghetto, I saw a terrible scene: the blueberries which I had brought were scattered, and the pan with starchy jelly was overturned. All of my relatives – 36 people – perished that day, including Aunt Asya and her children.

Now I started to live at Collectornaya Street, near to my friend Bebochka Lapidus. We were good friends. In the spring of 1943 a fellow called Fain, who studied in school together with my brother, came up to me and said, 'Get into Nikolai's truck. You must.' I asked him, 'What about Beba?' He told me to get Beba and climb into the truck. This vehicle was the one that Nikolai drove for a brigade that collected pieces of iron from the ashes of burnt-out houses. However, I didn't get into the truck on that occasion and, that day, Nikolai left for the partisan detachment.

A while after, when our column was going into the ghetto, David Mazo was walking beside me and he asked, 'Why are you hanging your head, Polya?' I told him that I was thinking how I hadn't got into that truck, which had gone to the forest. He suggested, 'Tonight come to house 81.' So I went, and I saw the strange sight of a number of people carrying bundles of firewood. Why did they need firewood in summer? It turned out that inside the bundles were sawn-off guns! I now discovered that, in old houses at the outskirts of the city, and in other places where prisoners from the ghetto were sent to work, they sometimes came across weapons. They collected them together in a certain place, and then somehow got them into the ghetto. I later discovered that groups were being formed for partisan detachments. It was in that very house, that I myself became part of a group which would leave the ghetto to face its fate. Not right away, of course, but we did get out. A Russian messenger led us to the First Minsk Partisan Brigade. The messenger's name was Polina, like mine. We were all armed. When we left, early in the morning, I was carrying a sawn-off rifle in an overcoat specially altered for it.

We went in single file towards Kolodishchy, trying not to attract attention to ourselves. By the evening we reached the village of Grebenka and waited there for another messenger. Eventually a fellow arrived and introduced himself to us as Lyosha Lozovoi. He asked if everyone had weapons. It turned out that we all did. 'Then everyone follow me.' We discovered later that Lyosha 'stole' us from the First Minsk Brigade.

Commander Kostya Sidyakin's *Avenger* detachment was independent. It had already fought well and crossed the front lines. The commander was decorated with an Order of Lenin for military deeds during the first year of the war. Now the detachment was returning from Moscow. We were very lucky to become part of such a detachment. In the village of Tovarskiye, we were met by Commissar Nikolai Dyagilev. He was a cheerful and smart person. He registered the reinforcements from the ghetto like this:

'What is your patronymic, girl?'

'Sholomovna.'

'Put down Semyonovna,' he said to the chief of staff.

And that is how I became Polina Semyonovna.

Sidyakin and Dyagilev were waiting for a messenger from Minsk, but she didn't come. This gave me an idea. When we left the ghetto, I had told Beba that I was going to the forest and I promised to come back for her; so now I had a good reason to go back to the city to free my friend. I told the commander about my plan to return to Minsk and to come back with a group from the ghetto which would reinforce the detachment. Sidyakin and Dyagilev talked things over with each other, and they made a decision: I was to set off on my first partisan assignment.

It was a hard campaign. I had an escort while we were still in the partisan zone, but then I continued on my own. Although the road was quiet, when I entered the city, I saw policemen and Germans in SS uniforms near Surazhsky bazaar. It was terrible. Pinning the hated yellow patches to myself, I entered the ghetto and headed straight to Beba Lapidus.

In just a few days, early in the morning, I set out for the detachment, together with Beba, David Mazo and those who had been equipped by the ghetto underground for leaving. There were several groups going along the road. Suddenly we saw that the road ahead was closed with a barrier, and that documents were being checked. Going forward was impossible, going back as well. Luckily, David Mazo noticed that a little bridge crossed the road, and there was a pipe under the bridge. We managed to dive under it and went along the stream one at a time, trying not to be noticed. Even though there were about twenty people, the whole group got through that way. Lyoshka Lozovoi met us at the appointed place and took us to Tovarskiye. They had been very anxious about us. At that time, we did not know that Kube [see glossary] had been assassinated on the very day we left Minsk, 22 September 1943. Had we delayed our departure for a few hours, it would have been all over for us.

We built a winter camp for the detachment in the forest near Lipniki. Muscovite Komsomol athletes formed the backbone of our detachment. They were strong and good-natured, and there was never any display of anti-Semitism. Moreover, they tried to make us forget about the ghetto and its horrors. We were immediately included in military activities. *Avenger* was a sabotage detachment, and mostly worked on the disruption of enemy communications. I became the platoon medical instructor. Once, I even went to the railway to blow up a train and, in the winter, I participated in operations to disrupt communications…

We set off on a raid in a new area of military activity. At the village of Yalovka we crossed a gravelled road. We knew that it might be mined, so we went in single file. I was always rushing forward. Fear ruled me from behind; I was afraid that I would be shot in the back. While I was jumping from one tussock to another, I was grabbed by Dolmatovsky's big iron hand. 'Where are you flying off to? There could be mines there.' With these words he threw me behind him; but it just happened that Dolmatovsky was the one who stepped on a mine. The explosion rang out and the detachment stopped. We put a tourniquet on Dolmatovsky, gave him something to drink, and put him on a horse. He could not walk; his leg was badly wounded. Now Commissar Dyagilev gave me a pistol and a horse without a saddle. He said, 'Return to the village with Dolmatovsky. There, a messenger will tell you how to get to Rokossovsky Brigade; they have a doctor.'

We only got to the brigade because Dolmatovsky knew the road well and didn't lose consciousness. As for me, that night was very fearful. At the brigade, it was as if they were expecting us. The explosion was so powerful that they had apparently heard it there. Everything was prepared for the operation. On the next day, we learned about the heroic death of Marat Kazei. He was only fourteen years old. The young scout had been caught in an ambush, but when the Nazis surrounded him to take him alive, he set a grenade off over himself...

They amputated Dolmatovsky's leg because gangrene had set in. Members of the detachment tried to support me all the time. One would bring an apple, another nuts from the forest. Even when I was at my post with a rifle, Olya from Vileika always brought me something tasty. Like a child, they tried to cheer me up and make me smile. I had forgotten how to smile in the ghetto.

They sent Dolmatovsky to Moscow on the very first plane, and offered to send me with him as the accompanying person, but I refused. The plane had barely taken off when a blockade of our zone began. Our detachment was driven into the swamp, but we burst through the ring of fire...

I finally met with Beba Lapidus in a liberated Minsk.

**Polina in 1949 with her husband Michael Dobkin (d.2016 USA) with their first son Semen. Michael had served in the Soviet army throughout all five years of the war.**

**Polina (second right) on her 90th birthday in the USA, 2017. On the far right is grand-daughter Dina, (daughter of her younger son Arkadiy). To her right is daughter Sofia, and further to her right is another grand-daughter Yvgeniya (daughter of elder son Semen).**

**Editor's note:** After the war, in January 1948, Polina married Mikhail Dobkin in Minsk. They had three children Semen, Sofia and Arkadiy. She and her husband lived for many years in Minsk, before emigrating in 1992 to the USA. Mikhail died in 2016.

In total, 36 of Polina's close relatives were killed during the war. Polina was the only member of her family who escaped the Minsk Ghetto.

# Leafing Through the Pages of Memory
## Maya Guryevich

**Maya Guryevich**

My name is Maya Tevelevna Abramovich. My name at birth was Maya Gurevich, and I was born in Minsk in 1937. I belonged to a large happy family. My father, Tevel Gurevich Kalmovich, was born in 1898 and my mother, Emma (Etka) Moiseevna, in 1903. I had one older brother Chaim who was born in 1925. We lived on Internatsionalnaya Street. My maternal grandmother, Rubina Minya, and my Aunt Raya, lived nearby. My Uncle Lazar Gurevich Kalmanovich, lived just across the street, with my cousins, Roman, who was eight, and Maya, who was twelve.

The war began on the 21 June 1941. During the first days of the bombing, the whole city of Minsk experienced widespread panic, and it quickly became apparent, that we needed to escape. The trains had already stopped running, and, as we were a large family, my father and my uncle began to search for other methods of transport, that would enable us all to leave. But it was too late; the Germans had already entered the city.

We realised immediately, that the Jews in Minsk were of particular interest to the Germans, as they targeted us directly. They raided our houses and would shoot at us on the streets. In September 1941, all Byelorussian Jews were evicted from their homes and forced into a ghetto. The Jewish ghetto was surrounded by barbed wire, and had a gate and watch tower. An edict was issued to all families that said:

'All Jews to take what they need, leave their homes, and re-settle in the ghetto'.

The members of my immediate family, which included, my uncle, cousins and grandmother, were all forced to move into one room. We were required to wear a yellow patch stitched to our clothing, along with a square of fabric that displayed the number of the house in which we lived. Food was scarce, and I can remember always being hungry.

My father, mother and uncle, had employment in work details outside the ghetto and, each morning, would be led away to work at the railway station. When any of the adults left the house, I was in a state of constant fear until they returned.

The ghetto was frequently besieged by violent and unexpected pogroms. They arose in quick succession; the first was on 7 November 1941, the next on the 20 November. On the 25 November, my father and uncle were directed to a different work detail. My uncle later told us what happened that day. The work detail was taken to Shornaya Street where the Germans issued a command: 'Communists step forward.' My father was a communist. It's hard to imagine what could have been going through his mind at that moment. Maybe his ability to think quickly and logically had become paralysed, and he was blindly obeying orders, because, along with several others, he stepped forward. They were all immediately shot. My uncle Lazar fell to his knees and collapsed, horrified at what had happened right before his eyes. The people next to him had to pick him up and drag him along to work. My uncle miraculously survived, but I had lost my father.

**My father**

**Tevel Gurevich Kalmovich**

The largest massacre began on the 28 July 1942, and it raged for four days. People on work details left the ghetto as usual, and did not return for the whole of that time, having been tipped off to stay away. During that time, the Nazis looted and ransacked their homes. The house in which we lived had a large attic, and we children hid there with our grandmother. The soldiers raiding our house threw a grenade into the basement, but we remained silent upstairs and they didn't search the attic. When the work details finally returned four days later, we heard them screaming and crying. We crept out of our *malina* in the attic, and discovered a dreadful sight: everything was covered in blood, and there were dead bodies lying everywhere. The building was in ruins. Following this dreadful experience my grandmother became terribly ill. She never recovered and died in the arms of her daughter, Raya. Now uncle Lazar took care of us all.

My brother Chaim worked determinedly to source contacts who could help us escape from the ghetto and join the partisans. He was given a tip-off about an introduction. However, on his way to the meeting, it all went terribly wrong. He was confronted by a drunken policeman, who for no particular reason, shot and killed him. In that appalling manner, I lost my precious only brother.

On 2 March 1943, there was yet another great blood bath, killing innumerable people. The attacks were becoming so frequent that we lost count. Shortly after this, trucks began arriving in the ghetto. Every few days the trucks would appear, loading up with women and children. No one ever returned. It didn't take long for people to understand why. Finally, on 21 September 1943, the day came when my mother and I were also loaded into a truck. It was packed with women and children, and we truly thought the time had come to say goodbye, both to life, and to one another. We drove through deserted city streets and then out into the countryside. When the truck turned into a particularly narrow country road, one of the women suggested that my mother should jump out. Of course, it was a terrifying suggestion, but the very idea of it, gave us some hope. We knew that doing nothing would end in certain death. We also understood the risks. Landing badly when jumping from a moving vehicle was extremely dangerous, but there was a chance that we could be lucky. My mother, along with a few other women willing to take the risk, were lowered over the side, and we children jumped out after them. God helped us that day, and we all survived.

From the road, we made our way to the forest. Once we were in the woods, we wandered aimlessly, not knowing where to go or what to do next. We decided it was better to hide as best we could during the day, and walk at night, feeding ourselves only on what the forest had to offer us. Eventually, we came across a hut, but we hid in the bushes, too frightened to draw near. However, my mother was a brave woman, and eventually she found the courage to approach. The house was home to a forester and his family; they were kind people. They took us in, fed us, and allowed us to sleep there overnight. We left again in the morning, but they pointed us in the direction of a village called Smilovichi.

**Maya with her mother -**

**Etka Movshe-Ayzikovna**

Back out on the road, we came across a man in a German uniform. We had been through so much, that some of the women in our group felt desperate. They begged him for help, and the children began to cry. Although he barely understood what we were saying to him, he nevertheless, pointed out which way we should go to avoid capture by the Germans. It happened like that sometimes, we would unexpectedly come across good people, with whose help, we were given the opportunity to hide, eat and stay alive, up until July 1944, and the liberation of Byelorussia.

After the liberation, my mother and I returned to Minsk. The city was completely ruined, but our house had miraculously survived. My aunt Raya returned from the Partisan Division Number 106, and Uncle Lazar and cousins Maya and Roman from the Kotovsky Partisan Division. All the members of my extended family, which had been so large, were killed in the ghetto. They lie in a common grave called Yama [see glossary].

I now live in Israel with my children. My cousin Maya lives there too, but her brother Roman still lives in Minsk. I always want there to be peace in the world, and I don't want anyone to experience what I have experienced. People, you must look after peace. Losing it, is the heaviest price to pay in the world.

**Maya Gurevich and her daughter**

**Jerusalem, 2005**

# Everyone Looked After the Orphan
## Roman Gurevich

**Roman Gurevich**

Before the start of the Great Patriotic War, I lived with my family in Minsk. My father's name was Lazar and my mother was Hannah. I had an elder sister Maya, and a younger brother Semochka who was born in 1940.

Our family home was on Sverdlova Street, opposite the football stadium "Dynamo". Our house burned down on the 25th or 26th of June 1941. When the war broke out, both my sister and I were away from home at summer camp, but my parents brought us home on the 2nd or 3rd July to live with my paternal grandparents on Shornaya Street.

My family did not evacuate Minsk when the war began, because my father had faith in Stalin. The possibility that Minsk could become occupied did not enter his head. After the formation of the Jewish ghetto, we were forced to move again, but we lived in the same street, on the opposite side, which was inside the ghetto. Our house was near to a school and it is still there today.

The first pogrom that I remember took place on 7 November 1941. We were lucky that it didn't affect our area. The winter of 1941 was extremely cold. My father took a job at a meat processing plant near to Chervenskiy Market. He would bring home leftovers from food that was used to feed pigs. This helped us to survive. In February 1942, my father escaped from the ghetto in order to look for the partisans. My mother, sister, brother and grandparents stayed behind.

The mayhem of a pogrom on the 2 March 1942 brought about our family's first loss. We were all hiding together in the *malina,* when my little brother Semochka began screaming, most likely from hunger and cold. My grandmother picked him up, left the *malina* and sat down on a stool in front of it, with him on her lap, in order to conceal its entrance. The Nazis raided the house and took her, Semochka and my grandfather. They shot them all. Then, on 22 April 1942, the Lithuanian and Ukrainian Police carried out a pogrom in which my mother was killed. So my sister and I were now left alone to look after ourselves.

My sister Maya was about fourteen at this time, and to save us from starving to death, she took a job at the Myasnikov Factory which made automobile parts. I spent my days begging on the streets near to the station, where the trains arrived from Germany. I would pick up cigarette butts, bits of bread and anything I could find. We somehow managed to survive in this way until the summer of 1942. We had still received no news of our father, and my sister decided that we would not be able to survive much longer. She believed that we should try to escape from the ghetto and join the partisans.

We had heard rumours that there were partisans in the area of Pleshchenitsy and Logoysk, so we headed in that direction. However, on the way there, in Radoshkovichi, we came across a police contingent. My sister and I decided that we would have a better chance if we separated, and so we hurried off in different directions. We did not see each other again until February 1943.

Unable to reach the partisans alone, I found myself in the Krasnaya Molodechno District Ghetto at the beginning of September 1942 [see glossary]. Although technically, I wasn't an orphan, I owe my survival to the kindness and customs of the Jews there. They had a special law, believing that care of an orphan should be shared by everyone. So on the first day one family would feed me, the next day another, and so on as the weeks progressed. I stayed there until the beginning of February 1943.

In late February, I suddenly had word from my father, who was a partisan messenger, and I was sent from the Molodechno Ghetto to live with Adam Martsinkevich in Brizhdovo Village. My sister Maya was already living there, so I was at last re-united with her. Later partisans took my sister to the Voronianski Partisan Brigade, while I remained with Martsinkevich. I lived there until May 1943, when the Germans began to burn down all the villages in the partisan zone.

Despite this, I managed to stay with the partisan unit until December 1943, when a decision was made to evacuate me to Moscow, as I was very ill and suffering from severe malnutrition. After three months of waiting, I was eventually taken there at the end of March 1944, and I remained there until the liberation of Minsk in July. After the liberation, I returned to my hometown and, finally, in September 1944, I once again found my father and sister.

I recently discovered that, of 4,000 people who lived in the Krasnaya Molodechno Ghetto, where I was cared for as an orphan, only three people survived: me, another who lives in the US, and the third who now lives in Israel.

# I Was Left on my Own
## Felix Gerbovitskiy

**Felix Gerbovitskiy**

My name is Felix Gerbovitsiy and I was born in Minsk on 16 March 1931. After the war, I was in an orphanage where age was assigned according to appearance. I looked young for my age, and, consequently the birth date in my passport is given as 1933.

Early on the morning of 22 June 1941, at around seven o'clock, a sudden deafening explosion of bombs woke the whole family. I had recently moved with my mother, and sister Nelly, into a new apartment on the corner of Soviet and Komsomol Streets, in the centre of town. There was no time for us to take anything with us, barely enough time for us to throw on some clothes, and for my mother to seize her winter coat, before we ran out into the street.

I remember seeing the German planes flying overhead, and hearing the firing of anti-aircraft guns. Trying to flee from the explosions, we headed toward the Svisloch River, where crowds of people had congregated. We were spared that day, but when we returned home that evening, we found it, like many others, completely in ruins.

We headed out towards the house of Aunt Anna, my mother's sister, who lived on Tolstoy Street near Oktyabrsky shopping district. It was my mother's mistake that we had not left Minsk to the East prior to the bombing, but she was distracted because of all that was going on around. We had lost my father in December 1937. He had been shot by the NKVD [see glossary] after having been wrongly identified as an 'enemy of the people.' I feel certain that, if my father had still been alive, we would not have delayed our departure from the city. As it was, we stayed with my Aunt Anna. On the arrival of the Nazis, we were all forced to move into the ghetto.

On the morning of 28 of June 1941, I watched the advancing regiments of Nazis. They arrived in armoured personnel carriers and tanks, driving into town at high speeds. They would jump in and out of their vehicles, chatting and laughing cheerfully. They had taken off their helmets and rolled up their sleeves in the hot June weather. There were very few adults around; it was mostly just us children watching them arrive. We initially kept a cautious distance, but, being children, we were naturally inquisitive and eventually drew closer. The Germans gesticulated to us laughing. They filled the engines of their cars with oil from brightly coloured canisters, and then they sat down to eat. They ate bread, canned food and hot drinks from thermos flasks. All of us were hungry and undernourished, and we looked on in anguish as they ate, then they moved on, leaving just empty food cans behind.

Shortly after their arrival, the Nazis began persecuting Soviet prisoners of war. I have clear memories of this, and it was difficult to witness. Many of the prisoners were injured and exhausted, with rags tied around their feet. Sometimes as they walked along the street in work details, neighbourhood women would try to reach out and give them food. On one particular occasion, a woman tried to help by throwing pieces of bread and bacon into the crowd of workers. The starving prisoners tried to seize the food but inadvertently created a mass of chaos and confusion. The guards began firing into the air, and onlookers fled in panic. The guards took two prisoners out of the line and around the side of a warehouse near to the railway. Shots rang out. The guards then ran back to supervise the column with the prisoners.

A few weeks later, we began to see walls and gates plastered with posters emblazoned with swastikas. On them was written an order for all Jews to immediately sew insignia onto the back, and chest of all their clothes. This was the so-called *lata or laty* of yellow material that marked us out as being a Jew. I remember my mother sewing the badges onto our clothes. She hated the yellow patches and was embarrassed by them, doing her best to hide them with her hands whenever she could. Simultaneously, all the Jewish people were commanded to leave their homes and move into a dedicated area, assigned as the ghetto. I remember that the orders were signed by Wachmeister Richter, who was Commander of the ghetto, and Hauptwachmeister Gattenbach, the Chief of the German Police.

The district of the Minsk Ghetto was extensive, many streets, bordered by Nemiga Street, Obuvnaya Street and the Jewish cemetery. Barbed wire and watchtowers surrounded it. Initially, the ghetto was policed by officers from the local force and Ukrainians, who had been issued with guns and white armbands. They diligently performed their duties, which was to monitor the implementation of the Nazis orders. Later, they were supplied with special uniforms – black tunics with grey collars and sleeve cuffs. From all parts of the city and the surrounding area, tens of thousands of Jews began flocking to this enclosed space. The vast majority were elderly people, women and children. Together with my mother, Nelly and Aunt Anna, we moved into an apartment on Ratomskaya Street. Aunt Anna's son remained in the Russian quarter, as his father, my uncle Mikhail, was not a Jew. Within the ghetto, anyone disobeying the orders of the Germans, and appearing outside their homes without the *lata* on their clothing, risked violation and instant execution.

**Felix and his wife Galina Gerbovitsky**

In the early days of the war, before we became prisoners of the ghetto, my mother, tried to prevent us from starving by scouring the city for food. In those days, her actions were brave and defiant, undertaken with a spirit of anarchy, when the risks were not so life threatening. In warehouses, flour could sometimes be found, along with cereals, molasses and even sugar. Now times were very different, no food was available. We had few clothes and were extremely cold. People traded what little they could, and my mother was able to extend our supplies for a short while, by exchanging my coat for some flour.

The Judenrat [see glossary] was on Ratomskaya Street near to Yubileynaya Square and located close by, was the Employment Agency on Ratomskaya and Tankovaya Streets. The Germans had appointed a man named Epstein, to run the agency. A Polish national, he was regarded as a Nazi henchman, willing to supply the Germans with a steady stream of young and healthy workers from the ghetto. He was assisted by Weinstein, another fascist flunky, and they ensured that all able-bodied citizens were grouped together in work details. Accompanied by the German police, work units would leave on labouring jobs each morning, and be escorted back at night. My mother had been selected for one of the work units. I knew that the Germans systematically murdered people daily, during working hours. I was constantly terrified this fate would befall her, and that she might not return home.

The first pogrom was on 7 November 1941. The Nazis referred to it as an *aktion* [see glossary] It was the first of many raids that brought about the systematic destruction of the ghetto. We managed to survive by hiding in a secret room, a *malina*. This was a primitive hiding place with a double wall made out of plywood, and an entrance under the bed. Others were not so fortunate. Not everyone had somewhere to hide, and many Jews were murdered in the subsequent pogroms. On many nights, the Germans would bring specially adapted trucks into the ghetto. They were gas vans, designed to be mobile gas chambers on wheels. People would be loaded inside and killed by carbon monoxide fumes piped into the enclosed space. At nighttime we could barely sleep, listening in dread for the approaching hum of the gas van engines, waiting for death at any moment. In this way, the winter passed.

**Felix with his wife Galina on holiday in Dombay, Russia**

In the early spring of 1942, the day finally arrived when my mother did not come home from work. We assumed that she must have been killed. Many forced workers were failing to return to their homes, as the Nazis were killing them in ever increasing numbers. Inside the ghetto, they were using the police to drive people from their homes during raids. Despite the frequent pogroms, Nelly, Aunt Anna and I managed to stay alive. During one raid, we hid in the *malina,* which had been made by my mother before she disappeared, but an old man and a young woman and her small child were discovered hiding in the loft, and dragged out of the house. We expected to be exposed at any moment. However, on this particular occasion, the Germans believed a thorough search had been conducted, and we were not discovered.

With my mother gone, we no longer had access to even the meagre amount of food that she used to bring home from work. Mostly, this was unfit for human consumption and had consisted of rotten frozen potatoes, bread crusts, peelings and debris from the Germans kitchens and garbage pits. Me and Nelly faced the prospect of starvation, and I was reduced to eating the grass that grew in the yard. Every day, the prisoners of the ghetto were entitled to receive a single portion of soup from a distribution point on Respublikanskaya Street. Barely enough to sustain life, it was vile, prepared from rotten oats, unsuitable even for horses, but it would be always devoured there and then.

In the autumn of 1941, Jews deported from cities across Germany had begun to arrive in the Minsk Ghetto. Although they had come from different places, we referred to them all, as the 'Hamburg' Jews. They appeared to have led affluent lives, with more money and personal belongings than the rest of us. They were held and housed apart from the local Jews.

Nevertheless, they were eventually removed from the ghetto, and driven in trucks to their death. When this occurred, they would divest themselves of the possessions they would no longer need, by throwing them over the barbed wire fence. I once managed to acquire twenty-five marks and some extra items of clothing in this way.

In May 1942, I fell ill with typhoid fever and was taken to a hospital on Sukhaya Street. It barely met the description of an infirmary, as no food, medicine or medical supplies were available. While I was there, a rumour began to circulate that the Nazis planned to kill all of the patients. When I heard this, I decided to break out. Despite having a fever, I climbed out of a window and down a drainpipe from the second floor into the yard. I hid in the bushes until it was dark, and then crawled under the fence. I'm sure that escaping in this way saved my life.

**My sister Nelly and my grand-daughter Olya**

July 1942 brought a terrible pogrom that lasted for four days. The ghetto was under continuous attack, and it was impossible to find escape routes under the wire fences. Nelly and I managed to hide in a storage warehouse on the corner of Ratomskaya and Opanskogo Streets. It was mostly used for the storage of rotting food and waste from the sugar industry. Somehow,

Nelly and I were not spotted by the two Jewish guards who kept watch over it. When the massacre was finally over, we crept out of the warehouse. We had escaped death once again, but still felt that our days were numbered. We had a sense of impending doom. The total destruction of the ghetto was drawing closer and the numbers of its inhabitants was decreasing daily.

**My grand-children, Olya and Serezha**

The winter of 1942 – 1943 was particularly harsh. Nelly would regularly risk her life by sneaking through the fence, to go into the Russian area. With her blond hair, Nelly didn't look particularly Jewish, and was desperate enough to take this chance if it meant the possibility of returning with some bread or potatoes. However, on a cold day in February, I waited in vain for my sister to return to the ghetto. She never came back. I was left alone.

In late February, I made up my mind. I would not survive any longer on my own, and I needed to try and escape. I finally managed to slip under the wire and into the Russian district. A few days later, I found myself in a suburb of Minsk known as 'The Exhibition.' It was here, near to the station, that I met a young man to whom I owe my life. He was sixteen, and worked as a railroad conductor. When a train bound for the town of Molodechno came into the station, he risked his own life by giving me a key, and letting me hide in one of the boxcars. In this way, I travelled first to Molodechno and then to Lida. Once there, good people sheltered me. I also believe that being an impeccable Russian speaker helped my escape. I spoke without an accent, and pretended to be a native of the Bryansk region. I had traded with refugees from this region before my escape from Minsk, and acquired some clothes from them, which made me seem like an authentic migrant from the east.

In Lida, I stayed at the home of Stanislav Ivanovich Vershilo doing chores, until the autumn of 1945. My hosts probably guessed that I was a Jew, but we didn't talk about it. I'm infinitely grateful to them for taking me in and saving me. They had risked their own lives, since hiding Jews was punishable by death. After the war, I returned to Minsk. Looking back, I know that I did everything I possibly could to survive, but, despite that, I'm still surprised, even now, that I managed to stay alive.

N.B.  No further reference is made in Felix's story to the fate of his sister Nelly or Aunt Anna. They are presumed to have died in the ghetto. However, a photograph from after the war, shows an adult Nelly. This indicated that she did indeed survive the ghetto, and was, sometime later, reunited with her brother. Subsequent investigations by the translating/editing researchers of this book revealed that Nelly did survive and in 2018 was still alive.

# How I Took People Out of the Ghetto
## Lev Kravets

**Lev Kravets**

I was born on the 11 May 1930 (although according to my passport it was 15 August 1930), in Minsk. My father, Abram, Leibovich Kravets worked as a cook in a military training school, and my mother, Lisa Israelevna Kravets was a nurse in a clinic. My older sister Hanna was born in 1928, and my two younger siblings, Maya born in 1932, and Boris in 1936, completed the family. Before the war, I went to school number 21 and finished third grade.

When the war started, we were living in Minsk at 37, Furmanova Street. In the early days of the war, our house caught fire during the bombing. My father was not in the city at the time, but my mother managed to grab the important documents that we needed, and we ran with them to hide in a bomb shelter. When the shelter was also bombed, everyone panicked and started scrambling in different directions. We went with my mother towards Logoysk. By the time we were halfway there, it was evening, but it was as light as day because the fires of Minsk burned so brightly.

When we arrived in Logoysk, a Jewish family sheltered us, but, a few days later, Logoysk was captured by the Germans, who ordered all the Jews to assemble in the main square. My mother gathered us together and, after a brief consultation, we decided that we should go back to Minsk. The roads were choked full of people and no one paid us any attention. We managed to get back without any incident.

Arriving in Minsk, we learned that the German commander had issued an order for all of the Jews to move from their homes and live in the area of Yubileynaya Square and the surrounding streets. It is possible that all the names of the streets on the order had been listed, I just don't remember. This designated area was called the ghetto.

In the ghetto, we lived on Flaksa Street, at my aunt's house. After a while, my father found us. His plan was to get me out of the city to join the partisans. It was expected that I would go first and that I would later come back and help get the rest of the family out of the ghetto. My mother didn't want to let me go. On the day after we were supposed to leave, my father was captured in a roundup. We never found out where he was taken.

After we lost my father, we moved to Dimitrova Street and we lived there until the massacre on the 2 March 1942. In that terrible pogrom, I lost my older sister Hanna and my younger brother Boris. My sister Maya and I would certainly also have died if we had been in the ghetto, but at that time we were in the Russian area. To get there you had to crawl underneath the barbed wire, and we would come back the same way, making certain that the police didn't detect you. During the pogrom, my mother was also away from home. She had been sent under supervision in a work detail to clean the tracks and to load the wagons. I often went with her to work but hadn't gone that day.

After the pogrom, we moved house again, this time to Tankovaya Street, which was close to the Yubileynaya Square area. Twenty to twenty-five people lived there, crowded together in one room. We slept close to the floor on a bunk. We had no choice about sharing our space with men, women or children. Everyone was packed in together, so there was no privacy.

We lived there until October 1942. During this time, there had been more pogroms, but somehow, we managed to escape without them directly affecting us. Then, one day, my mother didn't come home from work. Rumours began to spread that her work detail (labour force) had been loaded into trucks and taken to Trostenets [see glossary]. At the time, we had no idea what Trostenets was. It was only later that we found out.

When my sister and I were left without a mother, we wondered how on earth we would be able to survive on our own. There was nothing to eat, and people were dying of hunger. The likelihood and hope that somebody would be able to help us, were not enough to keep us alive. I took my sister with me and we ran away from the ghetto. We travelled from village to village begging, and it saved us from starvation. When the winter came, we had to return to the ghetto because there was nowhere to spend the freezing cold nights. I would leave my sister there and go in search of food. I went to the railway station where German soldiers, departing for the front, would sometimes give me dishes and cooking pots to wash, and these contained scraps of food. I would take anything I could find home for my sister. These meagre amounts were our salvation.

It was at the railway station that I first heard stories of partisans living in the woods. They would come to Minsk in secret, in order to set explosives, so that when a train passed through the railway station, it was derailed into a ditch. The station then became impassable, and daily raids were carried out.

During one of these raids, I was at the station, but miraculously survived. That day there were boxcars full of German troops going to the front. I was suddenly snatched up and thrown into a boxcar by a soldier. He put his hand over my mouth, and his finger to his own lips to indicate that I should be quiet. I blinked my eyes to show him that I understood. It was then that I heard a policeman coming towards the boxcar. It was the *Bahnpolizei* [German: Railway Police].

They regularly made searches, looking for *kleine junge* [German: young boys] like me. The German who was holding me, then showed me a way by which I could creep around the side and crawl under the boxcar, remaining out of sight. After the policeman left, the German gave me a loaf of bread and some jam, along with a warning about the direction the policeman had taken. So, I was saved that day, and I still have no idea if my saviour knew whether I was a Jew or not. I later heard of several similar incidents occurring at the same station.

During another raid, I was chased by a policeman and his dog. I ran a long way, with him shooting at me. Eventually, I sensed that the dog was catching me up, and I fell over. The dog put his paw on me and waited for his owner to arrive. I lay completely still, and the policeman, probably thinking that I was dead, withdrew the dog. After he had gone, I stayed where I was and continued to lay motionless on the ground until nightfall. After that, I decided to never go back to the railway station again. I went back to the ghetto to visit my sister, and then went off in search of the partisans.

**Lev Kravets, 1950**

When I left the ghetto this time, I was stopped by two police officers. One of them took off my hat and patted my curly hair. He said, 'You're a Jew, come with us!' On the way to the Police Station, one of them held me by the collar of my shirt so that I couldn't run away. I thought that this time it was all over for me, that I was about to die, but once again I was saved. We met a German officer. Seeing that I was being pulled along by the collar, he asked the policemen: 'Where are you taking this boy?' They replied: *'Das ist ein Jude'* [German: this is a Jew]. Then, as I understood it, the officer told them that he would take me himself. Near to the square, he pointed to a one storey house and said: *'Das ist eine Kirche'* [German: this is a church]. He then told me to go and ask for the pastor by name. (Unfortunately, after so many years, I have forgotten what it was). He left me there, but no-one answered my knock and the door of the house was locked. After a little while, I returned to the ghetto. I am so thankful that, among the occupiers, there were some good, honest people, who saved my life.

After that, I left the ghetto with a friend, and together we managed to navigate our way to several villages in our quest to find the partisans. No one showed us directly where the partisans were, but we were given enough information on which direction to take, and where we might be likely to find them.

One day in the village of Ptich, we were stopped by two riders who had red ribbons on their hats. We were scared, thinking that they may be policemen, but they turned out to be partisans. They began to question us, asking who we were, where we were going, whether we had any weapons and so on. The partisans then presented us with a proposition. They asked us to return to the ghetto, to a specific address indicated by them. Once there, we were to collect a group of men in secret and lead them to the village of Skirmantovo. If we succeeded, we would be accepted into the squad. We decided to accept the mission.

Once back in the ghetto, I found the address I had been given and collected four people. I then went to get my sister. Together, we all made the forty-kilometre journey safely to the village of Skirmantovo. The partisan who had sent me to Minsk on this initial assignment was Lenya Openheim, who was from the Parkhomenko Division. (This was the division that I joined, and my service in this unit is historically documented).

Following that preliminary success, I was given a further task. I was to return to the ghetto and was required to find another specific person and return with him and his colleagues. Again, I was keen to prove myself. Arriving in the ghetto, I found the man, However, he was not ready to leave, and told me that we would have to wait a few days. During this time, I was hidden away in a secret underground cellar, called a *malina* [see glossary] and wasn't allowed to come out. Apparently, he was afraid that I wouldn't be prepared to wait and may try to leave without him, so he made certain that I was given food and drink during that time. Eventually, after a few days underground, people began to appear. Altogether there was now a group of about thirty people. This increased number, meant changing our plans if we were to ensure that everyone successfully managed to leave the ghetto. After talking it through, we decided to leave at night, in the direction of Kalvariyskoye cemetery. We had chosen a spot at the end of Tankovaya Street, where it was easier to pull apart the barbed wire, and then climb over it.

I made it through the wire first and approached the railway line, which we had to cross, waiting there until all the others had come out of the ghetto. It was pitch black and silent all around us. As I walked right up to the railway line, preparing to cross over it, something unexpected happened. When I touched the wire in front of it, to step over it, I received an electric shock and cried out loudly! Panic broke out. I had even scared myself. However, I then came to my senses and began to shout: 'Don't be afraid, it's not soldiers!'

Everything calmed down, but we realised that we had to return to the ghetto and go back to the *malina*. We needed to plan more carefully how we could leave successfully, in such a large group. We couldn't really delay much longer, but the size of our group and the problems at the station, meant we had to change our route. We knew that every morning, the Germans rounded up people from the ghetto for work details. They were arranged in columns, accompanied by guards. Our new plan entailed joining a column that was going to work at the railroad station, and this was how we eventually left the ghetto.

It was very risky. We had discussed the route in advance and had decided that we would be travelling through the villages of Medvezhino to Staroye, and then to Skirmantovo. Two to three people from the group, would walk together at some distance apart from the rest. I would walk about thirty to forty metres in front of the first group and in the case of danger, I was to stop or signal by waving a hand. Passing near a brick factory, I witnessed just such an attack. From the gates, the guards from the brick factory began shooting. It was fortunate for us that nearby there was a field planted with tall rye. We all rushed into the rye field to hide, and then ran through it, towards the nearby forest where we all assembled. We discovered that some of our original party had been killed, but people joining from the work detail, had swelled our numbers from 30, to a much larger crowd. We continued making our way through the forest, skirting the village of Medvezhino, and avoided taking the road. With some difficulty, we finally reached the village of Skirmantovo where the partisans were waiting for us.

At the time of our escape, in July 1942, there was a universal partisan blockade. The roads were blocked by German troops. Because of this we couldn't reach the squad, and from Skirmantovo we had to re-route, crossing the Neman Canal, where several people drowned. With the partisans helping us, we travelled through the woods and the swamps. Shooting could be heard all around and people fled in all directions. We stopped in one of the marshes, looking for cover, because the Germans were close by. We heard their dogs barking. We lay down in the swamp between the grassy hummocks, keeping still and quiet for five days. They were long, hot days and we were extremely thirsty. I shovelled the moss aside, pushing my hands underneath it trying to find a little water. I drank it, despite the fact that there were mosquitos everywhere. When the gunfire finally died down and the dogs stopped barking, partisans on horseback began to appear and we all felt enormous relief. Now, we gradually began to leave the marshes. Back on the road we saw dead horses and cows. Those of us who had knives scrubbed off the maggots, cut off pieces of meat, and put them on sticks to cook on the fire. It's strange that no-one had a stomach-ache from the meat. We also ate blueberries that were plentiful and growing all around.

I was brought initially to the Parkhomenko squad, which was for adult males who were able to fight. As I was still a child, I left shortly afterwards for the Zorin Brigade Number 106, which was for families, women and children [see glossary]. It was there that I met up again with my sister, and found other people, including Misha Stoler, the carpenter. That is how I began my partisan life. I built dugouts and helped prepare for winter. I lived with the Tumina family, and also the partisan, Lenya Oppenheim who had given me my first assignment. His wife was the sister of Tumina Leni Opengeyma. My adventures saving people from the ghetto were over. Not everyone from our group had made it through. Some had died along the way and others had joined up with other partisan units.

I stayed with the partisans until the liberation of Minsk. After that, there was a census of all the children, and I was sent first to an assessment center in Minsk, and then to Orphanage number 12 for boys (my sister was sent to number 11 for girls) The war was over for us.

None of my relatives from before the war were left alive. My grandfather Zendel Israel, lived in the village of Berezino, but, during the war, the Nazis killed all of his family. When I grew older I went to Berezino, thinking that I may find at least some trace of my family, but different people lived there and they didn't know my grandfather. I stopped searching for any more family members. I believe, however, that I had an uncle living in America, but it was forbidden to talk about it at that time. Among those who left the ghetto, I remember the Tumina family, who I lived with in the forest. Their son Garik and his sister Genia, who was born after the war, settled in Los Angeles.

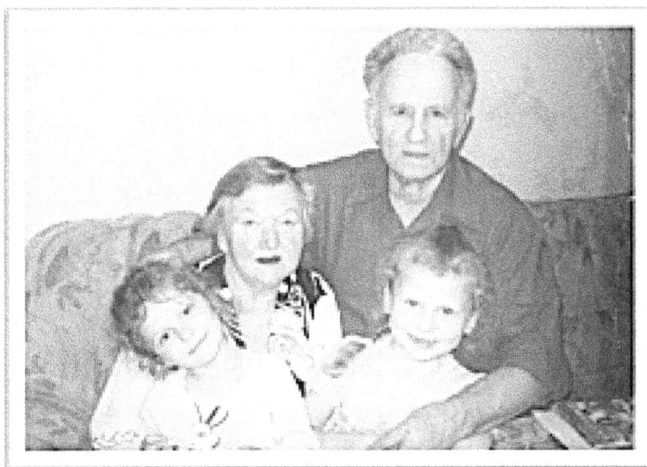

**Lev Kravets with his wife (Raisa Ivanovna) and his granddaughters**

# How We Joined the Partisans
## Yakov Kravchinskiy

**Yakov Kravchinskiy**

Following the declaration of war and the imminent attack by Germany, my father was called up and stationed in the fortified area of Minsk. My mother was pregnant at the time, and I had a broken arm, so we stood little chance of being able to leave the city. Shortly after the occupation, the order came for all the Jews to relocate to the ghetto. My mother wanted us to stay where we were, but we were forced to make the move by "good people".

We went initially to a former kindergarten on Sanitarny Lane. Several families, sometimes with six or more people, lived in every room. Sheets suspended on ropes divided up the living quarters, and we slept on the old desks. It was constantly noisy, with people crying, shouting and swearing. Arguments would frequently break out regarding the allocation of chores, such as who should mend shoes, who should fetch water, and so on. It was a difficult environment in which to live. Rumours frequently circulated that we would be liberated by the Red Army, but it did not happen. Our meagre food supplies quickly ran out, and we had to try to exchange the few possessions we owned, for food.

My father was captured by the Germans while on his way to join his battalion. Miraculously, he managed to escape and came back to Minsk to look for us. On his return, he became a member of the ghetto's underground organisation. He would often disappear for several days at a time, and then come home, bringing us food.

By late summer, the pogroms had begun. The Germans would round men up during the raids, and those they took away, never came back. The residents of the kindergarten built a *malina,* or hiding place. Along the side of the building was a large pile of firewood, and the *malina* was built underneath it. From the street, the entrance was concealed by logs, so it couldn't be seen. The entrance was through a hole in the toilet. During times when people were hiding, a waste bucket was fitted into the hole, pulled up and down through the hole by a rope.

After that first pogrom in November 1941, we moved from the kindergarten to a different location. Although, we regularly changed our place of residence within the ghetto, each apartment had a *malina* in which we could hide. One of our apartments doubled as a safe house. It was often used by smugglers, and well-known leaders of the underground (such as Misha Gebelev, Hersh Smolar and Nahum Feldman) when it was forbidden to move around the ghetto after curfew.

Life became increasingly difficult. In addition to the yellow patch, which we were forced to wear stitched to our clothing, we were also issued with white material patches bearing our street name and house number. These too, had to be visible at all times. Everyone was required to be registered. If anyone was found not registered, found hiding, or simply brought to the attention of the police, then all the inhabitants of the house would be executed. This would be in order to discourage others from violating the Nazi's commands.

Following the pogrom in March 1942, we relocated again, and settled in Novo-Myasnitskaya Street. It was a two-storey house. On the second floor was a hidden door leading to the attic. This allowed access to an exit over the rooftops, in case of danger. Just one other family and two young people lived there.

In April 1942, my father left to join the partisans. The Gestapo was beginning to close in around the underground, and nearly all of the leaders had left. In order to try and survive without his help, my mother would approach the fence surrounding the ghetto to try and barter for goods. She managed to gain the trust of the 'Hamburg' Jews [see glossary]. They lived separately from the other ghetto residents and were reputedly more affluent. My mother would negotiate with them for their belongings. This was a risky business: the 'Hamburg' Jews were cautious and reticent to take anyone at their word, and they took extra time to check all transactions in the finest detail. The German command obviously forbade such interactions. Raids regularly occurred when people gathered for such exchanges. It was not unusual for people to be shot at, and have dogs set upon them.

My brother was born on the 25 June 1941. Following my father's departure, my mother would find someone with whom to leave the baby, and she and I would try and find a route into the 'Russian' area. I would collect the stubs of half-smoked cigarettes and try to barter them for bread. It was around this time, that Vitka Feldman and Natasha (Tatyana Matskevich), dispatchers from the partisans, came to the ghetto. Vikta was taken immediately, and they arrested his entire family. We thought that our time had come, and that we would all be killed, but Vitka did not betray us.

We lived on Novo-Myasnitskaya Street until the pogrom on 28 July 1942. The labourers in work details left the ghetto as usual, but once they had departed the violence began. There were cries and mayhem in the streets. All of the children who lived in our house rushed upstairs into the attic shouting "Pogrom" My mother grabbed hold of me and followed them. In the attic, underneath the sloping roof, disguised as part of the wall, was the *malina*. No more than sixty centimetres high, we could only lie down inside it. Once we were all crammed inside together, the terrifying sound of hobnail boots thundering up the stairs indicated that a mob was already upon us. It had been unbelievably close, we had only just managed to shut the door, before the police were already kicking their boots against the walls, shouting out and yelling, in their brutal search for Jews.

It was July and terribly hot. The heat was like a red-hot iron over our metal roof, but we couldn't make a sound. We waited until it was dark, and then crept out. The house had been turned upside down, everything broken and trampled underfoot. The work details didn't return to the ghetto and we went back to the malina. The next morning at first light the police reappeared, shouting: 'All Jude, get out!' Once again, there was the sound of everything being smashed up, accompanied this time by shooting. We stayed hidden. We discovered afterwards that anyone who had come out of hiding, or resisted arrest, had been shot.

**My parents - Dora Tevelevna and Yosifovich Kravchinskiy**

We stayed in the *malina* for four days. At the close of the fourth day, the work details eventually returned to the ghetto, and those of us who had managed to stay alive, finally emerged from our hiding places. Screaming and crying could be heard everywhere. Outside in the streets "doubles" appeared (two people who had to carry dead bodies). The bodies were buried in the old Jewish cemetery, in a common grave. This time, our family had not managed to escape heartbreak and tragedy. My baby brother, who had been with us in the *malina*, died during that pogrom.

Following the pogrom, we sought a new place to live. My mother met with Rosa Lipsky, with whom my father had worked in the underground, and she helped us to find shelter. We settled on a place to live on a side street, near to Tankovaya Street and the site of 'Yama' [see glossary]. With us were two young men (one who had come from Rostov but got stuck in Minsk, and another one from a shtetl near Minsk) and another two families. Together we settled in that wooden house. After the massacre we had virtually nothing, only what we could carry, but survival was imperative. We were able to barter for potatoes or flour, and every now and then, for the various handmade things that were made in secret unbeknown to the Germans. These included carbide lamps, lighters, parts for stoves and various other essentials, such as soap and salt. We were sometimes able to trade saccharin, stamps, tobacco and other supplies, with which we could earn between two to three marks. Those caught trading, were always shot, but, due to the threat of starvation, the risk taking, smuggling and bartering for food continued.

My mother managed to obtain potatoes, at first on credit, but later she was able to pay for them. She scraped, grated and baked teygratz [Yiddish dialect: potato pie]. In the evenings, when the workers returned from the work detail, my mother would sell them the potato teygratz. When they had all been sold, the money was used to purchase more potatoes, and the whole process was repeated. As a result of this laborious process of scraping and grating of up to ten kilos of potatoes, we were able to afford our own portion of teygratz, which kept us from starvation. In the summer it was possible to pick nettles in order to make soup from them, but in the winter, we relied on the potato.

A barely edible lunch of soup was distributed daily to the workers at the ghetto gates.

In late summer and early autumn, the *Judenrat* began to organise the distribution of bread for children and the elderly. Many people would always turn out for this meagre offering. Later, when those turning up for bread became more numerous, the Germans and the police began round ups of everyone who came for bread handouts. They would swoop in, grab them, and take them away in vans. They would later be shot.

By the spring of 1943, rumours of the ghetto's demise, abounded. Dispatchers from the partisans would again begin to appear, to recruit young professional people, such as doctors. My mother knew many of the dispatchers, who promised her that they would come back and take us too, but these promises were not fulfilled.

**Yakov and Bella Kravchinskiy**

The round ups continued, including the removal of patients from the hospital. I had been admitted to hospital with typhoid fever, but I was discharged one day before a raid took place. If I had lingered there an extra day, I would have been taken. Everyone was expecting a pogrom to take place on 1 May. We knew that the Germans often timed them to coincide with the dates of Jewish, or Soviet holidays. It became clear that we had to make an attempt to leave before this occurred. My mother decided that we should make our escape as part of a group. We would travel with the group only as far as necessary and then we would try to reach the partisans any way possible. That evening, when a group with a guide, was attempting an escape, we were also at the wire, and ready to go. Once we were beyond the wire, we rolled into the ditch that surrounded the fence. As we peered up over the edge of the ditch, we saw a man in a leather coat walking along the street, and we all froze. When we had checked the street, the coast had been clear! Now we were dumfounded and it seemed that all was lost. We could not just go back the way we had come, and crawl back under the wire. However, miraculously, when we looked again, the man had suddenly disappeared, and we were able to press on.

We tried to follow a group that had left before us, but were unable to catch up with them. There were about a dozen in our group. We had escaped the ghetto safely, but now there was confusion over who was leading the group, and in which direction we should be heading. Some wanted to go back and wait for a leader, whilst others were undecided. My mother stood firm and said: 'Whoever wants to, can go back to the ghetto, I'm going to look for the partisans. I'd rather be shot on the run, than be buried in a pit.' With those words, she led us on our way. My mother was familiar with the names of villages she had heard from stories about the partisans. She also knew that it was necessary to cross the railway and to pass the brick factory on the outskirts of Minsk, in the village of Medvezhina, a favourite place for police ambushes.

When we had successfully passed the brick factory, without incident, we came to the railway. We had to wait a little while, for two trains to pass each other at the same time. We then quickly crossed the tracks to the other side. The heavily guarded railway station was the most dangerous place on the way to forest. But we were lucky; the crossing trains had assured our protection.

On entering the forest, all the others hid in the trees, while my mother and I approached a hut to ask for directions. We asked the way to Koidanovo and other villages mentioned by the leaders. The woman in the hut directed us towards village Staroye Selo. She told us: 'Go without worry there is a partisan zone there.' Staroye Selo had been the village in which my father had joined the partisans and here, we were indeed met by a partisan patrol. We were all interrogated and sent to the Zorin family squad [see Zorin's Brigade in the glossary]. It was nightfall by the time we reached the squad. News reached us that my father was definitely alive and that we had missed each other by barely an hour! He had come in search of us, hoping to hear news of what may have befallen us.

The next morning, my father was informed of our arrival. Following our reunion, he took us to the Stalin's Budenny Squad. After our incredible deliverance from the ghetto, our lives as partisans began from 2nd May 1943 until the squad was integrated into the Ponomarenko Partisan Brigade which was dissolved on 4th of August 1944. We went back to liberated Minsk, but my father stayed for another two months by order of the Soviet Army to search for Nazi spies in the forest as he knew the area very well.

**The Kravchinskiy Family**

# The Whole Village Deserves the Award of 'Righteous Among the Nations'
## Maya Krapina

**Maya Krapina**

Orphanage documents issued after the liberation of Byelorussia recorded my date of birth as 1937, but I was actually born in December 1935. Despite being such a small child, I nevertheless remember many pre-war events and, of course, the war itself. I remember as though through the eyes of an adult. I once suggested to my brother Joseph, who is six years older than me, that he should record his own memories of the war, and he replied, 'I have read your books and I think that you remember it better than I do.'

Before the war we lived on the 2nd Northern Lane. Many Jewish families lived in our district as well as in other areas of old Minsk. We had a large private house and our own farm with two or three horses. We were not a poor family but we were a large one. My grandfather had seven children and my parents had five. My grandfather, Borukh Levin was a master craftsman and cabinetmaker. He made beautiful furniture and there were many standing orders. The house and farm belonged to grandfather and all of us lived there together. Before the war we built an extension, but despite this, the house and yard was always crowded and noisy. Nevertheless, we managed to get by and live together well enough.

My grandmother looked after the farm and my father Isaac Borukhovich Levin was a cab driver. The eldest of my siblings was my brother Joseph, born in 1929 and I had three sisters - Valya born in 1932, Sarochka in 1938 and Lyubochka who was born on the eve of the war in 1941. We had a German shepherd dog named Ava, whom I loved to play with, although once I teased her and she bit my hand. We also used to have a goat that we would put out to graze in the meadow. What else do I remember from before the war? In the place where the technical college is now located, there was a big hill, which seemed like a mountain to me as a child. In the winter, we would go sledging. One day I went with my sisters and there was a horse passing by, so we sledged right underneath it! When my father found out about this he was very angry that we would do something so dangerous and punished us by forbidding us to ever sledge down the 'mountain' again. Another time I somehow managed to push a *baranochek* [Russian: small bagel] up my nose. No matter what I tried I couldn't get it out. I was taken to the hospital where I suffered and sobbed as they tried to remove it. Suddenly I sneezed and out popped the *baranochek*. My pre-war memories like these, are innocent and happy.

My father's brother, Uncle Misha was a very pious man who read Hebrew. He would always come over to spend Shabbat with my grandfather. Prior to Shabbat each week my parents would go to Storozhevskiy Market to buy fish and other tasty food. My mother was an excellent cook who always made delicious food and we always waited eagerly for them to come home and for her to start cooking.

**My mother - Sima Levin**

**My brother - Joseph Levin**

My mother's name was Sima Ioselevna. Before she got married her maiden name had been Friedland and she had lived in the town of Smilovichi [see glossary] but when she married my father and moved with him to Minsk, she left behind all of her relatives. During the war, every single one of them was killed in the Smilovichi Ghetto.

At home, the adults spoke constantly amongst themselves about the possibility of war. They spoke in Yiddish, and in a way that they hoped the children would not hear, but we all knew. Our grandmother tried to reassure us that we had nothing to fear from the Germans, because during the First World War not one Jew had been killed. I was not yet six years old, but I said: 'If a German comes here, I will hit him on the head with a hammer.'

When the war started, Minsk was bombed within the first few days. At first our family did not want to leave, but one day after the bombing had begun my father loaded us up into a cart and off we went. My grandmother refused to come at first, but by the time we were ready to go, she changed her mind and decided to come with us. My parents thought we should head towards Smilovichi. They thought that it would be calmer there and that the Germans wouldn't bomb such a little town. As we left, the raids were becoming heavier and the roads were clogged with people and vehicles. We couldn't even reach Smilovichi, so we decided to go back to Minsk.

We lived as best we could, like everyone else did, until the order came for all of the Jews to move into the ghetto. Our street did not fall into the territory of the ghetto so we exchanged houses with a Russian woman who lived on Sukhaya Street, which was inside the ghetto. She moved into our house and we thought that we would live in hers. However, when we saw how many Jews there were inside the ghetto, it became clear that the entire house wouldn't be allocated to just us.

When the day came to move, we were walking up the Kollektornaya street carrying as much as we could manage: a big iron bed, along with linens, pillows and blankets. We were all carrying bundles and our mother hung an extra one around each of our necks. She also put a lot of clothes on us, so we were wearing many layers, including our winter clothes. As it was the middle of July it was very hot and we were so thirsty. We managed to take only salt and matzah to eat. After the Passover we had much matzah left.

When we arrived in the ghetto, our whole family ended up living in just one room, which was half filled up by a bed. Several of us slept in the bed and the others on the floor. My mother had to care for the baby that she was nursing, who was only seven months old at the time. Finding enough food to eat was extremely difficult. The city was full of anarchy and the shops were being looted, but my brother would sometimes manage to bring something home. Things were better in the summer when there were nettles and quinoa to gather, but, in the winter, we would only eat if my grandfather and brother were able to bring us food from work.

My father was not taken into the army and stayed with us, but I think he died during the first pogrom on the 7th of November 1941; I don't know precisely. My grandfather continued to work in the furniture factory but in 1942 his hand became trapped in a machine and his fingers were cut off so he couldn't work any longer. My brother worked there too, in the boiler room. He now became the main provider and would bring food for all the family.

My mother also went out to work. She would take my little sister with her. On one occasion however, she witnessed Germans ripping nursing babies away from their mothers and smashing their heads on the pavement. After that she no longer left the house.

Those who did go out to work were fed and were given so-called soup and pretend bread. Half of this food they would bring home to their families. There was no special food or allowance for children. We children would go under the wire, to the Russian side to beg for food. We took whatever was given to us.

Like many other families we had a *malina* in the house. Ours was in the cellar and had been dug by my grandfather, father and brother secretly during the night. They would remove the excavated soil and throw it away, as far from the house as they could. They knew that if the Germans saw fresh soil they would immediately realise that someone had been digging and start to investigate. Our *malina* was accessed through a closet in our room that had been left there by the previous owners. Its rear wall was taken out and could then be replaced. It also had a second entrance and exit through the bottom of the Russian stove. In the oven, was a shutter and through that there was an exit. Inside the *malina* it was completely dark, with no windows and no light.

During a pogrom, everyone in the house would go into the *malina*. It was a time of terrible distress. My mother would hold my baby sister and, if she cried, she would either breastfeed her or give her milk that she had expressed to help quiet her. Once when we were hiding, the baby began crying and would not stop. Someone put something into the baby's mouth to make her stop, and my mother didn't notice that and held her tightly against her chest. The pogrom went on and on for two days and still did not end. All this time we sat in the *malina*. When the end finally came, and we went out into the light, I heard my mother begin to scream. This cry is still in my ears. My darling little sister had suffocated. We buried her in the Jewish Cemetery; we made a small mound of earth for her. I still visit it.

Some pogroms lasted a day, some two days. The longest one was four days sitting in the dark in the *malina*. We lived on dry food. We all wanted to stay alive, so we had to suffer it. If we left, we would be killed. We were only children, but we understood this well.

During the first and second pogroms, the police were unaware of the existence of the *malinas*. Then somehow, they found out about them. They would go into houses and throw grenades and spray bullets into the corners of the rooms. The death toll was particularly high during the last pogrom on 23 October 1943. Many people hiding in their *malinas* died that day.

Initially, the pogroms were on the streets. For example, the first pogrom was in the bakery area. Here on the street, people were herded together, loaded into trucks and taken to Tuchinka [see glossary]. As soon as a pogrom began, rumours of where it had taken place swiftly spread through the ghetto and people quickly got off the streets and began to hide in their *malinas*.

During the first days of the riots and pogroms, people were taken to Tuchinka where all of the dead bodies were thrown into a pit [see glossary: Tuchinka]. We lived in the centre of the ghetto on Sukhaya street. There was also an infectious diseases hospital and a Jewish cemetery where I remember big and deep ditches being dug and corpses were brought there.

In 1942 gas vans appeared in the ghetto for the first time. They would throw people who had been gassed out of these vehicles. In their haste to kill as many as possible, many of the people they threw out of the vans were still half alive. Some people went insane after being in these gas machines. We lived close to the cemetery and would hide and watch as corpses and those still half alive were being thrown from the vans into the ditches in the graveyard. Those who were still living would scream and tear at their hair. The Germans and the police then came and shot them with machine guns, killing all who were still breathing. They would pour bleach over the dead bodies and then cover them with soil, ready for the next batch.

As children, we tried to make escape attempts from the ghetto into the 'Russian district' every morning. Despite warnings from our parents to stay at home and not go there, hunger drove us under the wire. Once there we had mixed fortunes. Some people drove us away saying, 'Get out of here you little kike' but others would help us by giving some potatoes or porridge. We always brought this home to our mother, who despite scolding us, was happy to cook and eat the food we had brought. I never liked to venture very far, but my brother would sometimes disappear for three or four days a time and then come home with some potatoes or potato peel for my mother to boil or cook in the oven.

One day, as she was preparing food, some policemen and Germans unexpectedly arrived at the house. They said to my mother, 'Get dressed. Let's go.' I was standing nearby watching with my sister Sarochka and my brother Joseph. My mother said, 'Let me take Maya with me', but my brother stepped forward and said, 'Let Maya stay with us. She is older, how will I manage with Sarochka?' My mother nodded, dressed Sarochka and they left together.

Shortly after they had left a rumour swept through the ghetto that Jews had been hanged in Yubileinya Square. My brother and I ran there. We saw straight away that ten people had been executed. Ten bodies hanging from the gallows. My mother was the first one. She had long, long black hair and it was moving in the wind. On her chest and the chests of the others were signs bearing inscriptions that stated they had been executed because they were working with the partisans. I don't know if my mother had any ties with the partisans. Maybe, it was because we were children, that we were not told about it? We do know however that the GeneralKommissar for Byelorussia Wilhelm Kube was assassinated in Minsk in September 1943 and we know that these hangings were in retribution. What happened to Sarochka, we never knew. We still don't. This was in October 1943, and on each cold day afterwards my brother and I went back to ask to take my mother's body down. We were not allowed to do so, and three days later, she, along with all the others, was dumped in an unknown pit.

Joseph left Minsk to look for the partisans with Misha Pekar and Zhenya Mazich. They entered villages and asked if there were Germans there. There had been cases where Jews had purposely been told that they would find partisans in the village but instead of partisans, Germans were located there. At least some people showed them the way to Porechye [see glossary] where the boys did find partisans. Misha Pekar and Zhenya Mazich stayed with the partisan battalion, but my brother returned to Minsk, for me. My elder sister Valya was taken in by some Russians who were willing to hide her. When they were no longer able to do this safely they put her in a children's home. These good people saved her life, but unfortunately, we didn't even know their names. When my brother left for the partisans, he asked a woman named Dora to look after me while he was away. She was one of the few people left in our Minsk apartment. She was very beautiful. Dora went out each day to work and I stayed in the house. One day she did not come back, she had died. I was the last one in the apartment, there was no one left to look after me. My stomach began to swell with hunger and I could barely go on. My body was crawling with lice, the skin on my head was covered with scabs and I thought that I was about to die. Fortunately, it was then that Joseph returned to Minsk.

His plan, now that he had found the partisans, was to fetch me and take me away with him. However, on his way back to the ghetto, he passed through the old Jewish cemetery where he met two strangers who asked where he was going. They said, "Don't go home. We will feed your sister and look after her. We'll arrange to have you admitted to the hospital; it will be safer that way. We can help you leave with your sister and go to the woods, to the partisans". My brother agreed to the plan and was admitted to the hospital, to a ward on the second floor. These strangers would come to the house and feed me. I still do not know who they were. When I was a little bit stronger I ran to the hospital and talked up to my brother through the window.

The windows of the house where I lived overlooked the central ghetto gates. Not long afterwards I saw a large group of Germans, policemen, gas vans and other vehicles. I ran to the hospital and shouted to Joseph, 'Ioska, there's probably going to be a pogrom. There is no time to wait. We need to get out now'. He climbed down a drainpipe from the second floor and we began to look for somewhere to hide. The *malinas* in everybody's homes were full and we could not get in. I was still weak and barely able to walk, so my brother carried me on his shoulders.

We went to the far end of the cemetery. There was no one around, the Germans and the policemen had been sent to take part in the last pogrom. We climbed underneath the barbed wire. Behind us were a few others of a similar age to my brother who were also escaping from the ghetto. Once we were outside the ghetto we immediately ripped off our yellow patches, which were sewn to the front and back of our clothes. My brother decided we should make our way to the train station, it would be easier to become lost in the crowd. When we arrived at the station we purposely remained in full view, but tried not to stand around or walk along the platform, trying to decide what to do next. Close to the platform were large tanks with pipes. We hid inside them and stayed there for three days. My brother was the eldest and took charge. He would send other children out on missions to find out if the ghetto still existed or not. The boys returned and said, 'Everyone has died, no one is left.'

My brother said, 'If you listen to me and help carry Maya on your shoulders, taking turns, I will get you all out of Minsk and show you the way to the partisan battalion. She will not be able to walk by herself.'

Early the following morning we left Minsk. My brother split the group into pairs who walked along the highway at a certain distance ahead, in order to see what possible dangers lays farther on. But German convoys passed by and no one paid any attention to us. At nightfall, we went into the woods to sleep and at dawn we would carry on. In this way, we walked one hundred kilometres to Porechye.

Our group, consisted of about fifteen or twenty people, and in Porechye at that time there were other Jewish children who had escaped from Minsk, around forty people in total. Close by the village was the partisan battalion under the leadership of Israel Lapidus.

The question for the village was - what were they to do with such a large horde of children? To begin with, we were grouped together and moved into one large hut, making beds of straw on the floor. In an attempt to feed us, we were given kneaded dough from flour with water from the trough. When food was available, we all lived from hand to mouth, very much as before. I remember very well the first time that we all ate together. We collected potatoes in a wicker basket and then baked them in the Russian oven, shook them and spread them out onto a very big table. Whoever could, grabbed a potato. In the ghetto we had been used to grabbing food whenever we had the opportunity, so therefore we grabbed food here as well.

After a short while the villagers decided that it would be better to move us into the huts with families. Each family or hut took only one child. Nastya Khurs took me in. She couldn't take my brother and he lived at the other end of the village. Nastya was born in 1923 and lived on her own. Her husband was a partisan and they had no children of their own at that time. She cried when she saw me for the first time. I was covered in scabs and blisters, with wounds on my arms and lice crawling in my hair. She washed me, combed my hair and put me to bed. I think that I probably slept for three days. My brother came to visit me every day and Nastya said to him, 'I've heard that in the partisan unit there is a doctor called Podolyako who has ointment. Please bring it for your sister.' My brother brought back the ointment from Dr. Podolyako and I was treated with it. It contained lard and gunpowder, and after sometime, the blisters and scabs began to disappear. However, some still remained after the war. Once Nastya had cleaned me up a little and I began to recover, I began to go out to play with the village children. They brought some rags, and we sewed dolls. We wanted to play.

One week the partisans stayed in the village, next week the village was occupied by the Germans. At any moment we had to be prepared for the unexpected appearance of Germans. If they arrived, we would have to run and hide in the swamps and bogs in and around the forest. The partisans would try and warn us when the Germans were approaching and the villagers would gather some of our belongings into baskets and take us across the river into the swamp. Nastya and I would usually go to the same place, sometimes hiding there for two or three days. In the winter, it was terrible and we almost froze.

In our village there were no policemen, but there were some in the surrounding villages. Despite this, and the close location of the German garrison in Pukhovichy [see glossary] no one betrayed us and neither the police nor the Germans knew that Jewish children were hiding nearby. We believed that the Germans were afraid of becoming stuck in the swamp. Even with dogs, they were reluctant to venture any distance into it.

Once, when Nastya was hiding with me in the swamp, my brother stayed in the village. The Germans raided and all the young people were sent first to Pukhovichy and then to a concentration camp. My brother was included in this roundup. They did not know that my brother and the other people from the Minsk Ghetto were Jews; no-one had identified them as such.

Joseph managed to escape from the concentration camp, reaching a farm where he began to work. Shortly afterwards he was captured and returned again to a concentration camp, this time in Germany. After some time, he was liberated by Soviet troops and became the son of the regiment. Colonel Novikov, who was childless, then adopted him. The colonel gave Joseph his family name. After the war, Colonel Novikov served in Germany and Joseph lived with him.

After the war was over, Nastya Khurs's father told her that everyone had died in my Minsk home and that she should send me to an orphanage in the hope that relatives would find me. I was transported on three separate occasions to the Talkovsky orphanage, but I escaped, staying no more than two or three months each time. I wanted to stay and live with Nastya.

My father's sister's husband, my uncle Colonel Leo Novodvorets, happened to be in Minsk at this time. He had been wounded when the city was liberated but recovered and was appointed head of the water utilities. Before the war he had a paralyzed son. During one pogrom policemen dragged him away by the arms to be shot. He cried out so loudly that we, hiding in the *malina,* heard the anguish of his cry, but no one could help him. Leo Novodvorets' wife and three more of his children were all shot. He had an assistant whom he now sent around Minsk to search for members of our family. All of Leo Novodvorets immediate family had been in the Minsk Ghetto and had been killed there. Nevertheless, he said to his assistant, 'Look for my family, and the Levins'. The assistant found me in the orphanage and I went to live with my uncle.

**Villagers from Porechye, with a group of former ghetto prisoners - 1992**

The Russian people who had hidden my sister Valya during the war died in an outbreak of typhus, so she was also sent to the orphanage in Minsk. My maternal grandmother had been evacuated and in 1945 she returned to Minsk and lived there with her daughter, my aunt. She died soon afterwards, but before her death she said that Valya and I, as sisters, should live together.

Before long Leo Novodvorets acquired a new family, so Valya and I began to live in the 4th Orphanage on Kollektornaya Street. It was there we grew up and were educated. Valya lived there until 1950 and I lived there until 1953.

On the whole, they treated children nicely in homes and orphanages after the war. There were difficult situations that I had to face, but I was strong and tough and it helped me to survive. If something unpleasant was said to me, I was able to answer back. For example, a teacher once said bad things about me, and I responded by telling her that she was a Fascist.

On one occasion, as a punishment, I was separated from Valya and sent away to an orphanage in the countryside. We wrote a letter to the Minister of Education, and shortly afterwards, both of us were moved to Orphanage Number 7. This was a special orphanage for children of deceased war veterans. German Prisoners of war were employed there to do building repairs. At first, we treated them very badly, there was a lot of teasing and pushing. After a while, however, they made us toys and we began to stop teasing, and treated them more respectfully. In our games, we played mostly make-believe families; someone was always the father, mother, and children. We played games that reflected what was lacking in our real lives.

**Hand written letter from the Secretary of the Regional Komsomol Organisation to the Orphanage concerning children being sent there.**

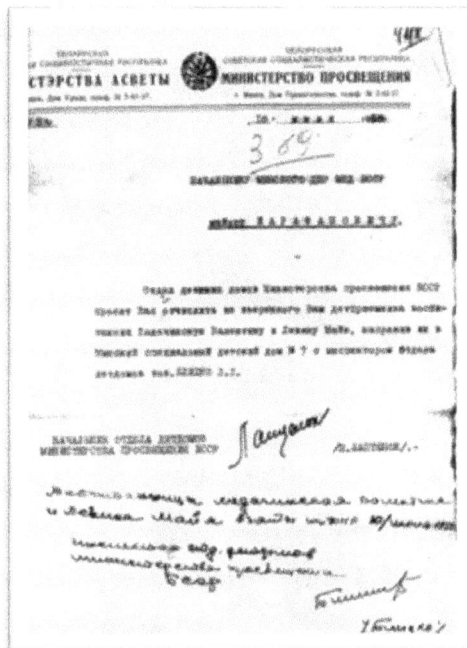

**Letter from the head of the Department of Orphanages of the Ministry of Education to the Department of Detention Centres for Minors, Ministry of Internal Affairs – to transfer Valentina Hodachinskaya and Maya Levina to Orphanage Number 7.**

Colonel Novikov, who had adopted Joseph, now arrived in Minsk after serving in Germany, and Joseph began to look for members of the family. Joseph and I each thought that the other was dead. However, he eventually found an aunt, and she told him that Valya and I were in fact still alive. He came to find us in the orphanage. Joseph found a job in the print shop at the tractor factory. He now lives in the United States. Valya went on to study at teacher training college after graduating from high school. She then began studying to become an accountant. All her life she worked as an accountant. She also now lives in the United States.

Meanwhile, I graduated from the Physical Education College and then *in absentia* from the Institute of Physical Education. I worked as a trainer in children's sports school and in 1961 my husband and I won the USSR Acrobatics Championship. I then went on the stage and worked there for nearly twenty years. Now I am deeply engaged in social work.

**Former juvenile prisoners of the Minsk Ghetto, (left to right Maya Krapina,**

**Mikhail Novodvorsky, Serova Vera and Frieda Reizman).**

**Porechye**

**Anastasia (Nastya) Khurs**

**At the grave of Anastasia (Nastya) Khurs**

**(photo: A. Kleschuk)**

In 2000, a monument was unveiled in the village of Porechye, dedicated to the courageous people who saved the lives of Jewish children during the war. However, in addition I would like the whole village to be awarded the title it truly deserves: 'Righteous Among the Nations.'

**The unveiling of "Monument to the Righteous' - Porechye, 2000.**

Story recorded by Arkadiy Shulman

# I Saw for Myself but I Still Don't Believe
## Ura Kaplan

*Ura was a survivor from the Jewish ghetto in Novy Sverzhen, a village approximately 50km south of Minsk. This ghetto was, like the Minsk Ghetto, fenced by barbed wire.*

**Ura Kaplan**

People, look at me and listen to my story. I am 87 years old, but I do not feel the weight of those years. I love life and I am young at heart. I have many friends, and everyone knows that I am always willing to help in difficult times. I love cheerful holidays, and I am happy if everything is going well for my close friends, relatives and for all people in general. However, during my life there have been many difficult trials. I remember every day of them, every moment. There were times when I did not believe what I saw with my own eyes; what people, and not animals, did to each other. God forbid that it should happen again.

I was born in 1925 in the town of Novy Sverzhen. The town was situated in the Stolbtsy district, a suburb of Minsk, which in 1925, was still a part of Poland. My father, Jakov Yosifovich, born 1902, worked at the sawmill, and my mother Rachel, born 1903 was a housewife. I had two younger sisters, Yosl (she was 14 when war began) and Raita (who was 12 at the beginning of the war). Our family observed all the Jewish traditions and celebrated all the holidays. We spoke Yiddish, but we all knew perfectly well how to speak Polish and Byelorussian. We were friends with our neighbors of all nationalities.

I studied at the local Polish school, and at *cheder*, [see glossary] where I learned Torah and Yiddish. In 1935, I went to study at a Jewish school in Stolbtsy, where they taught Hebrew, Polish and Geography. I stayed there until 17 September 1939, the day of the liberation of Western Byelorussia by the Red Army. After that I went to Byelorussian School.

When the war began I was 16 years old. German troops marched into our town on 27 June 1941. However, on 22 June my father and I had already decided to try and leave Byelorussia and attempt to reach Russia. We had heard talk that the Germans were killing all the men but left the women and children unharmed. When we reached the bridge over the Neman River, in Novy Sverzhen, my father began to have second thoughts. He said to me: 'Urele, how can we do this? Your mother and two sisters will be left without any help? What will happen to them?' So, we returned home. Father continued to work at the sawmill, and I found work in a bakery, chopping the wood for the ovens. That is the way that life continued until 1 August 1941, the day the Novy Sverzhen Ghetto was set up. A terrible, black day.

The ghetto was situated next to the Novy Sverzhensk timber-processing factory. Jews were transported there from all the surrounding towns. My grandmother, along with my aunt and cousin Ida, who, up until that time, had been living in Stolbtsy, also arrived in the ghetto.

**Ura Kaplan with his father**

The former owner of the bakery where I worked, had been a Jew. He had been shot when the Germans occupied the town. The new owner's name was Pan (Mr. in Polish) Mostovsky, and he was a wonderful man. During the time I worked for him, I would take bread home with me, two or three loaves, hiding it under my jacket. Pan Mostovsky would avert his gaze and pretend not to notice. He would exaggerate excessive harshness and mutter 'cursed Jew' under his breath. However, furtively, he wiped away tears and treated me as kindly as would a father.

Then came the dreadful day that changed my life, 5 November 1941*. On returning home from work the day previously, I discovered that the Germans had herded together the inhabitants of the town. They had been forced to spend the day digging an enormous pit in the cemetery. That night our family spent the hours of darkness in fearful prayer, anticipating the worst. So it came to pass. The following morning, trucks arrived in the ghetto. Into these they pushed the sick, the elderly, women and children. I was bundled into a truck, along with my mother and sisters. The trucks then moved in the direction of the cemetery. No one had any doubt about what was happening, that we were being taken to our death. My mother decided that at least one of her children must be saved. She said to me, 'Ura, jump, and run!' With the truck hurtling at full speed, I fell out. The truck drove on, and I somehow managed to pick myself up, uninjured, and sprinted towards the woods. From the other trucks, German soldiers were shooting at me, but apparently my mother's prayers for my safety were stronger. Miraculously, the bullets didn't touch me. I was the sole survivor of that brutal massacre.

Meanwhile, healthy adult men, including my father, continued to work at the sawmill. It was to the mill that I ran that day. I found my father and broke the awful news about the death of the whole family. After that, the two of us continued to live in the ghetto for more than a year, until January 1943.

About this time, I established contact with the partisans. On 29 January 1943, two armed partisans arrived secretly in the ghetto, explaining the urgent necessity to organise an escape. It had become known that the Germans were preparing to kill the remaining ghetto residents. Together with the partisans' preparation, help and planning, we tore down the wire surrounding the ghetto, killed the guards and engineered the successful escape of around 200 people. We then headed in the direction of Kopyl. Not everything went smoothly however. Nearly all of the escapees, fearing the extreme cold and starvation, abandoned the escape attempt and went back to the ghetto. It was clear that they were returning to certain death. On the 31 January 1943, everyone who had tried to escape and then returned, was executed in Stolbtsy. As for my father, he had been ill at the time of the planned escape, and instead of going to the partisans, went to a village, where he had contacts. This was a disaster for him. People in the village betrayed him, and gave him up to the Germans. That is how I lost my last family member. Of the 200 people who escaped from the ghetto, only eight, including me, survived.

**My wife Rosa Yosifovna Barash, and myself**

I joined the partisans and became a fighter in the Shchors Squad, Chapayev Brigade. I was an assistant machine gunner in the troop from the 23 January 1943 to 23 June 1944. I took part in ambushes, shootings and the mining of the railway line, which resulted in derailed German trains. Within the unit, I was treated very kindly and with respect.

I particularly remember the Lavsky Battle. We were ambushed, and many partisans were captured. I was wounded in the leg by a shell fragment, but my friends carried me from the battlefield.

For the most part, fate kept me safe, but I do remember one incident. I had a fever and tonsillitis. I can't remember exactly how or why, but I was lying underneath a tree. Suddenly, there was an eruption of gunfire and a battle began. The Germans had broken through, and there was I, lying on the ground, with a temperature of 39 degrees. The retreating partisans had to carry me on stretcher, on foot, from Kopyl to Pinsk, a distance overall of almost 150 kilometers, through swamps and forests.

During this period another memorable incident occurred. I was sent with other fighters on a combat mission. We were tasked to collect food from villagers who had collaborated with the Germans. We were presented with the details of the farm, where one such German henchman was supposedly living. On discovering the farmhouse, we found a rich Polish man living there. We decided the best course of action would be to 'redistribute' his much-needed livestock. To our surprise, he pleaded with us, saying: 'Please, don't touch me. I'm hiding a Jewish woman.' Cautious, in case it was an ambush, we said, 'Show us the Jewish woman.' The man led us to a barn, where, underneath the floor, was a hiding place covered with a bale of hay. Who should come out of the hiding place, but my cousin Ida! I hadn't known that she had survived, because her family had been taken away on the same day as my own family. Ida took one look at us and began screaming. To disguise ourselves, we were dressed in German uniforms, and she thought we were policemen. In her fear, she did not even recognize me. No matter how we tried to persuade her to leave with us, and return with us to the squad, she flatly refused. Eventually, I had to leave her on the farm, in hiding, and go back to the detachment. I relayed the story to my commander, and he appointed a group to return to the farm, and bring Ida to the squad. After this, my cousin was finally convinced. She remained with us, contributing to the squad fully, as a cook, until Byelorussia was liberated.

**The Kaplan family, (from left to right) my son Leonid,**

**Ura Yakovlevich Kaplan, my daughter Raisa, and my wife Rosa**

Our partisan unit, connected with the Red Army and participated in the liberation of Minsk, where I was fortunate to become a member of the famous Parade of Liberators.

Soon, I was taken into active service (with the 5th Army Byelorussian Front). On 14 January 1945, I participated in the liberation of Warsaw. As I spoke Polish, the commander invited me to take part in the negotiations, and, in 1945 I attended the interrogations of arrested Poles who collaborated with Nazis during the war. On Victory day, close to Hamburg in Germany, our army troops met our American counterparts. This was the first time that both sides had mingled freely together. Along with the Americans, we shared celebrations and talked easily, like old friends.

**Ura Kaplan (survivor of the Novy Sverzhen Ghetto) and Vladimir Rubezhin (survivor of the Minsk Ghetto)**

**February 2012**

I was awarded thirteen medals and the Order of the Red Star of the Great Patriotic War.

After the war, the command sent me to military school in Balashov, near Saratov. I was later discharged from the school for health reasons. Following that, I served in the Saratov Department of the Ministry of Interior. In Saratov I met my future wife, Rosa. She and I moved back to Minsk in 1950. In 2008 we celebrated our Diamond wedding anniversary.

Several years ago, I went to visit relations in Israel. Whilst I was there I was fortunate enough to see 'The Jews of Novy Sverzhen and Stolbtsy: Book of Memory.' Imagine my surprise, when I discovered photographs in the book of my entire family, my father, mother and grandfather, and even pictures of me as a baby. There, in the land of Israel, the land of my ancestors, a miracle happened. After the terrible pogrom on the 5th of November 1941, I had thought that I had nothing left with which to remember my family. Now the pictures that hang on the walls of my apartment ensure that my mother, father and sisters, Yosl and Raita, will remain forever young. Truly, those whom we love will remain alive as long as we remember them.

\* In the Novy Sverzhen Ghetto, Ura Kaplan's story tells us that a major pogrom took place on the 5th November 1941. We know that one of the four major Pogroms in the Minsk Ghetto took place around the same time, on November 7th 1941.

# I Live and I Remember
## Saveliy Kaplinskiy

**Saveliy Kaplinskiy**

I am Sanya (Saveliy) Kaplinskiy. The book '*The Avengers of the Ghetto*' by Grisha Smolyar mentions me. I belonged to the group Nonka Markiewicz, along with Sholom Grinhaus, Yasha Lapidus, that came out of the Minsk Ghetto and with the help of Byelorussian school comrades, Vitya Rudovich and Kolya Prischepo, we dug out 540 bullets, machine gun tape, twelve rifles and two grenades in the area of the Mogilev Highway.

Before that, I lived with my family, in House 6 on the 2nd Opanski Alley. The enclosure of barbed wire around the ghetto was just two metres from our house, and our road separated the ghetto from the Russian area. My father, Isaac Kaplinsky, was a blacksmith and my mother Berta, a housewife. I had three brothers. By June 1941, my eldest brother Elijah, had already served in the army (he served for 25 years including the war and now lives in Brooklyn). The next oldest, Shay, was on the eastern front working in a military factory in the Urals. The youngest brother, Yasha, was with us in the ghetto.

During the pogrom of 7 November 1941, I hid with Yasha and other family members in the *malina* belonging to David Kaplinsky. The Germans arrested my father during the pogrom and we never saw him again. My mother was sick, so the Nazi's took her into the back yard and shot her. My grandfather was also taken into the yard and shot in the head. During this time of frequent pogroms, my brother Yasha was also killed. I still reproach myself that I wasn't able to save him. I was thirteen years old and had now been left alone without family and friends.

In order to somehow survive, I had to work, and I managed to find a job in a work detail. I would be taken to Bel-Polk, [a Troop Regiment for the Ministry for Internal Affairs] on Grushevskaya Street where German soldiers were living in army barracks. The land between the buildings was planted out with vegetables, and it was my job to tend it. During the summer, I worked on these plots, and, in the winter, I carried wood to the barracks' rooms. The soldiers never stayed for long, as some would be sent to the front, and others to the rear, on rotation. As they came and went, I took advantage of this cycle to steal weapons and ammunition.

My family was dead, so I became friends with other boys, whose parents had also been killed. Nonka Markiewicz was the eldest in our group, and the leader. We actively collected ammunition, and distributed leaflets throughout the ghetto. Once, my friend Sholom and I dragged a large tube radio home to the attic where we lived, we repaired it, enabling us to listen to the reports from the Moscow news stations. One day, we came back to a terrible scene. Someone had informed on Nonka. He and his parents had been beaten up and taken away in a police van. Despite this, while in prison, he did not betray any of us. Nonka was shot.

We continued to pass weapons and ammunition through our Byelorussian contacts. Lyuba and Kolya Prischepo were reliable, and also lived near to the Telman Shoe Factory, which was close to the ghetto.

Those of us who left the ghetto daily to work, would carry galvanized steel cans for transporting food and drink. We would always try to procure food for those left behind in the ghetto, bringing it back in the cans. I was constantly on the lookout for the half-eaten remains of soldiers' porridge. I would scrape the porridge from their bowls and hide bullets under it. Of course, if this had been discovered, the whole work group would have been shot, but God spared us.

Then my friend Sholom escaped from the ghetto to join the partisans. He returned shortly afterwards to lead out of the ghetto our entire group, including his mother, brother and sister. I also joined the partisans and my unit was called Sholom Zorin. I carried out guard duties and was a fighter.

After the liberation of Minsk, I returned to my father's house. It was now occupied by people I didn't know, so I was given a small single room there. I went to study in FZO (Fabrichno Zavodskoe Obuchenie – trade school). They fed and clothed me. Following the war, my older brother Elijah, who had fought in the army all these years, sent a letter to our old address. He had hopes of finding someone in the family still alive. He returned home and found me! He continued to help me with my schooling, for which I am extremely grateful.

In January 1946, my friend Sholom was killed. As students of excellence, and former partisans, we had been invited to a Christmas party in the House of the Trade Unions. While we were there, a huge fire broke out, and Sholom was unable to escape. I escaped by jumping out of a third-floor window. Tragically, there were many lifeless bodies lying on the pavement, and I broke my fall by landing on them. For many days and nights afterwards, I visited all the local hospitals and morgues, hoping to find Sholom, but to no avail. Eventually, all of the victims who could not be identified were included in the general memorial at the military cemetery. Sholom Grinhaus, the name of my great friend, is now among those to be inscribed on the monument.

In 1947, I enrolled to study in the construction faculty at Minsk Polytechnic. I have warm memories of my friends and classmates from those college days. I remember the dining room where you could dine cheaply, and where I was able to eat plenty of liverwurst. Who does not remember the quality of liverwurst in those post-war years?

After graduation, I began working as a construction foreman in Minsk. In the evenings, I continued my studies at the institute, where I graduated in 1955. I then went on to gain my diploma in Leningrad. It was in college that I met my future wife, Zoe Roslabtseva. We studied, and later worked together: she was in the design institute, and I was in construction. We were married in 1956 and are still together, and in love, after more than fifty years.

I quickly progressed up the career ladder: Master, Foreman and then Section Chief. In 1957, I became Chief Engineer of Construction Management, and, two years later the youngest head of the 9th Construction Management Trust. I now have 43 years of building experience. Hundreds of buildings in Minsk have been built under my direct supervision.

In 1992, I emigrated with my family to the USA. I began to learn English, (already having a good command of German at the time of the occupation). In America, I joined the Association of Former Prisoners of Ghetto and Concentration Camps. After the death of its first president and founder, I became the new leader. The staff consisted of 350 members. Zhanna Berin (a former prisoner of the Odessa Ghetto), became Vice President, and its main task was to unite all the former prisoners into one association which would become a self-reliant, independent organisation. I am proud to say, that, along with my colleagues, we achieved this goal. The association has become one of the largest in New York, with over 965 members. They have developed and approved the program and the charter. There have been regular contacts with many American and Russian speaking institutions, whose goals and objectives coincide with our own. After five successful years, I handed the reigns over to another. Since 2003, I have been working with the American Association of Jews from the Former Soviet Union, of which I am the Deputy President. We have established relationships with many organisations in Israel, including associations of former prisoners, and the Belarusian community. The stone memorial in Brooklyn (NY) dedicated to the victims of the Minsk Ghetto, was set with my participation.

I often visit my native city of Minsk. I always try to time my visit for the 9th of May, the date of the annual commemoration at Yama memorial [see glossary].

**Saveliy Kaplinsky with his family**

# A Story of Salvation
## Eugeniy Machiz

**Eugeniy Machiz**

My name is Eugeniy Savelievich Machiz and I was born in 1932. I am a Jew and a former prisoner of the Minsk Ghetto. I was rescued by the Shashok family, Mikhail Stepanovich and Eugenia Yakimovna. Their son, Aleksander Shashok, who was born in 1930, still lives in the village Porechye in the Pukhovichy district in the region of Minsk.

At the beginning of the war, I lived with my parents in apartment number 4, at number 10 Pervomayskaya Street, Minsk. I had just finished the second grade in school Number 4, on Krasnoarmeyskaya Street. The war caught us by surprise. I was away from home, out of town at a scouting camp that was called 'Drozdy.' The camp was disbanded immediately at the announcement of war, and we had to walk back to Minsk. However, in the early days of the war, our house was burnt down, and my mother and my sister Olga were evacuated to the city of Ufa. My father had gone to the front to fight, so I now went to live with my maternal grandmother, Lisa Vigdorovich on Storozhevskaya Street.

In early August 1941, my grandmother and I were moved with my uncle and all his family, into the ghetto. We moved from apartment to apartment. At first, we all lived on Ratomskaya Street, then on Zamkovaya, and then on Sukhaya and later on Kollektornaya Street. The ghetto was constantly becoming narrower and more confined. In the first pogrom on 7th November 1941 my uncle and his family were killed, but I managed to escape by hiding in the Jewish cemetery on Sukhaya Street.

Although I was only ten years old, I now went to work on the construction site on Krasnoarmeyskaya Street, covering up the windows in the Lenin Library. I also had cleaning jobs, in a German garage and a German flying unit. The Germans would line us up and march us to work each day, under armed guard. On 20 March 1942, I returned home to find my grandmother gone. She had been killed in a pogrom while I had been at work.

In late September 1943, I was with a group of my friends by the barbed wire fence, when the German Commandant of the ghetto arrived with his dog (whose name we knew to be Epstein). We realised that this was a sign that a pogrom was about to take place. So, that night, we decided to run away. There was a group of us: me, Misha Pekar, Yosif Levin, Misha Novodvorsky, Monka Shapiro, Mustafa and Lupaty, plus a few other children whose names I don't remember. We slipped under the wire fence during the night.

While it was still dark, we hid in a concrete pipe on Chkalov Street, and, at first light we left Minsk heading towards the Pukhovichy district. We walked for about four days. We tried to keep to the most remote country roads, avoiding the larger villages, and sleeping in haystacks. We travelled mostly at night and in the early mornings. Sometimes we would arrive in a small village and be brave enough to ask for something to eat. Finally, we arrived at the village of Porechye. We stayed in an empty hut and discovered other children there, doing the same thing. For the first few days, local farmers came to the hut to bring us food, but then they began to assign us to families who were willing to conceal and look after us.

I went to the family of Mikhail Shashok Stepanovich and his wife Eugenia Shashok Yakimovna. They had a son Aleksander born 1930 and a daughter Vera born 1939. They were a poor family, undernourished themselves, and barely had any food.  However, they divided whatever they had equally, between everyone, including me. They treated me as their son. When the Germans staged a blockade in the area, the partisans gave warning to villagers to conceal themselves and anyone that they were hiding. I knew that, if I was found, the Germans would have killed me and the entire Shashok family. Mikhail Stepanovich was not afraid, and he hid me in the bushes. I lived with his family until the liberation of the area by the Soviet Army. Then, when Minsk was liberated in July 1944, I returned to the city. I will remember the kindness of this family for the rest of my life and I honour them for it. They risked their own lives to save me from the Nazis.

Mikhail and Eugenia are no longer alive, but their son, Aleksander, still lives in the village of Porechye. I visit him often. I believe that the Shashok family deserves to be immortalized in Yad Vashem, since their noble deeds are worthy of the gratitude of the Jewish People.

# I Typeset Partisan Newspapers
## Elizaveta Morozova (Lisa Moroz)

**Lisa Moroz**

My name is Elizaveta Morozova, but I was originally called Lisa Beynusovna Moroz. I was born on 14 December 1915 in Mogilev. When I finished school, I went to work at a print shop as an apprentice hand-typesetter.

After six months, I was working independently and in 1936, I set the all-Soviet record for hand typesetting 27,000 characters in one 7-hour working day. Articles were written about me in the newspapers, and people would visit the printing plant, just to look at my hands.

In 1937, I married Lazar Aronovich Trachtenberg, and we moved from Mogilev to Minsk where his parents lived. On 21 August 1938, our son was born.

In 1941, when war broke out, my husband went to the front as a volunteer. I was left behind with a two-and-a-half-year-old child, and my mother, who had moved to Minsk with us. When Minsk was bombed on 27 June, we were in the woods, about six kilometres from the city. We watched one German squadron after another flying over and bombing the city. This continued for the whole day. When it started to get dark we went back to Minsk and found that the centre of the city was already ruined, and that our house had been destroyed. We stood looking at the ruins, weeping bitterly, and then we went to look for somewhere to spend the night. My husband's parents lived along the street from us, in a single-storey wooden house with shutters, and so we went there. We found a note on the door which read: 'We were looking for you, but we couldn't find you and so we left without you.' The house had been left unlocked, so we began to live there.

On the night of 28 June, there was an enormous battle for Minsk. The Germans entered the city and captured it. From that day, a new kind of life began. The Germans introduced a new order. Everyone had to re-register and anyone who refused was shot. They imposed further orders to begin a clean-up of the city, as the whole city centre had been destroyed. They organised a Jewish ghetto, and every day, people were forced to labour for long hours in work convoys.

I was made to work near the medical institution. I was given a cart in which I had to throw bricks and plaster. A German guard would run behind me with a whip. Using any excuse to beat me, he would shout: 'Keep working, like you would work for Stalin.' To avoid the beatings, women would grab the cart and try to run with it. This went on day after day, and I would come home from work in agony and exhausted. At that time the ghetto was set up and people were made to go to work in labour groups.

In Minsk at that time, there were two large companies: KRIG and KRUPP. KRIG was a construction firm which the Germans made to build huts and barracks for their own use. One evening, when I came home from work, my neighbour saw my distress and said: 'Tomorrow you will join my work detail.' She worked at the KRIG company.

When I started to work there, I met three other young women: Lisa Livshits, Basia Melzer and Masha Hare. We were put to work as labourers with the motor vehicles. The driver was Russian, but as he did not want to go to the Soviet Army, he had remained in Minsk, where he worked for the Germans. I worked extremely hard, every day from morning until dusk. On 21 August 1941, there was a raid, and all the men were seized. The women were made to kneel down facing the wall. We were told, 'If anyone turns around, they will be shot.' The men were taken away, and never came back.

Each day brought a new misery to our lives. Each household living in the ghetto began to build a *malina,* a place to hide during raids. We dug a big hole under the floor of our one- storey house. We loosened a few boards under our bed and threw pillows over them. Our *malina* was then ready to shelter us in the case of a pogrom. If we were lucky enough to hide without detection, then maybe we would be able to postpone being killed, at least for a while.

The first big massacre occurred on 7 November 1941. Throughout the ghetto, there had been advance warning of the mayhem to be unleashed, and we didn't sleep at all the night before. At six in the morning, we saw through the cracks in the shutters, that the first snow had fallen. The street was white, and spaced every ten metres along it, stood policemen in black uniforms, with machine guns at the ready.

We went down into the *malina,* pushed the door shut, and threw rags over the top. A pillow had been taken in for my son. If he started to make a noise and cry, it would be used to smother him. There were many people hiding in the *malina* and by crying, he could give them all away. I took him in my arms, hugged him, and told him that he must be quiet. The poor thing, he clung to me all day, without making a sound.

At seven o'clock, the 'gas vans' arrived. Soldiers began to drive people out of their houses. Terrified, they began to shout and call out to each other. The children were crying and screaming. We had scattered around and upended all the furniture in the house, to make it appear as though the Germans had already 'turned the place over'. Meanwhile, we sat silently in the malina, with our teeth chattering. We remained in hiding for the whole day, the night, and half of the following day, consumed with fear and anguish the entire time. We eventually heard footsteps, the sound of somebody walking around above us. A voice called for us to come out. It was our neighbour. She told us that the pogrom was over, but that the street had now been divided into two sections. Our side had not been touched, but, on the other side of the road, everyone had been taken. Two days later, the barbed wire boundary of the ghetto was moved to just outside our window. The ghetto had decreased in size by half. At that time, more than 3,000 people had been taken away. We had been lucky this time, but still lived in fear every day.

**Lisa Moroz, (right) with her friends, Mogilev 1936**

Opposite our house was a bread factory that was guarded by German soldiers. One day, when I was walking with my friend Sonya on 'our' side of the street, one of the Germans aimed his rifle at us. Sonya ran to hide in a nearby yard, but I kept walking straight ahead. The German fired at me. The bullet hit the thick woollen shawl that I was wearing and went straight through it, avoiding my neck, and hitting a nearby building. Sonya, hearing the shot, began to scream that I had been killed. When she saw me walking through the gate, she rushed over and kissed me. I showed her the damaged shawl that smelled strongly of gunpowder. I was incredibly fortunate to have survived.

Another time, we were unloading a wagon of boards at the railway station, near to the hospital. I was standing by the truck catching the boards that were being thrown from the vehicle. One board hit me on the head and blood began to pour out. The German guard took me by the hand and led me to the hospital. The Russian doctors patched me up and for a month, I went around with a bandaged head. I still have a scar there, in memory of the Nazis.

The Germans were afraid of a typhus epidemic spreading through the ghetto, so they began to select people to clean the yards, streets and garbage dumps. My little son began to work with me on these clean-ups. He would drag buckets of garbage, sweep the streets and collect all sorts of rags and paper. The police would bang on doors and just order us into the street to do this work. On one occasion, when the police came with orders to carry out some of this work, my friend Sonya, who lived in my apartment, didn't want to go. She hid in the *malina*, and I began to close the house. A policeman began shouting at me: 'Who are you hiding? Open up, you Jewish pig! If I find someone in there, I'll shoot you both on the spot!' I told him that there was no-one in the house but, despite that, he came inside, looking into the living room and then the bedroom. I had my four-year-old son with me and was very frightened. He eventually finished his search and told me: 'You're lucky, I'm not going to shoot you.'

In 1942, during a pogrom, my mother was killed. She had been to visit a friend, and it was during the time that the Germans had started to snatch people and put them into the 'gas vans.' My mother and her friend were both caught that day. Now I was left alone with my child so I started taking him to work with me. When we were on work details we were always accompanied by German guards, so I would hide him underneath my skirt, and sometimes in my sack. I was eventually spotted, and the German guard saw him. He said to me: 'Don't take him on the job.' I began to beg, but the German said I would have to continue in the work detail without him. I quickly began to talk to my son. I told him to return home, and if there was any sort of disturbance in the ghetto, he was to hide under the bed, cover himself in rags, and sit very quietly until I came home. I then cried the whole day, until it was time for me to return home. However, our ghetto children were very clever and mature before their time. They were like little old men and women, and they all understood the conditions in which we were forced to live. They were all extremely vigilant.

I continued my work as a labourer on the trucks. Each day we hauled tons of cement, sand and bricks. On one occasion, we were unloading enormous logs, which were extremely heavy, and I sat down to rest for a few minutes. A German approached me and hit me in the face so hard, that I fell down and hit my head on a log. More than a month later, I still had the bruises from being hit.

One day, we were driven to work in Borovliany. During the time that I spent at work, there was a great massacre in the ghetto. Our street off Yubileynaya Square, had recently been excluded from the ghetto, which was constantly becoming smaller, so when I returned after the pogrom, I had no idea where to go so my neighbour took both me and my child into her house. On the second day, she said that the area I had wanted to reach was no longer guarded, so I went home to collect some rags, which I would be able to use to hide under.

Cautiously, I made my way down Ostrovsky Street, through which it was possible to access our yard. I met with a former neighbour who was very happy to see me, as she was afraid to go into her house alone. We went into her house together, and I will never forget what I saw there for the rest of my days. She had three beautiful children, two girls aged five and three, and a boy aged around one. The eldest child was lying on the sofa, shot dead. Next to her, her sister was also dead, and the little boy was in his cradle, his head split wide open, blood caked all around him. My neighbour ran out of the house screaming, and I never saw her again.

When I stumbled out of that house, I could barely remember why I had come there. I stood by the wall for a moment, trying to regain my senses and recall where I had been going. As it gradually returned to me, I forced myself to go as quickly as I could to my old house, grab a few things and run out. I hardly had time to take two steps on the return journey, before my heart began to sink. Coming towards me in the opposite direction, were three SS men, with big bellies. I forced myself to greet them, and told them where I worked, explaining that, after the pogrom I had gone home to get a change of clothes. They looked at me and gesticulated with their hands, saying: 'Go! Run faster!' I ran all the way to Yubileynaya Square, collapsing on the first bench I came across, and then I fainted. People gathered around and gave me water. I told them about what had happened, and yet again I was told that I was fortunate, lucky to still be alive.

**Former prisoner of the ghetto Lisa Moroz (right)and Lisa Livshits, Minsk 1953**

The pogroms continued. On one occasion, we were transported back from work by truck. We had driven about a kilometre, when we passed another truck carrying people from the ghetto coming in the opposite direction. The passengers on the truck began shouting to us that a massacre was happening in the ghetto and we shouldn't go back. We began banging on the driver's cabin, shouting at him to stop, but he kept on going. I quickly made a decision. I grabbed my son in my arms and jumped out of the truck while it was still moving. Other people followed us. We returned to the workplace, telling them about the massacre in the ghetto, and asking if we could wait it out there. Fortunately, the German running our work detail was compassionate. He told us to hide, and then left for the evening. They captured and rounded up many people in the ghetto that night. The Minsk Ghetto was still in existence, but not for much longer.

On 23 October 1943, we returned home after work, and were confronted by a group of Jewish boys. They ran out in front of us shouting: 'There was a final pogrom in the ghetto! Everyone's been taken in the gas vans! Soon the Germans will come here to pick up the last of the Jews!' Lisa Livshits and I grabbed our children. Lisa had a son called Abrash, who was my son's senior by two years. She also took him to work with her. Her youngest son had died in a pogrom, and she was afraid to leave Abrash on his own. Together, we ran through the allotments to one of the company buildings. Behind it, there was a yard in which there was a barn for cows. We went inside and climbed up to the hay loft to hide. Towards evening, the owner arrived, found us, and told us that we had to leave. If the Germans discovered us there, they would shoot us all and burn down the buildings and barns. We thanked him for not disclosing our presence and promised to leave as soon as it got dark.

As night fell, we left the hay loft and began to run. Not far from the company building was a ruined brick factory and kiln shed. We took the children into the ruined shed. We could hear, as soon as we got inside, that other people were already hiding there. Amongst them, were two sisters, Fanya and Riva, who worked for the company. They too had fled after hearing about the final pogrom. They began screaming at us and asking us why we'd come there. We told them that we would leave at first light. Our children were so exhausted that they keeled over and fell asleep as soon as we reached the shed. They hadn't even asked for anything to eat. Nevertheless, as soon as dawn broke, we woke them, tied scarves round their heads like peasant women, and made our way to the railway station. The station was crowded with people. The Germans were transporting labourers to Germany, and we joined in with the general crowds surging on the platform. We were looking for a goods train that would take us west. We saw that there were closed wagons loaded with cement and tiles, and we managed to climb on top; but a woman began screaming that the Germans were checking people's documents, so we climbed down and ran away.

Eventually, we found a train heading west that was carrying a large consignment of logs. We clambered up onto the timber, and a few minutes later the train moved off in the direction of Baranovichi. When I was still in the ghetto, my neighbour, Lazar Losik, had told me that in

Nalibokskiy Forest there was a Jewish partisan unit under the command of Zorin. I told Lisa that, when we came to the forest, we were going to jump off the train and look for the partisans. Fortunately, the train travelled for forty kilometres and then it stopped.

Nearby there was a farm house at the edge of the forest. We quickly got off the train, dragging the children with us, and approached the house. We told the peasant woman who opened the door that we were refugees who had escaped from the train. We were so worn out and bedraggled, that she believed us and took pity on us. She gave the children something to eat and we spent the night with her. We left bright and early the next morning and began walking. The dawn broke in the woods and we met no one, but it was the beginning of a long and miserable journey. We spent the next night sleeping in a ditch. The children were crying, and so were we.

We eventually came to a village and saw a woman in the street. She spotted us and started shouting that she was going to call the police. We began to run, and we kept on running for over five kilometres. I told Lisa that she should go to the police and let them shoot me, because I had no more strength left. She became exasperated and scolded me, and this gave me the incentive to carry on. So we continued for five days, travelling when it was light and spending the nights in ditches, until we finally reached another village. The first person that we saw there was a girl tending a cow. We asked her if there were any police in the village, and she replied, 'Yesterday, but not today'. She took us to meet with another woman, whose appearance and manner, were more in keeping with someone from the city. We related our story, explaining that we were refugees running away from the ghetto, who needed to find the partisans. She listened carefully, and then told us that there was a windmill in the village, where the partisans came to collect flour. She told us to rendezvous at the windmill when night fell, for further instructions. We found our way to the windmill that night, and the woman returned, bringing food for both us and the children. She informed us that, 20 kilometres away in Zhuk-Borok, the village chief had connections with the partisans. She explained how to find our way through the forest, making another stop along the way, at the home of another contact, whose children were also partisans.

We successfully found our way to the house belonging to the partisans' mother. She let us rest there and gave us a bite to eat. When we were rested, she told us how to find the rest of the way. When we finally arrived in the village of Zhuk-Borok, we saw and heard the police approaching in a cart. We ran and jumped into a ditch to hide, and we stayed there until they had passed. After that, we scrambled out and went in search of the village chief. The village consisted of a street of peasant dwellings backing on to a deep, dark forest. We found the home of the chief and told our story once again. He listened, then left us alone in his house, asking us to wait. Barely an hour had passed when the door was suddenly thrown open and a policeman strode in. 'Who are these strangers here?' he barked at us. We froze in terror but managed to stand up and stammer: 'We are the strangers'. The policeman led us, trembling, across the street into the woods. Once there, he revealed that he was actually a partisan in disguise. When my son started to cry, because he couldn't walk anymore from the pain of bloody blisters that covered his feet, the partisan picked him up and carried him in his arms. We walked together through the forest for about six kilometres, finally stopping near a burnt-out farm.

The partisan left us in the care an old peasant, in a dugout on the farm. He assured us that someone would come back for us. We stayed with the old man for two days, sleeping in the deep dugout. The Germans were no longer following us. The old man told us that, three kilometres away, at another farm, they baked bread for the partisans. On hearing this, we decided to go there. It proved to be a fortuitous decision. At exactly the time we found the farm, three partisans from the 'Chapaev' division were heading home after a raid. They had also stopped off at the farm for bread. We retold our story yet again and explained who we were looking for. They said they would take us with them to the 'Zorin' Squad. We began to cry with happiness, our suffering was at an end.

We were so happy when we arrived amongst the people of the 'Zorin' Squad. We thanked the partisans who had delivered us. They continued on their way, but we stayed. Some of the people in the 'Zorin' group recognized us from the ghetto. We were taken to the village gathering where everyone congregated around us asking questions. They all had someone close to them whom they had known in the ghetto, close friends or relatives. They wanted as much information as possible from us about these people. However, it was our sad task to relay the news that the ghetto no longer existed, that the last of the Jews had been taken away or executed. Everyone was crying, and we cried along with them.

We stayed in the forest with the partisan squad. It was around the eve of the October Revolution holidays. People came up to us and congratulated us on the holiday, and we were happy. After the Revolution Day celebrations, we moved to another camp about two kilometres away. We began living in a dugout, and I was appointed leader. Lisa and I fenced off an area inside for ourselves. We made our beds using fir branches and birch twigs. Each person living in the dugout chose a place for themselves in a similar manner. In each dugout, there were about forty people. Among them were lots of young Jewish boys between fifteen and sixteen years old, who had also escaped from the ghetto. We were given saws and axes and told to go into the forest to look for dead wood, in order to make ready for winter.

About three kilometres away from our camp was the 'Bielski' detachment [see glossary]. One day in December, we headed there on a visit. It had been snowing, so the children stayed behind in the dugout. We had hardly covered a kilometre of the distance when German Planes swooped down and began to bomb the camp. We ran back as quickly as we could through the snow, to get to the children. When we arrived back, the dugout was empty. Everyone had scattered. I started to search for my son and called out for him. He didn't have anything to put on his feet and had run out into the snow barefoot. When I found him, he was hidden behind a tree, standing knee-deep in snow. I quickly took off my scarf and twisted it around his feet, lifted him into my arms, and made a run for the dugout. We were fortunate not to be hit by a shell from the bombing.

About a month after that, Grisha Smolar [see glossary] came to visit the squad. It was agreed with the squad leader that he would take me to work for him in the print shop in the Interdistrict Center. Moscow was sending the partisans a printing press by aeroplane, but they didn't know of anyone who was a typesetter. Smolar had learned, by accident, that I could typeset, and he had come directly to the squad to pick me up. Of course, I went willingly, and took my son with me. The printing took place a hundred kilometres away from the Zorin squad, in a small house, in which one room was set up as an editing room, and the other held the printing press. There was a table, and on it stood the printing machine, a box containing a full set of letters, and all the accessories needed for manual typesetting.

Smolar said to me: 'Get familiar with it, as you are going to start typesetting the newspapers.' I set up a work bench and said to him: 'What should I type? Dictate to me.' When he began to dictate, my hands found the right letters by themselves and I began to typeset. Smolar called in the others to see how fast I was able to set the type. I typeset and produced five regional newspapers, including *Mirskaya*, *Stolbtsovskaya* and *Karelichskaya*, as well as posters and leaflets, and everything else concerning the frontline and the action of the partisans. Smolar was also the editor of the newspaper called *Golas Selyanina* [Russian: Voice of the Villager], as well as other newspapers in the region. Copies of my newspapers still hang in the Museum of the Great Patriotic War.

My son would take the newspapers and distribute them at the infirmary where partisans lay wounded. We had excellent doctors there: one male surgeon, and a woman, Dr. Zoya. She was very fond of my son, as were all the partisans, He was a good and clever boy. Dr. Zoya often took him with her when she went on her rounds tending the sick, and he confided in her his ambitions to be a doctor when he grew up.

On one occasion, we learned that the Germans were planning a large partisan blockade. It was suggested that, for his safety, I put my son on a plane and allow him to be flown to the mainland. I started to cry. My son was five and a half years old at the time, and I didn't want to let him go. However, I was eventually persuaded. They told me that that Stevchenko, the head of the special department, was also evacuating his son. After I heard that, I agreed. If I died, then at least my son would survive.

The day came when I gathered together his few belongings, and along with Stevchenko, travelled on a cart to the partisan airfield. It was a hundred kilometres away and it took us two days to get there. Partisans who had been seriously wounded were also taken there to be flown out, as it was impossible to treat them effectively in the forest.

On our first day at the airfield, the evacuation plane didn't arrive. However, on the second day, we heard the hum of the approaching aircraft, and the three partisans on duty lit a signal fire. The plane landed and the lights were hastily extinguished. Newspapers, paper, medicines, and supplies required by the partisans were quickly unloaded, and then they began to take the wounded on board. Stevchenko grabbed our two boys and passed them to the pilot. The doors closed and plane rose up and flew away. People hurried away from the airfield, as the threat of German planes bombing us, was always a brutal reality. They tried to persuade me to leave, but I stood there in despair and cried out my son's name: 'Vova!' Finally, it was Stevchenko who said to me: 'Come, I myself put the children into the hands of the pilot. Let's get out of here'. I was crying, and only allowed myself to be taken away from the place with difficulty. I had never been apart from my son before, and I felt as though my heart had been ripped out. When we finally returned to the squad, people asked if I was sick, so I told them that I had sent my son away. They then told me that it was for the best, and that the surgeon had wanted to send his own son away but had not been allowed to. Nevertheless, I began to cry. I felt reassured but not comforted.

Between 7 and 22 June the Byelorussian advance and offensive began and meanwhile, I was working day and night, typesetting newspapers, bulletins, leaflets and all the requests and orders of the high command. We had to keep up with our troops and inform them about our successes at the front. The Germans began to retreat through the woods and the forest. There were big battles and as a result, many partisans were killed and wounded. The Red Army began to liberate our cities from the Germans. On the 3 July, Minsk, the capital city of Byelorussia, was liberated.

When the partisans began to emerge from the forest, we were fired on from three sides. Each side thought the other side to be the Germans. We were caught in the middle, the cross fire was so intense and the battle was so harsh, that I thanked God my son was not there.

We were positioned behind a hill and could not raise our heads until the shooting had stopped and the confusion was over. After we emerged from the forest, we found that there were many squads from all the nearby areas. We assembled in Stolbtsy where we began to publish newspapers again. There was a big partisan parade on the 3 July, to which I was invited. We were given gifts and medals. I was awarded a medal which said: 'Partisan of the Great Patriotic War.'

Currently, I have fourteen awards, including the Order of the Great Patriotic War, and many certificates. My husband returned home from the front disabled, after being wounded twice. He also had many medals and awards. He died in 1981. My son did become a doctor and worked all his life as the head of radiology in Minsk, in the 3rd Municipal Clinical Hospital. I changed profession after the war: I studied and then worked as head of production at the Minsk hat factory called the 'Red Front.' I worked there from 1951 until my retirement. In 1990, I emigrated to Israel, where I still live.

# I Was an Orphan from the Age of Three
## Lidiya Petrova (Kompanets)

**Lidiya Petrova (Kompanets)**

The difficult memories from my childhood have never left me. At the beginning of the war, I was living with my parents in Minsk, but I don't remember the name of the street. In July 1941, all of our family moved to the ghetto, where the conditions were inhuman. By the time I was three years old, I was an orphan who had lost both of my parents. The word 'mother' had disappeared from my vocabulary forever.

My early memories are of the houses around me being on fire. People would sometimes still try to get back inside to find something to eat, a carrot or an apple. The Germans would pass by, all dressed up and wearing military uniforms. I remember asking for something to eat and being kicked with the edges of their boots. I was constantly hungry and swollen with cuts and blisters. My hair had been cut off because of the lice and the sores on my head. I often couldn't sleep from the pain and would sometimes lose consciousness.

In the ghetto was Children's Home (orphanage) Number 2, on Krasivaya Street. Children like me were sent there, who were weak, ill and orphaned.  Orphanage staff tried to hide children who looked particularly Jewish. Those whose appearance was not especially Jewish, tried to be baptized. I remember that, in the orphanage, there was a large portrait of Hitler on the wall, and in the morning, we would stand in front of the picture and sing. Once we sang, 'O Tannenbaum, O Tannenbaum' (a German Christmas song). The priest would arrive, and, when he did, all of the children would crowd around and listen to him. He gave us small pieces of bread and glasses of water. He also gave us crosses to wear around our necks on a piece of string.

One day, a truck arrived at the orphanage. The truck windows were covered up and two pipes came out of the roof. Children were taken from the orphanage, put inside the van and taken away. They never came back. The van was a mobile gas chamber. I don't remember exactly how it happened, but a few of us were taken to a dark room and made to hide in there. We were hidden to prevent us being taken away. Hidden from death.

After continual heavy bombardment, Children's Home Number 2 was destroyed. Our teachers posted an advertisement. They asked if anyone willing to take a child from the orphanage, even temporarily, would come forward. No one took me. Still sick, swollen and lice infested, I would hide under the bed. The teacher's found me and pulled me out of my hiding place. Eventually I was taken in by a family of railway workers.

In 1945, the forty-five children who were survivors of Children's Home Number 2 were distributed to other children's homes around Minsk. (This was confirmed by the Yad Vashem certificate of 11.02.1995). I was placed in Orphanage Number 7, along with children whose parents had been killed at the front.

The memories of the time I spent in the Children's orphanage number 2 will never leave me - the constant fear, hunger and persistent disease. In post-war Minsk however, conditions were barely improved. Left half-starved, half-dressed, without any visible means of help and support, I still had to survive on my own.

Without having experienced any childhood, I spent my youth graduating from a trade school in Riga. Following that, I worked in Siberia, Kolyma and Magadan, before studying at medical school. After receiving a small pension, I was able to return to where my parents were buried, my homeland, Byelorussia, now Belarus.

**Former prisoners of the Minsk Ghetto, Lidiya Petrova and Eugeniy Machiz**

**23 February 2012**

# It Will Never Be Forgotten
## Maya Radashkovskaya

**Maya Radashkovskaya, born Maya Smelkinson**

**Maya and her sister, Celia, were prisoners in the Minsk Ghetto**

I will never forget the pain and suffering of that time. Pain was caused by the loss of relatives and friends, and constant fear for the children and the elderly. All this was combined with a total sense of insecurity, hunger and cold. It is impossible to convey in words from the heart, how much grief the prisoners endured.

My sister and I were sent to the ghetto directly from the Pioneer Camp in Kolodishchi.

We had been in the woods at camp when the war began. A bomb fell on the camp and burned everything. Most of the pioneer leaders fled, but Dr. Halperin, who was a senior person in charge, made a decision to follow the refugees who were already fleeing the city to the east. Our parents did not give us up as gone; they had been told that we had been evacuated.

There were people of many different nationalities on the road, Byelorussians and Russians alongside Jews. On the highway, low level German planes fired at us. Eventually we caught up with the German Military Field Gendarmerie near to the village of Smalyavichi. Dr. Halperin approached them and requested a pass allowing orphans to return to the orphanage in Minsk. She was given the pass and we returned to Minsk. We walked for a very long time without anything to eat.

When we arrived back in Minsk, it was under curfew. Dr. Halperin brought all of the children to her house and the next morning told everyone to go in search of their homes. In the event that they were unable to find anyone they were to come back to her. There were only two children who came back to her - me and my sister Celia. I was 7 years old and Celia was 13.

On 19 and 20 July an order had been issued to create a 'Jewish District in Minsk', and on 1 August the ghetto was created. All Jews had to leave their homes and move there. The ghetto was fenced in on all four sides, and was guarded day and night. As soon as the ghetto was established, it was described by the authorities as a 'divorce from the local population.' The Germans were trying to set the local Byelorussian population against the Jews.

We were on our own.

Later, the *Judenrat* [see glossary] managed to open a children's home on Zaslavskaya Street. It accommodated 150 children. A smaller centre for orphans and sick children was later set up, but that only took around 68 children. By then I was suffering from malnutrition, anemia and frostbitten hands and feet, so I managed to acquire a place there. Conditions were grim, I would lie on the floor beside the unlit Dutch stove and, once or twice Dora Losik, would bring a bucket of soup. Everyone would ask: 'Auntie Dora, can I have some.... even a little bit?' However, she would reply, 'My dear little children, I have to share this bucket of soup, between sixty-eight children.' [For more on Dora Losik, see Frieda Reizman's Story].

On 7 November 1941, the first major pogrom began, and it was terribly frightening. Countless people were thrown into vans to be taken away and shot. The vehicles returned time and again for more victims. It is impossible to forget the screams and tears of the mothers and children; they broke my heart. After the pogrom, orphans who had no shelter quickly matured. They grew wise, hiding wherever they could. The children would sing this song:

> 'November seventh was a day of trouble,
>
> The Jews were attacked by German thugs,
>
> They were beaten with whips and hacked with swords,
>
> And mocked as much as was possible'

Adults sang in Yiddish:

> *Ir zayt dokh yidn*
>
> *Ir zayt tsufridn*
>
> *Tsu undsere tsores*
>
> *Vet kumen a nes.*
>
> *Un Got zol gebn*
>
> *Az mir ale zoln lebn.*
>
> *Tsu undsere tsores*
>
> *Vet kumen a nes.*

> And yet you are Jews
>
> You are satisfied

That to our troubles

A miracle will come.

And may God grant

That we shall live.

To our troubles

A miracle will come.

On 2 March 1942, on the feast of Purim, two vehicles arrived at the orphanage. One of them had a gramophone in the back and was playing music. They began to load up the children and take them away. I was in the isolation ward, lying in the corner, on the floor. When I heard all the noise of the children crying, I quietly crawled under the stove. It was never heated, and I soon lost consciousness. Sixty-seven children were taken away and killed that day and I was the only one to survive. Hours later, Dora Losik came back and heard my hoarse, cat-like cry from underneath the stove. I was the only one left alive. She took me to her home and then later she took me to Malke Kaufman, asking her to take care of me. Malke already had four children, but despite abject poverty, she fed me like one of her own.

The surviving prisoners of the Minsk Ghetto will forever remember days of 6 pogroms in the ghetto. 21- 23 October 1943, was the date of the last pogrom. During those days the ghetto was completely liquidated, drawing a line underneath the twenty-seven months of its existence.

Hitler had systematically attempted the extermination of the Jews. Among the victims of Nazism were our fathers, mothers, sisters, brothers and children. Despite that, however, we are still here, alone with our memories of the past. We were prisoners of the ghettos, and of the concentration camps, but we are survivors, living with the memory of the suffering of our people. From our tears, our pain, our anguish and our hopes, there emerged the State of Israel.

# The '*Zvezda*' Newspaper Was Printed in Our House
## Alla Rakovshchik and Irina Golubeva

**Alla Rakovshchik**

My name is Alla Davydovna Rakovshchik. My maiden name was Sussman and I was born in Minsk in 1937. My father was David Sussman and my mother was Fanya Davydovna Kivovich. My older brother Anatoly was born in 1932, my younger brother Heinrich (Henry) in 1935, and my sister Irina (Ira) was born in 1939.

**Irina Golubeva**

Before the war, we lived in a private house, at number 4 Izdatelskaya Street. It was on the outskirts of Minsk, in the area of Komarovsky Market. When the war started and the bombing began, the home of our friends, the Yakovenko family, was burned down, so my father invited them to come and live in our house. Calistrat Yakovenko came from the same hometown as my father, and they also worked together. However, shortly afterwards, our family was forced to move into the Jewish ghetto in Minsk.

In June 1941, my older brother Anatoly was away from the city at a pioneer camp in Zhdanovichy. The camp, along with all the children, was evacuated to the Stalingrad area. Anatoly was put into an orphanage there, where he stayed until the end of the war.

My father died in 1942 under mysterious circumstances, and the three of us children remained with our mother. We moved in with relations of hers on Sukhaya Street in the ghetto. My mother went to work, to try and earn some money for food, leaving us two little girls in the care of our brother, but he too, would sneak out of the ghetto in search of food. When he left the house, my mother's relations would look after us. My brother was only seven years old, but he knew how to leave the ghetto without being seen. He would beg on the streets for food and bring it back to us.

We lived in the ghetto until the spring of 1943. The Yakovenko's son Alexander, occasionally managed to procure food such as potatoes, beets, carrots and onions, from the garden of our old house, and he would bring it to us.

My younger sister Ira, was often ill in the ghetto, because of the harsh conditions in which we lived. One day my mother went to work and never came back. The three of us were left without parents. We cried long and hard, and our mother's cousin, with whom we lived, consoled us as best she could.

**Our mother - Fanya Davydovna Sussman in 1932**

Shortly after our mother disappeared, a Byelorussian woman, who had been a friend of hers, began to sneak into the ghetto. Her name was Anna Fedorovna Shirpo, but we called her Aunt Nura. After the war, we learned that she was a member of the underground organisation set up by the Communist Party. We also discovered that our previous home on Izdatelskaya Street, had been recommended as a suitable place to set up an underground printing press. In our old house, three issues of the newspaper 'Zvezda' were printed, and various flyers were also produced.

**Our father (centre) - David Sussman**

When she arrived in the ghetto, Aunt Nyura told our relatives that she had been sent, at our mother's request, to help us and take care of us. My brother told her that it had been my mother's wish for us always to stay together and not be separated. Aunt Nyura told us not to cry anymore. She convinced us that we would be able to remain together, if we kept quiet, listened to her, and did as she told us. She took my sister Ira out of the ghetto first, and then managed to take both my brother and me.

It happened like this: one night we were taken outside and bundled into in a small cart. A tarpaulin or blanket was put on top of us and off we went. We were shaken up and down inside the cart when it passed over a stone bridge. We groaned from the vibrations, forgetting that we had to remain silent. Eventually we arrived at a house which may have been Aunt Nyura's home. Hidden from prying eyes, we were given a straw mattress to sleep on and fed with bread and milk. I remember that there were curtains which we had to keep closed, and we were not allowed to walk around the house. We felt lost and disorientated, still constantly asking: 'where is our mother?'

The house we stayed in with Aunt Nyura was on Tolstoy Street in Minsk, close to Orphanage Number 2. Now she took us there and we were registered as three Russian orphans, under the name of Davydov. This may have been arranged by private agreement with the director of the orphanage. We stayed there until 1946. During our stay in the orphanage, all I can remember is fear. My sister Ira was often sick and would frequently be placed in the isolation ward. My mother had always told me never to leave Ira on her own, so I often went to the ward to check if she was still there. For this vigilance, I would receive a slap.

**Older brother**

**Anatolia Sussman, 1960**

Once the bombing started, Ira and I would hide together sometimes in a dark pantry located in the basement. I remember this particular episode with clarity. A commissioner came to the orphanage. He was a tall, thin German with a woman assistant. All the children had to line up, while the staff stood behind a glass door watching. The commissioner went along the line checking the status of each child's health (their eyes, throat, hands, stomach) They picked out the healthier children and made them stand to one side. I was in this group. However, I needed to use the toilet and I kept hopping about, showing how impatient I was to go. One of the staff told the Germans that I needed to use the toilet, and, with their permission, I was removed from the line. Instead of being taken to the toilet, I was pushed into a dark storage room and told to hide there and be quiet. I didn't understand why I was being punished and cried. However, this noble act from the member of staff saved my life. The children who had been selected and pulled out of line, were taken away and never seen again. We believed that their blood was to be used in transfusions for German soldiers. Six children were taken that day. The staff was crying. They had feelings too and were sorry for the children they had lost.

**Younger brother**

**Heinrich (Henry) Sussman, 1960**

Another memory is of a religious festival. We were seated at tables, around which a priest was walking dressed in a smart cassock. The priest sprinkled us with water, then placed a cross on a narrow ribbon around each child's neck. The girls later turned them into dolls and played with them. During the next bombing, I found that I had left my doll-cross underneath my pillow. There was an order for us all to hide, but despite the roar of bombs and broken glass all around me, I went back into the bedroom to retrieve my doll-cross. I was afraid to lose her.

All around the orphanage were houses with fruit trees in the gardens. After the fires, caused by the bombing, had subsided, we would search the gardens for fruit. Collecting and eating the apples baked in the heat of the fires. My brother Henry was smart and would often run away from the orphanage. He would bring back food, such as a baked potato, carrots or bread, which he would share with all the children. Most of the time, however, we were cold and hungry. All three of us had fleas and were covered in scabs and sores. It was hard for us without my mother and, despite everything, we kept waiting for her and never stopped hoping that she would find and rescue us.

**Alla (15 years old) in the centre, with her cousins Michaile and Lyuba, 1952**

**Irina Golubeva**

**With her husband and daughter**

Then Aunt Nyura was killed. Her daughter Galya however, had saved our birth certificates and other documents relating to our house that Aunt Nyura had given her. When the war ended, Galya went to Flat 1, Number 4, Izdatelskaya Street, and handed all the documents over to my aunt Elizabeta Efimovna Sussman. She told my aunt where she could find her nieces and nephews and informed her of the names we were using. Aunt Elizabeta found us and took us out of the orphanage in 1946. Thanks to the documents that had been kept by Galya we were able to go to court, and eventually we returned to our home. Our aunt now took custody of us and we lived in the house on Izdatelskaya Street until 1970 when it was demolished for the construction of Komarovskiy Market.

Nowadays, there is a sign just opposite the shopping centre on Kulman Street. It is the place where our old house used to be. The sign reads, 'In this place, Izdatelskaya, 4/1, (Vidavetskaya, 4/1) during the Great Patriotic War, the newspaper '*Zvezda*' was published.

**Alla (second left) with her daughters and Irina (far right)**

# Memories Must Be Preserved
## Frieda Reizman

**Frieda Reizman**

On the day that Frieda Reizman recounted this story to Arkady Shulman, she had just returned from the annual memorial meeting at Yama in Minsk. This commemoration takes place annually on 2 March. On this day in 1942, over 5000 Jews, including many children, were shot and killed in a punitive action carried out by the Nazis and their 'henchmen-policemen' [see Yama in glossary].

We lived in the ghetto near the pits on Krimskaya Street. At that time, Krimskaya linked Zaslavskaya and Tankovaya Streets. Now it no longer exists. On the corner stood a synagogue and on the same street, there was a children's home which my mum sometimes visited. She tried to help the orphans who lived there and sometimes took them food. Four of us lived together at that time: our mother, my father's uncle, my middle brother and me. The uncle began to live with us after the first progrom of 7 November 1941, when his entire family was killed.

I will start by saying a little about the pre-war years and telling you something about the lives of my parents. I will also describe a few of my memories of childhood, memories which even the war could not dim. Before the war, our father Wolf (Velvl) Sholomovich Losik had worked in a shoe factory called Kaganovich. He had been orphaned at a young age and was raised by his grandmother. However, she also died when Wolf was only ten years old. He was the only male left in his family, and life forced him to be strong and independent. While his grandmother had been alive, the little boy would go to the synagogue regularly in order to read the *Kaddish* [Hebrew: memorial prayer] for his father. His first job was as an apprentice shoemaker in the town of Pukhovichy and over the years, he became skilled at his trade. In 1920, at the age of 17, he moved to Minsk and got a job in a factory. However, he travelled often to Pukhovichy in order to visit relatives. He was a taciturn young man. In 1932 he joined the Party and around that time, was sent to further his studies in some kind of school of further education for workers. However, he was unable to remain there due to illness and he always deeply regretted this. (I believe that the illness in question may have been a stomach ulcer for which no effective medication was available at the time). His older sister was serving as a maid in the house of a wealthy family and she lived with this family in a box room, so Wolf moved in there with her.

Our mum, Dora Kuselevna, worked, as a young woman, in the Lower Bazaar in what is now called March the 8th Square, in Minsk. The Lower Bazaar was a small department store and she served at the counter selling fabrics. She liked to call herself a *manufacturshitsa* [Russian: a textile dealer]. Mum had perfect dress sense. Whatever fabric she chose to wear just looked amazing! My mother was one of seven children, and each one of these siblings had their own children. It was a huge family. For example, my mother's youngest sister had six sons. I remember that, when the remnants of this *mishpokha* [Yiddish: family] gathered together for a photograph in 1965, there were thirty people in the picture: cousins, second cousins, brothers and sisters. My mother was born in the town of Shatsk, and her maiden name was Shatskaya. Her father Kushe-Leiser died at the young age of 38. He was a *balagula* [Yiddish: drayman or driver of a horse-driven vehicle].

**Frieda Losik 1944**

My mother lived in Shatsk for the first 23 or 24 years of her life. Dad met her at a party when she was just 18 or 19 years old. He told me that, when he first saw her, he was literally dumbfounded because she was so beautiful. After they were married, my mother stayed in Shatsk while my dad lived and worked in Minsk, only coming to stay with her at weekends. In 1926, my older brother was born in Shatsk and was named Kushe-Leiser in memory of his grandfather. It was after his birth that my mother moved to Minsk. A second son Avrom-

Meyske soon followed and I, the youngest, was born in1935 and named Frieda in memory of my grandmother.

**Losik Family, 1945**

**From left to right - mother Dora, brother Lazar, Frieda, father Wolf, and a family relative**

My family rented two rooms on Myasnikov Street and I remember this apartment well. The house was small and the windows almost touched the pavement. We could easily see the people walking by outside. The household was poor and spoke mainly Yiddish. Mum was a deeply religious person, but dad was a communist and not religious at all. I recall one particular occasion: it was at the time of the High Holy Days and my mother had cooked a special meal. When it was time to sit at the table and recite the prayers, my father flatly refused: 'No, I will not!' he said. My mother responded: 'If you don't say the prayer – then there will be no food!' At that very moment, we heard a knock at the door and, when mum opened it, there was an old man standing there. It was a cold autumnal evening, but he was wearing such threadbare clothing that you could almost see his thin body through the fabric. My mother was a very kind person and she asked the old man to come into the house, even as she continued to argue with my dad. Hearing the conversation, the old man said: 'Please don't argue. Shall *I* say the prayers?' So, it all ended peacefully, and we were able to sit at the table and eat. Mum gave the old man a shirt and a bed for the night. She suggested that, in the morning, they would go to the department store and she would get him some clothes, maybe even a corduroy suit. At that time such a suit was a rarity. However, in the morning, when we all awoke, the old man had gone from the house. Everything was closed and he had just disappeared. From that time on my mum had a favourite saying: *Fun fenster, un fun tir.* [Yiddish: from windows and doors.] Around that time some good fortune befell us. This was when the new Soviet stores called Torgsina shops were opening, and my mum was asked to work there. The location was good and mum was able to get clothes for our family, and now we always had butter on the table. Mum put our luck down to our mysterious visitor. She would say, 'That old man was the great *Moyshe-Rebeynu*' [Hebrew: The prophet Moses].

**My brother Lazar Losik**

We lived in Minsk until 1940, when dad got a job in a factory and was transferred to Bialystok [see glossary]. He went to work there as chief engineer in a shoe factory and the family also moved to be there with him. We got a two-room apartment and my mother found work in a store. I had a Polish nanny and it was from her that I learned to speak Polish. I remember that one day she took me to church with her. When I told my dad that I had visited a church, he reprimanded the nanny, 'Manya, don't you ever do that again.'

When we lived in Minsk, my brothers studied at the Jewish School Number 12. They were naughty boys and I remember that, on one occasion, my mother was called to the school by the Hebrew teacher who reported to her that they had been playing truant: '*Nisht gekumen, nisht gekumen, efsher hundert mol...dan yo gekumen!*' [Yiddish: They didn't come, didn't come for maybe a hundred times! And then they turned up!] However, once we had moved to Bialystok, Avrom-Meyske went to school there, while my older brother Kushe-Leiser stayed at home with us – at least for the first month. However, one day he took me outside onto the porch and told me, 'Tomorrow, I want you to tell our dad that I have left and gone to Minsk.' And, with that, he left. That night, I was awakened in the night by a loud cry. It was mum screaming, and shouting 'Lazar has disappeared!' I realised that they were looking for Kushe-Leiser, so I found my dad and told him that Kushe-Leiser had left and gone to stay at a relative's house on Vitebskaya Street in Minsk. I remember that not long after that incident, Kushe-Leiser found work there as a plumber!

On 20 June 1941 Dad went into a sanatorium in Drushkininkai, probably due to pulmonary emphysema and for attention to his stomach ulcer. My mum, Avrom-Meyske and I stayed in Bialystok. However, it was on the very next day that the war began, and Mum quickly realised that we would have to go back to Minsk to be with Kushe-Leiser. We started out by truck with Masharsky, a friend of my dad, and his family. However, we had to finish the journey on foot, walking for about two weeks. At one point, a convoy of Germans overtook us and when we reached Minsk, we discovered that they were already in control there. We settled down, not in our old apartment, but in the one opposite where there was an empty room. Here we were re-united with Kushe-Leiser.

**With husband Albert and granddaughter Anna 1980**

One day a woman came to see my Mum. She told her that Losik, our father, had been seen in the forest near Minsk. It seems that he had left Drushkininkai, which is situated in a natural forest reserve, and had walked far enough, under cover of the woods, to get close to Minsk. My mum was 39 years old, a young and brave woman. She now went alone into the area of the forest described to her in order to search for my dad. At this time, there were various groups in these dense forests, including Nazis, partisans, and others who were simply homeless. It seems a miracle that my mother actually found my dad who was indeed hiding there. She told him how things were in Minsk and brought him home.

Soon after this, orders were issued by the Germans for the resettlement of Jews in the ghetto. We obeyed the order and, once again, moved to a new place. Our group consisted of Dad, Mum, me, my two brothers and four of our relatives: my father's aunt, Rayful Sukhman, her husband Leib, her daughter Fanya and her little granddaughter Lyuba. We all moved into a tiny one-room apartment on Vitebskaya Street. In this room there was just a sofa and, opposite that, was the door. We all slept on the floor. I remember that Dad buried his party membership card in that apartment and then recovered it after the war. He was a Party member for fifty years in all.

My dad Wolf-Losik went out of the ghetto daily, walking with a work detail to an abattoir in Krasnoye Urochishe. (Now it is a car factory). As soon as the underground movement [see glossary] was established in the ghetto, he joined it. At the very first meeting, he discovered that Gebelev, a friend of his from pre-war years, was a member of the same group. They had both been actively engaged in public work in their neighbouring home towns of Pukhovichy and Uzlyany. Hirsh Smolar [see glossary] was also part of that group. Smolar was a writer and academic who had formerly been a leading member of the illegal communist party in Poland, and would soon become a leader of the resistance in the Minsk Ghetto. He later became commissar of a partisan group operating in Byelorussian forests.

In the first pogrom of 7 November 1941, the inhabitants of Vitebskaya Street were moved to Respublikanskaya Street. However, my father's aunt Rayful Shulman was killed. She had been in a work-detail which was taken away and herded into a mobile gas chamber. Her husband, my uncle, was at work outside the ghetto at that time. His work detail was not allowed back in while the pogrom was in progress. He therefore survived.

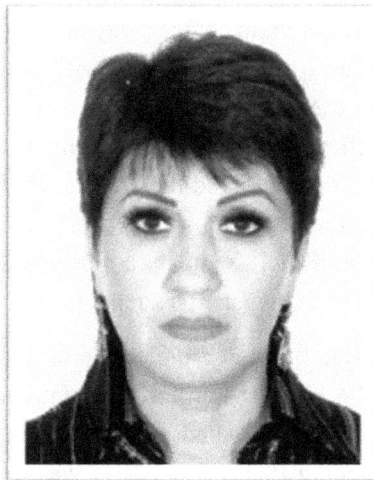

**Frieda's daughter Maria**

The apartment at Respublikanskaya Street was a large one. Nevertheless, it was crowded as there were four families living there. Our group was allocated one room and we all lived in the same seven square metres. There were two beds and a desk. My uncle slept on the desk, my brothers were together in one bed, and the rest of us slept on the second bed. I remember that apartment and how jealous I always felt when Dad held little Lyuba on his lap. Children are children wherever they are – even in the ghetto!

**Son Michael Reizman**

I also recall that Dad brought revolvers and cartridges into that apartment. He hid them under a mattress, and I slept on top of them. After a day or so someone would come and take the weapons away. Food was short, as we had no money with which to feed ourselves. Somehow, Mum still managed to get horse meat, which she cooked with cabbage leaves. She also made groats. In the early days, soon after the Germans had captured Minsk, there was looting in the shops and, on one occasion, my brother joined the looters. He brought home a crate of vinegar, which really helped us. My mother used it to flavour potato peelings mixed with cabbage leaves. It was a masterpiece – *a maykhel* [Yiddish: a mouth-watering delicacy]. I remember the children's reactions to this day. That vinegar was such a tasty treat for hungry people!

At this time, my mother and brother did not go to work, but Dad was working in a slaughterhouse. However, this did not last long, maybe until January or February 1942. It was winter time and there were severe frosts. I had blisters on my feet, and I recall Dad heating a needle in a candle flame and piecing them. The house was so cold. However, there were still wooden sheds and toilets, so at least we had something to burn!

One day, one of my father's underground group was caught by the Gestapo, and the captor led the Nazis directly to our house. The ghetto underground found out about this and managed to warn Dad just a few minutes before the Gestapo arrived. He took one of the weapons that were being stored at home and managed to escape. I remember how the Germans burst in. One of them immediately hit my mother in the face. I was hiding under a stool. When they started to search, I was able to run out into the hallway and started for the door. It was open, and through the crack I saw a soldier walking up and down outside. While he was facing me, I was afraid to move, but when he turned his back, I ran out and hid in the lavatory which was located in the yard. I was there for a long time and it was so cold. I discovered later that members of the underground were watching our house all the time and it was they who saved our family. Someone eventually pulled me out of the toilet, but I never discovered exactly who it was that rescued me. Apparently, I was ice-cold, had lost consciousness, and my hands were blackened and swollen. I remember finally waking up in a large building on Respublikanskaya Street.

**Husband Albert Reizman**

The building had been a doll factory before the war. It was now just a huge empty space in the middle of which stood a big table (something like a billiard table). There was a dead woman lying on it and I saw that rats had gnawed part of her face away. The sight just terrified me. I crawled under some blankets and lay hidden in that room for some time. Finally, the underground came for me and took me to my Mum, but the effects of that trauma would be with me for a long time. After that episode, I started to wet the bed, and this continued for many years until I was 14 years old.

You may wonder how my mum was saved. When the Germans questioned her about the whereabouts of her husband, she told them that he was at work. When they asked where he worked, she replied, 'I don't know where he works. I have never been there, but I could take you to the home of one of his workmates.' She went with them and directed them to this man's house, but when the soldiers went to the house to fetch him, she managed to get away. Now the Germans set a trap at the house where we lived. They searched it and then watched it continuously. Although they allowed people in, they stopped all of those who tried to come out.

Now, sometime earlier, my mum had been visiting a friend who was also called Dora – like her. In that same house, there lived a Polish Jewish lady who was about 90 years old. This old lady was lonely and my mother had befriended her. She always wore a belt into which she had sewn some gold, and one day, during one of my mum's visits, she had pulled off the belt and said to my mum, '*Dveyra* [Yiddish: Dora] take this and hide it away. You might need it sometime.' My mum had taken the belt home with her, and hidden it in a small sack of flour which she had been saving. Although this sack had been lying on the table in full view when the Germans had first searched the house, they did not check or even touch it.

**With former prisoners of the ghetto and Nazi concentration camps in Germany, at the home of Manfred Cableav in Germany. He is a supporter of the ghetto survivors. (Frieda is second from the left in the front row)**

Fortunately for us all, we had a *malina* in our house. My mum told her friend Dora to go into the house and tell the children to take that sack of flour from the table and then escape with them through the *malina*. This escape route was through a trap-door concealed under the bed and it led straight into the room of the house next door. Of course, that other house was not being watched by the Germans, so my brothers and I went with Dora and escaped.

We found my mother and went to stay with her in Shevchenko Street with some of our distant relatives. The Germans continued to look for us, but we were living in the ghetto under the name of Sukhman and were not discovered. However, we did not know where Dad was. To make it worse, our elder brother Kushe-Leiser was now really traumatised. He was so shocked by all of the events going on around him that he seemed to have sunk into some kind of trance, and my mother could not let him out of the apartment. Our middle brother Avrom-Meyshke, (we called him by a pet name Mishka), was the one who took care of me at this time. He was such a kind person. I remember that I had very little appetite and he was always the one who could coax me into eating. He was a real *mentsch* [Yiddish: decent human being].

We managed to survive like this until the spring of 1942 when finally, on April 9th, a young boy, a stranger, came to visit us. He told my mother that he would return on the following day and take her to her husband. My mother decided to take me along and, on the next day, we accompanied the boy to a place inside the ghetto where two old pre-revolutionary homes had once stood. (A fashion house stands there now). The buildings were very dilapidated so that only the frame remained. We went into the ruins. The boy whistled and a ladder was lowered from above. We climbed up and the ladder was immediately pulled up after us. At first, I did not recognise our dad. He had grown a large moustache to make himself look like a Tatar. He told us that on the following day he would be leaving to join the partisans in the forest. Mum asked: 'Are you leaving me here with three children? At least take Lazar with you.' Dad considered for a while and then replied, 'Tomorrow I will send someone to fetch Lazar and I will take him with me.' After that we heard no more of Dad or Lazar until the following year.

So now there were just four of us left: me, mum, Avrom-Meyske and little Lyubochka. Dad's Uncle Leib Sukhman had gone to work one morning and got caught up in a raid. He was sent to the concentration camp at Trostenets [see glossary] and, as far as I know, he died there soon after. His son, Mikhail Sukhman, still lives in Minsk.

In the winter of 1943, my brother, Avrom-Meyske, was working with a work detail. The work involved gathering firewood. One day, they were taken to the workplace and their convoy was attacked by partisans. The Germans fled, and many prisoners escaped into the woods, but Mikhail decided that he would return home and stay with us. We asked him why he had not escaped like the others. 'How can I leave you?' he replied. He continued his work gathering firewood. However, late one evening when his work detail returned to the ghetto, Mikhail was not among them. Mum immediately sensed that he had been in a roundup. She was so distraught that she tore a tuft of hair from her scalp in grief. She ran to Gotenbach, the head of the Gestapo, and fell on her knees, begging him to save her son. My mother was a very beautiful woman and Gotenbach told her, 'If your son is still alive, I will try to save him.' But he already knew that no one who was caught in the raid had remained alive.

I learned after the war that, on 29 and 30 January 1943, all those who were captured in the raid were taken into the prison yard on Volodarsky and shot. The bodies were taken to Trostenets. Meanwhile, in the ghetto where the police were Jewish, one of them, Isaac Hayot, told our mother, 'I saw your son in the prison yard, he is in the sixth chamber of the prison, in the basement. He has asked that you send him a small parcel.' Mum did what she could, and sent her son parcels on three occasions. Only then did she learn that Isaac Hayot was taking those parcels for himself, and that Misha was, as she had suspected, no longer alive. After the war, Hayot was jailed.

Now my mother and I were alone. We lived on Krimskaya Street in the synagogue. There were many other people also living there. We two were located in the hallway, and next to us was a Jewish family from Poland with five beautiful daughters. Their father and mother seemed so old to me then, but after the war I learned that they were only in their fifties. My mother worked in the courtyard of the Government House. If you walk from Miasnikov Street today, you can see that the same house is still there. Mum would take me to work with her. Next to the house lived Max the German who bred rabbits. I used to clean out their cages, tearing up the grass and feeding them.

**Excursion to the former Minsk Ghetto**

One morning in the summer of 1943, there was a rumour in the ghetto that the Germans were going to liquidate the children's home on Zaslavskaya. Sometimes the orphans would visit us, and my mother would feed them as best she could. As soon as she became aware of the rumour, my mother rushed to the orphanage. As she walked around the two floors of the old brick house she heard a child crying, and discovered a little girl hiding in the oven. She could not understand how this girl had managed to squeeze into that small space. She brought the child back to stay with us. Her name was Maya Radashkovskaya [see Maya Radashkovskaya's story]. We took a door off its hinges and that door became her bed. Maya was older than her years, and she soon left us to go the Russian district [see glossary]. She warned us not to wait for her to return, but we did manage to stay in touch. After the war, she continued to live for a time in Minsk, and now she lives in Israel.

One day, in 1943, when my mother was on her way to work on the Russian side, she was approached by a stranger. He told her that he had been trying to find her for a long time. 'I have come from your son Lazar. I will take you to him.' Mum spoke to him in Russian. She spoke it well, but with a strong Jewish accent. She suggested that he take me to Lazar first. They agreed on a meeting place and it was then that my mother gave me the news that tomorrow I would have to leave.

**Former prisoners of the ghetto**
**Maya Krapina, Rimma Halperin, Frida Reizman**
**with the Ambassador of Germany in Belarus.**

The next day, I went with my mother to the wire fence which surrounded the ghetto. On Flaksa Street there were gates. We sat and waited for a moment when there would be no Germans or police around and, as soon as the opportunity presented itself, I crawled under the wire. As Mum said goodbye to me, she pointed: 'There is a small cart over there. Go quickly and run over to it.' On the cart sat a dark skinned young man, maybe 15 years old. This was Misha Schneider. He now lives in America. There was also a Byelorussian peasant who put me in the cart, and off we went, all three, in the direction of Minsk. I did not look Jewish as I was light haired and blue-eyed, and my mother had dressed me in a headscarf as worn by the local girls.

Somewhere just outside of Minsk we heard shooting. The peasant took us off the cart and left. Misha Schneider and I ran, but I was unable to keep going for long. I had a stabbing pain in my side, so Misha took me in his arms and carried me. We found a barn and hid inside the hay. The sun had already set. Finally, the shooting ended and, eventually, the farmer found us and took us back to his home. At his place in Uzlyany, he fed us and let us sleep in the hayloft. Later in the evening Misha's brother Fima Schneider arrived on horseback. He was in a partisan unit with my own brother. It was Fima who took us to the village of Ozerichino. He told us that this was where my brother was staying. He was in charge of explosives, and was currently planning an operation on the railways. However, at the time of our arrival, he was asleep in a cellar. Fima took me to him and woke him up, saying: 'Lazar, I've brought your sister.' At first Lazar told him to go away and not to bother him. But then I said something and, when he heard my voice, he opened his eyes. Now he saw me, grabbed me by the shoulders and began to shout: 'Mishka our brother is no longer with us.' He was crying! This was such a bad experience for me.

Lazar was a fighter with the partisans in the Kutuzov 2nd Minsk Partisan Brigade in Lapidus. A squad was staying near the village of Porechye. He could not take me along with him, as he was part of the fighting force. However, he asked the cowherd in Ozerichino to look after me, and so I stayed there for a time and helped him to take care of the cows. I recall that, during that time, I was plagued by scabies. The itching was so severe that I used to tear my hands to pieces. The only thing that made me feel better was to go to the river and plunge my hands into the water. Meanwhile, Lazar returned for a short time and agreed to leave me with the same farmer while he went off again. This time, he was gone for about a month because he went all the way to Minsk and brought my mother back with him. Lazar had discovered the details of her whereabouts by partisan post. He brought her back on horseback, and I remember that they talked all through the night. The next morning, he took me and our mother, in a partisan detachment, to Porechye. I recall how we had to walk through a swamp for about five kilometres. I was jumping from hummock to hummock, and my mother found it very hard to keep going. It was not until the evening that we finally left the swamp behind.

Mother looked after the wounded in the hospital in the unit, and I was placed in the village called Sviatoye with a Byelorussian woman called Paladya. This was in the Pukhovichy area, in a village of just nine houses. On the other side of the river was another village called Porechye, where forty Jewish children lived during the war. Here in Sviatoye, the partisan doctor, Podolyako, finally cured me of scabies by mixing lard with gunpowder and rubbing it into my skin. And it was here that I finally regained my childhood. I was mischievous, rode around on horseback and played with the boys. I remember fighting with Paladya's son, even though he was older than me.

On 5 July 1944 we returned to Minsk. Mum was eager to go to the city. She still wanted to know what had really happened to Mishka. Hayot had told her: 'Your son said that, if something were to happen to him, and if you are still alive, he will leave a message for you on the wall in the sixth prison cell.' She had to be sure. Luckily we knew the prison guard. He was our pre-war neighbour Ruva. He went with our mother into the sixth chamber which, as I now know, was called 'The Jew Cell'. There was a lot of graffiti on the wall but, of course, nothing from Mishka. Hayot had invented everything.

We now settled on Respublikanskaya Street, in an apartment previously occupied by a policeman. He had finally escaped after living there in hiding from the Germans. Here we hosted almost all of the Lapidus partisan unit. These guys were young and always hungry, so they often stole chickens, or even a goat. They would bring the food back to us to cook and eat. My brother Lazar also lived there with us. He had been responsible for the derailment of 18 enemy trains during the war and was later presented with the Order of Lenin. He was also awarded the Order of the Red Star and the Order of the Red Banner. He was one of the first in Byelorussia to be awarded the Partisan Medal of the First Degree – an award of which he was particularly proud.

Finally, Dad returned to us a few weeks after the liberation of Minsk. He had been working in some covert position, and his work was shrouded in secrecy. He was also presented with a military award, but nothing has ever been said about it.

In September 1944, I went into the first class of school number 12, and Lazar began to work as a plumber. Dad was sent to rebuild the shoe factory named after Thalmann, and soon Lazar went to work for him. I was given a photograph of the partisan unit in which Lazar fought. They would often get together after the war. Reunions were organised by Haim Kaczynski who, in those years, worked as a driver and delivered bread.

Eventually my mother fell ill with typhus and was taken to the Hospital for Infectious Diseases. When she came home, she was very weak and, very soon afterwards, she died. Dad worked in the Thalmann shoe factory until he retired. He lived to the age of 88 and died in 1991. Lazar died three years after our Dad – whom he had loved very much. Meanwhile, I graduated from the technical high school, and then studied at the All-Union Institute of Textile and Light Industry in Moscow. I then worked at the knitting factory which was housed in the building which is now the Jewish Community Centre on Khoruzhey Street. Now I am the head of the ghetto prisoners' charity called GILF and I have held the position for more than 20 years. Every year our numbers decrease, but our memories of the terrible events of the war years must continue to be told. It is our duty and our responsibility.

# A Boy Aged Thirteen
## Vladimir Rubezhin

**Vladimir Rubezhin**

An article entitled 'Ghetto Tragedy' by Ilya Erenburg appeared in the magazine *Belarus No.6*, dated 1946 and issued by the National Archive of the Republic of Belarus. The article told the story of Vladimir Rubezhin, a young man who was then studying at The Suvorov Military School, but had not long previously, at the age of fourteen, been a bomber with the partisans. He had even participated in combat, having also been a member of a clandestine ghetto organisation.

Mikhail Burshtein (Mihas Bury), who was gathering information about young Minsk ghetto survivors, read the article and determined to find out more about this extraordinary young man. Burshtein writes, 'I had already heard a lot about this person. My wife used to work with him at the Kirov Plant. She told me that he was a good specialist and hard-working development engineer. So when I came across him at an event organised by the Union of Jewish War Veterans, I decided to become acquainted with him. Holders of the Order of Glory were being honoured, and Vladimir Semenovich Rubezhin was one of them. However, it was not easy to get him to talk.

'I fought as everybody did,' was all he was prepared to say about himself.

'But, at the time, you were only thirteen years old...'

To which he replied, 'And at thirteen years old, you still had to defend the Motherland.'

So Burshtein began to search further in archival materials, scouring the memoirs of ex-partisans and underground fighters. It seems that 'Volik' Rubezhin, as his friends and relatives called him, was just 13 years old when the war broke out. He was away from home at the time, staying at the pioneer camp at Medvezhino. However, when Volik tried to leave the camp to get back to his family in Minsk, there was no transport available, so he had to find his way across country alone and on foot.

On 25 June 1941, when Volik approached his house on Stepyanskaya Street, he was informed by neighbours that his mother and younger brother Marik had fled the city, and his father had left to join the army. Volik found a note fixed to the door of their apartment: 'Volik, my son, I was at your camp this morning but you were not there. We waited for the whole day. So now Marik and I are leaving. We don't know ourselves where we will go. When you get this message, go to Auntie Natasha. She is a good woman. She will help you. Let's hope the war will end soon. Kisses Mum.'

Volik lived alone in the family flat for about a month. Then one day, coming back from Komarovsky market where he had been to exchange clothes for bread, he saw the so-called 'good' Auntie Natasha. She and a police thug were breaking into the flat together.... so Volik did not go home any more. By August, he found himself in the Minsk Ghetto, together with thousands of other Jews.

**Vladimir (Volik) Rubezhin - 1941**

Фото Л. ЛЕОНИДОВА.

**Commander of the Harkov Military District headquarters, Lieutenant General Buhovets, after handing out orders and medals to the children-participants of the Great Patriotic War.**

Volik spent his early days there going from house to house in search of his parents' friends and his own comrades. Finally, he was befriended by the Goland family who gave him a home. Sara Goland watched the lad closely and one day she asked if he had been a member of the Young Pioneers. Volik was indignant. 'What do you mean? Of course I was a member of the Pioneers – and I am still a member now! Nobody ever threw me out... and my Dad is a proud Communist. He is fighting at the front.' Sara admired the boy's spirit and understood that he was growing up early. She also began to realise that he was someone who might be of use to the partisans. In the Ghetto, he was already proving helpful and reliable. She knew that his father had been an activist, and that he had taught his son to treat his studies seriously and love the Motherland. Sara Goland was an active member of the Ghetto underground. She would have been very aware that there were some in the Ghetto who were very different from Volik, young people like the local police thug Kolya, who strutted about full of self-importance, even though he was, in truth, an idler, a drunkard, and a thief whose true character was clear to everyone. Kolya, by contrast with Volik, was untrustworthy and personified the arrogance of those in power.

Sara brought Volik to the attention of the partisan leadership, and a few days later two men came to the Goland house to meet him. That's how Volodya Rubezhin became acquainted with Mikhail Gebelev [see glossary] and Hersh (Girsh) Smolar [see glossary], leaders of the underground in the Minsk ghetto. Before allotting him any particular tasks, they discussed the need for vigilance and prudence, and spoke of his duty to the Motherland. They were addressing him as if he were an adult and not a 13-year-old teenager. He assured them that he understood and would not let them down. After that, Volik's life of secrecy began. On the orders of Gebelev and Smolar, Rubezhin went to safe-houses. These were locations where secret meetings took place, and were mostly at Gertsen, Yasinskyaya, Internatsionalnaya, and Kolosa Streets. He usually carried secret communications and he quickly became acquainted with senior underground members like Sofia Sadovskaya and Sara Levina. By September, he was ready to follow elaborate plans and began to lead people out of the ghetto to the Dzerzhinsky Partisan Detachment.

**The young Vladimir Rubezhin as an officer in the Soviet Army**

**Vladimir Rubezhin with his father Semen Borisovich**

The time arrived when, very late one night, Sara Goland woke Volik to inform him that vital medical materials were needed by the detachment. The following night, Volik led a group of underground members out of the ghetto. They carried their precious cargo to a nearby rendezvous where a horse and cart were waiting to take them to their destination. Here they were met by the detachment commander. Their much needed cargo included not only medical supplies, but also a typewriter, charging materials for the portable transmitter, three sets of German military uniforms, salt, tobacco and paper.

A month later, Volik was given the order to get a group of ten people out of the ghetto and to the partisan detachment. Before his departure, he was ordered to call at the home of Roza Lipskaya where a printing press had been hidden. They dismantled it and put it into two bags. Volik carried this heavy cargo and led the group to the suburbs of the city near Petrovschina where his partisan communication agent Zavala was waiting. She now took over and led the people further on her own. In all, during his stay in the ghetto, Rubezhin took fifty people to the partisan detachment, as well as delivering weapons, medicines, cartridges and other much needed cargo.

In the middle of January 1943, a communication agent came to the ghetto from the detachment. He had come to warn Volik that he was under observation by the authorities and would have to leave the ghetto immediately. Police thugs started searching for Volik the very next day, but he had already escaped into the forest. He was called Vilik by partisans. Many of the partisans were shocked by his appearance. After his time in the ghetto and several wintry days hiding in the forest, the boy they saw before them was a bedraggled and starving child.

**Vladimir standing by the former temporary quarters of the Frunze Partisan Brigade**

However, the detachment commander was well aware of the worth of this 'child' who had behaved with the fortitude of a man. The division was lined up and an order was read aloud. One of the paragraphs stated that 'the partisan Rubezhin Volik will be enrolled in the 1$^{st}$ division of the 1$^{st}$ squadron. He will be at the commander's personal disposal to carry out special tasks.' Then Volik was presented with a special rifle, cut to size for his height.

In a book called *The Ghetto Avengers*, the author, Hersh Smolar, devoted a whole chapter to this period of Rubezhin's life. Describing one particular incident, Smolar writes: 'The partisan group headed for the high road leading to the main railway station at Negoreloe. The Nazis were not on full alert, but the weight of traffic rushing in both directions made it difficult for the partisans to seize an appropriate moment to set a landmine. The group was stretched out close to the road, but they had to go to earth and lie down flat, not even lifting their heads. Volik crept on all-fours to the road-side, and finally, when a vehicle approached at the head of a work detail of lorries, he drew himself up to his full height and threw a grenade in the direction of the vehicle. That was a signal to the waiting group of partisans. They started firing on the whole convoy and created such a 'porridge' (confusion) that it took the German field ambulances several hours to take away the dead and injured. Farmers from the nearest villages reported afterwards that 47 Nazis had been killed, and there were an unconfirmed number of injured.'

During his time in the detachment, Volik Rubezhin was a communication agent, a spy and a bomber. Thanks to his active participation, seven enemy echelons were destroyed.

**Vladimir (left) with other former ghetto prisoners in Nalibokskiy Forest**

After the liberation of Minsk, his mother and brother came back to their native city. Not long afterwards he also heard from his father, now an officer in the Red Army. Volodya (Volik) began making up for lost time, studying hard at school, joining an aero-club, and entering the Bataiskoe Military Aeronautic School. However, after more than two years of cadet life, and despite achieving high grades, he was excluded from the school. This occurred when his father, the director of one of the administrations of the Byelorussian military district, was arrested after a false denunciation. It was not until the beginning of the Kruschev 'thaw', that his father was finally rehabilitated and restored to the Party. Vladimir (Volik) became apprenticed to a fitter at the October Revolution Machine-Tool Plant in Minsk. He worked and studied at an evening school and later at the Vehicle-and-Tractor Faculty of the Byelorussian Polytechnic Institute. Finally, he became a construction engineer and secretary of a research and technology society.

Vladimir Rubezhin was awarded two medals: The Order of the Patriotic War, and the Order of Glory – awards for military service as an underground member and partisan. A copy of the commendation list is held in his personal archive. The commander and the commissioner of Frunze brigade interceded with the higher command about the possibility of awarding Rubezhin the Order of the Red Star [see glossary]. An authorised representative of TSK KPB [Central Committee of the Byelorussian Communist Party] and the Byelorussian headquarters of the partisan movement approved the request.

The document states: 'On 7 July 1943, Rubezhin took part in an ambush on the highroad Shnek-Stolbtsy, when a passenger vehicle and three lorries were destroyed. The *Hauptman* (the captain), two junior military officers and 20 German soldiers were killed. On 19 July, he took part in an ambush on the Volma-Ivenets Highroad.' Once again, there was a list of the Nazis who were killed and military equipment destroyed. However, Vladimir did not receive the Order of the Red Star. The reason for this is unclear. *

Vladimir Rubezhin eventually became a grandfather and, even when his health deteriorated, he did not complain. Mikhail Burshtein, on whose report this account is based, describes how Rubezhin, a man of few words, smiled at the conclusion of their talk, saying 'Everything is alright.' Burshtein comments: 'Yes, everything is indeed 'alright', because Vladimir Rubezhin had an honest life under his belt.

* Soviet Passport - Fifth Paragraph: It has been pointed out to the editors that a possible reason for Vladimir not having been awarded the Red Star may be related to the official information obtained when a Soviet citizen applied for a passport. Holders of a Soviet passport were required to complete a declaration of personal information with details such as full names, date of birth and social status (e.g. worker, peasant, serviceman, etc.). The fifth category requiring completion was the declaration of nationality. Under this heading, Jews were obliged to enter 'Jewish'. Such state discrimination inevitably impeded the advancement of Jews in education, work and other official forms of recognition or achievement.

# From the Ghetto to the Nalibokskiy Forest
## Pavel Rubinchik

At the start of the war in Byelorussia I was at a Youth Camp near Minsk, so I was separated from my parents. In fact, the whole family was split up. I was 13 years old. My three-year-old sister had been sent to a kindergarten in the country, my mother had gone to Essentuki, and my father was away on a business trip. Not for a moment had any of us imagined that we were going to be apart for so long. Unfortunately, fate had its own plans for us all.

On 22 June, the normal daily routine of the youth camp was continuing as normal, but we were a little surprised to notice that all the male attendants seemed to have disappeared. Then, on the evening of that day, the mother of one of my school friends arrived and took him away. She explained that his father was intending to take him on a trip to Artek, so his leaving did not strike the rest of us as particularly unusual. We all knew that his father was the People's Commissar for Construction in the Byelorussian Soviet Socialist Republic.

Then, on the following day, we were outside playing football, when two planes flew over us, one marked with a star and the other with a strange black cross. They were firing their weapons, but we just assumed that they were carrying out shooting exercises. Even on the twenty-fourth, when the sky grew dark with dozens of aircraft, we did not understand what was going on. A number of people now started to appear on the road that ran alongside the camp. They seemed weary and were dragging suitcases and bundles. Then troops also began to appear on the road. Finally, we were all gathered together in the dining room and told that we were at war with Nazi Germany, but that our troops were winning and were already approaching Warsaw. A cry went up, 'Hurrah!'

It didn't take look for us to realise that our innocent joy had been premature. The roar of planes continued and we could now hear the distant thunder of explosions. A strange glow appeared on the horizon, and it stayed there. It seemed as if the sun was no longer setting each night. Parents started to arrive and were hurrying to take their children away with them. That was when we learned the cause of the constant glow in the sky: Minsk was being heavily bombed by German planes and the city was on fire. The parents were taking their children and heading off in the direction of the Minsk-Moscow Highway.

No one came for me, and eventually I left the camp with the family of a schoolmate, Peter Golomb. The road was jammed with crowds of refugees. Many had already become exhausted and some were just discarding their belongings on the road, so that we had to step over bags and bundles as we trudged on. When we got to the Minsk-Moscow highway, the German planes caught up with us. Machine gun fire caused the terrified crowd to disperse in all directions - but to no avail. When the planes flew off, all I could see around me were dead and injured men, women, and children – many of them very young. Some people were crying, and all around there was thick black smoke. The tar which covered the highway was burning where the Germans had dropped incendiary bombs. There were also some burning vehicles of retreating military.

We wanted to get to Borisov, which was 60 kilometres from Minsk, but it was now nightfall and we were exhausted and traumatised. We simply did not have enough strength to continue, so we crept into the woods to rest, but we were soon awoken by the sound of German voices shouting "*Raus*!" We had no choice but to obey their commands. The men in our group were immediately separated from the others, and checked to see if they were carrying weapons. The rest of us were then sent off in the direction of Minsk, and so for two days we walked under the fire of planes. When we finally reached Minsk, the city lay in ruins. There were no Germans in the city yet. Of the house which had been our family home, only ashes remained. I was in shock. I remember that I naively began to search for my collection of ancient coins. All I found was a few coins fused with glass. Eventually, I was discovered by some Russian relatives of my mother's brother, and they took me back to their home in the outskirts of the city. My grandparents were also taking refuge there. There was nothing to eat and we all survived on whatever food we boys managed to scavenge in the basement of a bombed-out cake factory – flour, biscuits, left over molasses, together with seeds which we discovered at the railway station.

On 30 June the Germans entered the city. They were self-confident, armed with machine-guns called *Schmeissers*. They travelled in trucks and would sing loudly. On 15 July the German commandant's order appeared on the walls of the surviving houses and on fences. All Jews were to move into the area of Minsk which had been reserved for them. My relatives wanted to avoid this prison by leaving Minsk for some country retreat Ostrashitsy town where things might be calmer. However, we stayed there for a short time as a rumour was going around that, in the nearby town of Logoysk, any surviving Jews were being thrown alive into the ravines. So other means were sought to avoid incarceration in the ghetto. I was sent to Minsk and into hiding with a Russian family. We hoped, in such a big city Germans would not kill people on the scale was soon to unfold. At first, I was concealed in a cellar, but the danger was too great, both for me and for the family, so it was decided that I should be baptized and resettled. Accordingly, the baptism took place and I was moved again, this time to a Russian orphanage in the Minsk suburb of Zhdanovichi, and my name was changed to Matusevich. By now, not only was I pining for my family, but I was really missing school and wanted to study. The administration was approached and I was finally allowed to go back to school.

I was so happy to be accepted into the seventh grade. However, on my very first day, just as I was entering the classroom, I was horrified to see someone I knew. She was sitting at one of the nearest desks. It was my pre-war classmate Galya Misyuk! Of course, she recognised me too. The teacher started the day's proceedings by calling the register, and when she arrived at the name 'Matusevich', I stood up and waited for the inevitable denunciation. However, Galya remained silent. During the break, she came up to me and whispered, 'Pavel, don't be afraid. I understand everything.' Despite this kindness, I was unhappy there. Every day, we had to listen to the teachers praising the Germans. What is more, they were constantly telling us that the German army had brought liberation to the people of Byelorussia from the Communists and the Jews.

On 5 November, we were taken to the cinema to watch a documentary about the victories of the German armies. When we emerged from the cinema after the film, a terrible sight awaited us. There were men hanging from lampposts and trees, and on the chest of each man there hung a sign which read: 'We are guilty of firing our weapons at German soldiers.' I was still in shock when I arrived with the others at the orphanage, only to be immediately summoned to the principal's office. There were some strange people there: a policeman accompanied by a boy and a red-haired girl. The policeman was starting to interrogate me, when he suddenly grabbed my arm and slashed my hand with a knife, announcing: 'Here it is, Jew blood!' The three of us children were then taken out and driven into the ghetto. We were kicked and pushed over the wire fence, while the Jewish guard was ordered to take us to the children's quarters. I just remember that there was a terrible stench and it was bitterly cold. Hungry children were wandering around like living skeletons. This was to be my new 'home'! We were each allocated jobs of work to do. I was given a two-wheeled cart and told to walk through the ghetto daily. My job was to find any children who had died, load them onto the cart and take them to the ghetto cemetery, which was on the territory of the ghetto.

And then there was an incident. On 6 November, on my way back from the cemetery, I saw that the SS and their Ukrainian and Lithuanian collaborators had surrounded the whole area, including the children's quarters. I abandoned the cart and ran across the ghetto to where the Dzulyas, friends of our family, lived. I found only Grigoriy Dzul. He had sent his wife and children to the other ghetto area, as he hoped it would be calmer there. Next morning a pogrom began. The Nazis and their accomplices, drove everyone out of their houses - men, women, old people and children. They were forced to line up, and most were taken away. In just two days, 7 and 8 November, about 29,000 people inhabiting one-third of the ghetto were taken away. The Germans left only essential workers and professionals such as carpenters, plumbers, mechanics, and lathe turners. They were placed in other parts of the ghetto. I was only saved by the fact that Grigoriy Dzul had a certificate for one of these professions, and he said that I was his son.

The area of the ghetto which was cleared in this way remained empty for only one day. On 10 November about 30,000 German Jews from Hamburg, Berlin, Vienna, Bremen and Düsseldorf were brought in. Their situation was even worse than ours: they could not speak Yiddish or Russian like the rest of us, and they were forbidden to communicate with us in any way. Nevertheless, although the area into which they were driven was fenced with barbed wire, those poor people disobeyed the order. Starvation forced them to barter clothes in exchange for food. However, their ultimate fate was the same as the others. Of the thirty thousand German Jews brought into the Minsk Ghetto at that time, only one woman survived. She alone managed to escape to the partisans.

My own existence in the ghetto continued. I eventually found my friend Peter Golomb, with whom I had left the summer camp on the third day of the war. Even though many families inhabited the flat, the Golombs sheltered me for a time, allocating me a sleeping place on a Russian stove. From them, I learned that there were some Jews in the ghetto who had been brought from nearby suburbs and neighbouring towns including Ostrashitsy. So I then started rushing around looking for my grandparents. I hoped that they might be among the most recent arrivals: those who had been placed in the area near Nemiga Street. I searched frantically, even though I knew that many of the Jews in that area had already been killed and the street became a part of the so-called 'Russian district' which was another area of Minsk. Nevertheless, I risked my life and found my way to the place where these Jews had been. The area was full of looters, and in one apartment I found several dead men wearing bloodied prayer shawls, and lying side by side on the floor. They had been bayoneted. It was there that I finally understood what the adults had realised from the very beginning… that there was a plan to destroy us all.

Back in the ghetto, I set out to visit the *Judenrat* in order to register and get a job, but I ran into a round-up. We were caught, pushed into a vehicle and taken to jail, which for some reason was called the 'American Jail'. (Previously it had housed political prisoners). Next to this jail the new owners had decided to build another prison for guilty German soldiers – and it appeared that we were to be its builders! Now I had to learn how to prepare and mix concrete. We also had to transport bricks from the brickyard under guard. However, our first task was to pull the bricks directly from the furnace, and this meant scorching our hands. For this work, we received a bowl of soup in the afternoon and 200 grams of bread in the evening. We also received a little money – a few German occupation marks.

On 2 March 1942, after work, we were being escorted back to the ghetto in a covered truck. As usual, we were sternly forbidden to look out through the gap between the vehicle and the tarpaulin. By the time we arrived at the gate of the ghetto it was dark. We could hear some shouting and swearing. There was an argument going on between our escort and the SS, who were clearly demanding something which our guards were refusing. When we finally entered the ghetto, the senior guard, Corporal Kau, said to us: 'You should thank me. You should thank me very much.'

When we emerged from the truck, we understood why he was demanding our thanks. There were hundreds of corpses lying in the streets. It turned out that a huge massacre had taken place there. All of those who were unable to work had been taken away to the death camp at Trostenets [see glossary], and those who resisted or tried to hide had been shot on the spot. Returning work groups like ours had also been taken away, so Corporal Kau really did deserve our appreciation. Fortunately, my benefactors, the Golombs, survived. They had hidden in a dug-out shelter under a large Russian stove shelter. This hiding-place saved 15 people. But David Golomb, their 25-year-old son, did not come back from work that day.

Four months later, on 20 July 1942, the same guard, Corporal Kau again prevented us from returning from work and for three nights we slept on the construction site. Finally, on the fourth day, we returned, and discovered the results of another mass shooting. Now, only about 30,000 people were left out of the original pre-war Jewish population of Minsk, around 130,000.

The Germans once again reduced the area of the Jewish ghetto. It now covered only a quarter of the initial territory – the part containing the Jewish cemetery. One day, shortly after this last massacre, our team was taken to the gates of the cemetery. Here our vehicle was stopped by *Stürmbahnfürer* Richter. He demanded that the gates be opened, got in the car and ordered our driver to go to the cemetery. We were certain that it was now our turn to be shot. But by whom? There was no one at the cemetery when we arrived, apart from Richter and our guard. We were brought to a freshly dug mound of earth and just stood there. Minutes went by…. we were waiting for a shot in the head…. but Richter only handed our guard the sketch of a gravestone and said something to him. Realization dawned on us that this must be the place where Richter's dog was to be buried. I now remembered that, during the *actions* of the previous day, a high ranking officer had come into the ghetto to check on how well his orders were being carried out. This officer had turned out to be the General Commissar of Byelorussia, General Kube. He was accompanied by a large retinue of guards. *Stürmbahnfürer* Richter had also been there with his Alsatian dog, a so-called 'man-eater'! At one point, Kube had turned suddenly and waved his hand, whereupon the dog had rushed at him. However, one of the General's guards had immediately fired his weapon, shooting and killing the dog. So now we realised that this was to be its burial place! Once the burial had taken place, Richter ordered us to collect some of the Labradorite stones which had been used to adorn the richer graves. We were to construct a tombstone from them. The final touch would be an inscription: 'Here lies my beloved dog'. So for three days the whole team worked on the production of a monument for this man-eater dog!

In the autumn the pogroms continued. One autumn night, another pogrom began, this time under the pretext of a search for partisans and members of the underground. Soldiers started moving around the ghetto, throwing scantily clad people out of their homes and shooting them. On the first night of this pogrom, Tulskiy, the chief of the Jewish police, was at our house at 22, Stolpetskiy Alley, when the Germans rushed in shouting: 'Where is Tulskiy?' I remember that I was lying in my usual place - on the Russian stove. Tulskiy jumped up to where I was in an attempt to hide, but the soldiers drove us both outside and Tulskiy was taken away. Everyone else was now driven out into the yard, and we were ordered to stand facing the wall. Behind us stood the guards with guns at the ready, while other soldiers went into the house to carry out a search. They spent a long time in there. Once again, I was certain that, at any second, the soldiers standing behind us would shoot at our heads with machine guns… but again, it was not to happen. The soldiers finally left, having turned everything over in the house, but finding nothing. Our guards just followed them, ordering us to remain standing there, facing the wall.

It was during one of these night-searches that we learned, for the first time, about the so-called 'gas chambers'. These were big trucks with diesel engines and a sealed compartment. They would shove 40-50 people into the truck and start the engine, which had a pipe attached to the exhaust. Then they would drive out of the ghetto. After 15-20 minutes, the people trapped inside suffocated from the exhaust fumes. I understand that they died in terrible pain.

In late August, I was involved in yet another raid. Fifteen of us were caught and brought to the premises of the former garage of the People's Commissariat on the Chervenskiy dirt road (now Mogilevskiy). This was where the Germans carried out the repairs of weapons and small arms or *Gever-Wafenverkstadt*. We were lined up, split into groups of five people, and then every fifth person was taken and hanged on a nearby pole. Then the *Hauptmann* – the man in charge of the workshop – announced that anyone carrying out any form of sabotage, or disobeying orders, would suffer the same fate. Now they placed us in the barracks containing prisoners-of-war in three-tier bunks. These barracks were surrounded by barbed wire under high voltage. This was, in fact, a small concentration camp. We were forced to work here for 14 hours each day. My neighbour on the bunk next to mine was a German Jew from Berlin. His whole family had been killed. Eventually, he broke down and hanged himself.

My duties included clearing away the wood shavings, cleaning rust off of the rifle bayonets and other parts of the rifles and machine guns, and dismantling rifles into parts. I was always very tired and constantly tormented by hunger. Fortunately, I was eventually transferred to the *broneray*, as they called the weapons site. Here, NCO Urlyaub, my immediate overseer, had me wash and clean the cooking pots. Sometime the pots contained the remains of food, and I believe that it was these scraps that saved me from death by starvation.

After a certain 'probation period', we were allowed to go back to the ghetto once a month for a whole day, a Sunday. On the occasion of one such a visit, I spoke to Monya (Emmanuel), the son of our friend Dzul. Having learned where I worked, he asked: 'How would you like to have the opportunity to take revenge on the Nazis by working for the partisans?' I had dreamed about such a thing almost from the first days of the occupation, but I had no idea as to how it could be achieved. Emmanuel set two conditions: firstly – I would have to get one hundred springs from the breechblocks on which I worked daily, and secondly – I would have to acquire a sawn-off shotgun, or indeed any small gun, for myself. Quite apart from the danger of discovery, the risk would be great. Firstly, in order to acquire the springs, I would have to dismantle the breechblocks, leaving the rifles unusable. Secondly, I would have to find a way to hide the springs. Eventually, I decided to conceal them in my mess tin, something we always had to carry with us for those times when we were fed with Nazi gruel. We would be thoroughly searched at the exit from the workshops when we went back to the ghetto on a Sunday, but I wasn't discovered. In this way, over the course of a few months, I managed to take a hundred springs into the ghetto, each time risking my life.

Moving a shotgun out of the workshops, even in parts, was even more dangerous. I secretly took sawn-off parts of the barrel and hid them in holes drilled in pieces of wood. In the same way, I hid and carried several other parts. For some time, the security guards had not paid any attention to the branches and logs we would take away to heat our homes. Eventually, they banned this – but not before I had performed the necessary tasks! My only regret was that we were now freezing in the ghetto, since there was absolutely nothing left to burn - furniture, interior doors, and floorboards had long been consumed!

One evening in February 1943, while getting into the truck, I lost one of my galoshes. Seeing it on the ground, next to the wheels, I jumped down to put it back on, when suddenly I felt a terrible pain and lost consciousness. I woke up the next morning lying on the floor, covered in blood. My body ached, and my head and face were swollen. Neighbours were leaning over me and eventually told me what had happened. When I had jumped down from the vehicle, the guard and the driver had started kicking me and hitting me with their weapons. They had beaten me half to death, and were about to throw me back into the truck. However, the guards then decided that I was dead, so they ordered others in my team to take me to the cemetery and throw me into a mass grave which was known as 'the pit'. Then the guards left. My fellow team members were about to lift me, when one of them realised that I, the supposed deceased, was still moving and breathing!  So they brought me back to the house, and the Golombs and the other neighbours began to tend my wounds. They even called a doctor. However, the next day, they were all frightened by the appearance of a German and ran away to hide. This was our supervisor Urlyaub, who had arrived at the house with another worker. My appearance terrified both of them. Urlyaub had brought me a loaf of bread and a piece of sausage. He ordered everyone to leave and whispered to me: '*Paul, lauf in Wald!*' [German: 'Paul, run away to the forest!']. When I finally returned to work a week later, my 'killers' just grinned.

The late spring and summer of 1943 was a terrible time. There were frequent attacks at night. The gas lorries were used, and there was a lot of looting by the Byelorussian policemen. Every evening, on one side of the ghetto or the other, you could hear the sound of gunfire. In late August, Monya Dzul warned me that it would soon be possible to leave for the partisans: he was waiting for the leader to contact him. He had checked that I had carried out the task he had set, and had taken some of the springs that I had collected. I was advised to stop going to work and to leave the house. The work team and our neighbours were told that I was dead.

Waiting for the leader was very frustrating. I slept in some burned out ruins inside the ghetto. I was hungry and constantly afraid that I would be discovered. Finally, Monya rescued me from this hiding place and the dispatcher arrived. She was a girl called Katya, aged around 13 or 14. There were ten of us who were to go with her. She checked that the list of tasks had been carried out, gave us the route and provided details of meeting places to be used in case of emergency. Then it was time to leave: two of our group waited for a moment until the guards had moved away from the fence, and they then cut the wire with pliers. The rest of us cautiously began to crawl out of the ghetto, one by one. Suddenly, from another nearby shelter, more people appeared who also wanted to leave in order to join the partisans, and they came with us.

Finally, we crawled to a sufficiently safe distance and, surprisingly quickly, found ourselves out of the city. However, up ahead there was a heavily guarded railway and a dangerous crossing. As we approached it, we heard the sound of an approaching train, and so we lay down. Suddenly and quite unexpectedly, there was a powerful explosion and bright light was all around us as, and with a roar and screech, the wagons of the train toppled over. The guards opened fire and flares filled the sky. The people who had joined us, especially the women, started to run in panic, some directly into the path of the German bullets. Now our position was revealed. In all the shooting and the chaos which followed, I managed to flee into the nearby woods with Lenya Friedman, who was the same age as me. Others were not so fortunate. We heard later that, in the morning, the dead bodies of almost all of our group, including the leader Katya, were found and transported to the cemetery. In the ghetto, the Germans and their local collaborators carried out punitive actions.

Meanwhile, we hid for a time in a ruined Lutheran cemetery having lost everything we had been carrying for the partisans. When we attempted to move on, we just lost our way. We even started to consider the possibility of returning to the ghetto.... but not for long. On the third morning, we managed to attach ourselves to a large work group of ghetto workers which was passing us on its way to work. Now we were able to move with them into more familiar territory. Finally, we slipped into the next burned-out ruin, tore off the yellow patch and numbers, and off we went in search of the nearest partisan unit.

Three long days later, we found what we had been seeking all along, a certain large village, which, according to Katya's information, marked the start of a partisan zone. We also knew that it was called the Staroye Selo. But how to check? We were afraid to leave the cover of the woods, so we decided to watch from a distance. Again, we spent the night in the forest, but we hadn't eaten for three days and, by morning, we were desperate. We emerged from the relative safety of the forest and knocked at the door of the first hut we came to. The lady who lived there came out and, seeing two emaciated youngsters, she called us into the house and put hot potato, pancakes with milk and a loaf of bread on the table. We were amazed by all of this luxury. In my whole life, I had never eaten anything more delicious than that meal, not even food prepared by my mother. To this day, I still remember the taste of those pancakes with milk, and the bread. Best of all, we felt a huge sense of relief, when our good hostess confirmed that the village was indeed Staroye Selo. She told us, that partisan units had a presence, and that Jews from Minsk also gathered here to form their brigades and units.

However, it was not easy to make contact with the partisans. On the first day after our arrival, we went into the village and approached two men who were wearing red ribbons on their caps. We approached them with a greeting of 'fellow partisans' but they called us 'little kikes' and took everything that we had. With the muzzles of their rifles they forced us to run back into the woods. We later decided that we must have run into policemen in disguise. For the second time, I went into the village alone, as Lenya refused to follow me. This time I was lucky. I saw a lot of men in Soviet military uniforms with red ribbons and stars. Some men and women were like me: escapees from the ghetto. I also saw three Ukrainian legionnaires with whom I had worked in the weapons workshop. They recognized me, and led me to the captain of the partisan troop. I believed that I would now become a partisan and maybe join a new detachment. However, the captain said that youngsters without weapons were not wanted. Nevertheless, he assured me that his party would soon be going to the Nalibokskiy Forest, which was a hundred kilometres away. He had already agreed that, when the time came for the march, the Jews of the village would be permitted to join him. However, the captain also warned us that he would only take us as far as Nalibokskiy Forest, and no further. Then he would show us the way to a brigade named after Stalin, in which there was apparently a Jewish family squad. I ran with this information to Lenya, but he was not at the agreed meeting place. I searched everywhere for him, but had not found him. I was alone.

A few days later, the partisan detachment took to the road. We walked for four days – mostly at night, but sometimes during the day – and we covered more than one hundred and thirty kilometres. Then, in the forest, the Jewish group had to break away from the others, and now we continued our journey alone, moving towards the village of Rudnya. However, as we approached the area, we saw chimneys poking out of piles of ashes, and we realised that they were all that remained of the burned-out village. Rudnya had been obliterated along with all of its inhabitants. However, in some nearby fields, we came across many Jewish women who told us that they were from the family unit number 106, named after Stalin. We had discovered part of the 'Family Squad' of Jewish Partisans! We learned that the commander of this detachment was Sholom Zorin [see Zorin's Brigade in the glossary]. The brigade commander was General Chernyshev, a very honourable man. The Family Squad consisted of former prisoners from Minsk and other ghettoes, and had been created on the order of Chernyshev. Not all partisan units took Jews. Some attributed this to the fact that women and children hampered manoeuvrability. Others said that some Partisan units were simply anti-Semitic. However, in November 1943, Chernyshev created a general detachment of 620 people. After brief questioning and interviews, our whole group was enrolled in the squad and we were quickly allotted various tasks. Women were to dig potatoes in the abandoned fields and to tend the vegetable gardens. Men were to join the battle group; and so our days as partisans began. It was necessary to build a community, construct huts, prepare the winter dugout, and search for weapons and ammunition which might have been abandoned by the retreating Soviet forces in June 1941. We also had to repair any weapons we found, establish health units, stand watch, and destroy German communications. This meant cutting cables and wires, knocking down power poles, demolishing bridges and disabling railway stations. At last, I was participating in the defence of my country and resistance to the Nazis. I was even taught how to smelt TNT shells. It was dangerous work, but necessary in order to extract the explosives. In any artillery shells we found, we gently twisted the fuses and immersed them in a container of water, and melted the TNT over a fire, which was then poured into a square mould.

In the spring of 1944, we knew that we were finally approaching the end of the war. However, before this happened, many comrades would be killed in our final battle. In early July, Nazi groups were retreating through the woods. On the night of 10 July, a German military unit attacked our base and, in the battle that followed, many partisans were killed. The detachment commander Sholom Zorin was wounded by an explosive bullet and his leg had to be amputated. Many men, who were receiving treatment in hospitals, as well as doctors were wounded, and lay suffering in the brigade hospital. Nevertheless, we did not lose hope and continued to look forward with great anticipation to the arrival of the Soviet army. We were finally liberated three days later on 13 July 1944.

Military vehicles took us to Minsk. Soon after, the city held a parade of Byelorussian partisans, in which I am very proud to have participated. After the ceremonial march, I was recognised by a relative. He was overjoyed to see me, and gave me the news that my parents were still alive! They were living in Zelenodolsk near Kazan. We had not been in touch since our separation in the days prior to the outbreak of war. Now, at the age of sixteen, I would be reunited with my parents!

Moscow was 750 km away, but distance would not deter me from a journey where I was to meet with family. Kazan was to follow! I was demobilized and left for Moscow. I reached Yartsevo station ten days later by travelling in open carriages, on the roofs of carriages, and in coal locomotives. I saw how the war had left a terrible trail of destruction: abandoned homes, refugees, disabled people, even corpses left in full view...

At Yartsevo station, I finally got lucky. I found some space in a carriage, climbed up to the third shelf and slept peacefully on the last leg of my journey to Moscow. In the capital, it was as if I was in another world. I was struck by the colourful dresses of the women and by posters advertising the cinema and the theatre. I even travelled on the metro to my family's address. Everything seemed like a dream. My sudden appearance amazed my relatives – they had believed that I was dead. But before they were allowed to hug me, I had to visit a bathhouse. What a pleasure that was - hot water and soap were luxuries that I had not experienced for three years!

Joy gave way to grief when I told these members of my family about my experiences, and about the general tragedy of the Jewish people in the occupied zone. It turned out that they knew very little about it, and then only in general terms. However, in the evening, I once again experienced true happiness – I heard the voices of my Mum and Dad over the phone from Kazan. To describe our meeting there after that forced separation, when each of us thought that the other was lost, is just too difficult. Let all who read these words, imagine it for themselves.

# Letters from the Minsk Ghetto
## Nadejda Andreyevna Solovyova (Nadya)
## Leonid Grigoryevich Ruderman (Lyonya)
## Leah Merson Samuilovna Ruderman (Liza)

Facing certain death inside the ghetto, a Jewish mother (Liza) took the perilous decision to part with her only child (Lyonya) in order to save his life. Risking her own safety, she smuggled him to a trusted non-Jewish friend (Nadya) who lived outside of the ghetto. This is their story told through the personal accounts of Nadya and Lyonya. Liza left behind two letters which conclude this story.

## Nadya's Story

My name is Solovyova Nadejda Andreyevna (Nadya). My maiden name was Krezo, and I was born in Minsk on 12 March 1923. I studied at the Law Institute. I am widowed with no children.

I was friends with Jewish girls before the war. They were my neighbours and we developed very close friendships. In 1941 our street Oboynaya, became part of the Minsk Ghetto, and so my mother and I moved to Second Opanskiy Lane, in a Russian neighbourhood on the outskirts of the ghetto.

One evening during the Spring of 1941, my friend and schoolmate Maria, and her mother, crept under the barbed fence surrounding the ghetto, and came to our house. Several days previously there had been pogroms in the ghetto. They told us about dreadful things that had happened. People had tried to hide. They crouched in dark cellars for days at a time, forced to drink urine instead of water. In one small cellar, a baby had begun crying. To prevent it giving away their location, its mother had accidentally suffocated the baby. Maria and her mother needed our help. They begged us to hide a little boy, the son of her cousin – Ruderman Merson Leah Samuilovna (Liza). The child's mother knew she would die, but was prepared to take any means necessary, to save her son. We knew that the penalty for hiding Jews meant that we could be shot. But, since we had moved to the Russian neighbourhood where nobody knew us before the war, we agreed, and arranged with the mother to take her boy.

**Leah (Liza)**

**Leonid's mother**

Our house was on a hill and easily visible. Late at night, a few days later, Liza brought us the child, whose name was Leonid (Lyonya). With him, she left two letters, and a photograph of herself. In one letter which was addressed to her husband, she outlined her plan - to leave her son in the care of the Russian family, named Krezo. The other letter was for me, requesting that, after the war, I should try to find her husband - and give him the first letter - along with her photograph. At this point, I remember how she broke down and sobbed over her child, certain that this was the last time she would ever see him. Our hearts broke, overwhelmed with sorrow and sadness. This happened around the end of March 1943. A few days later, we heard that there were more pogroms in the ghetto. We never saw Liza again. She died in the Minsk Ghetto.

The police made searches of houses close to the ghetto, looking for Jews in hiding. Worried that they would find the boy, we took him to the woods for a few months, hiding him with my mother's relative, who was a woodsman living not far from Minsk. On our return, we concealed him from the neighbours by hiding him in a dugout in the cellar. My mother and I would alternate the time we spent with him there. Only at night could we go outside with him, so that he could breathe some fresh air. Following the liberation of Minsk, we commenced our search for Leonid's father, Ruderman Grigoriy Hanovich, but discovered that he had died during the war. After the end of the war, distant relatives wished to take the boy, but we had become very attached to him. Together we had survived the war and risked our lives. To my mother, he was like a son, and to me he was like a brother. In 1945, my mother became the authorised carer for the orphan boy Ruderman Leonid Grigoryevich. The records showed that his mother had died in the Minsk Ghetto, and his father had died in the war. Leonid retained his nationality and his surname, but continued living with us, in the same house that he had been brought to by his birth mother.

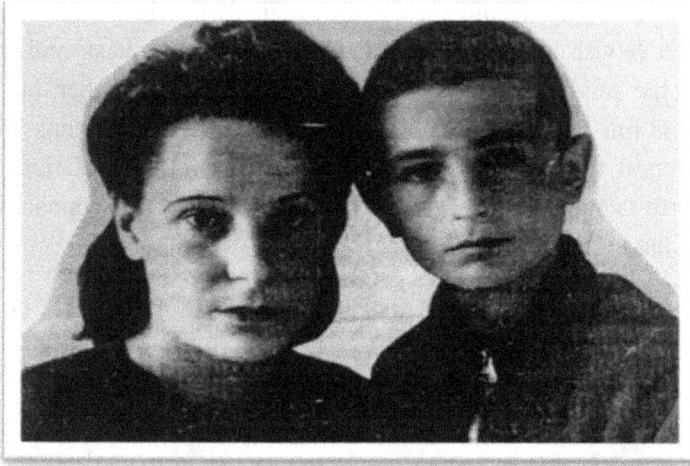

**Nadya Krezo with Lyonya (Leonid)**

Lyonya finished school, studied a profession, married and had a daughter. He still lives in Minsk. We have always lived closely, like one family. Even after my mother died, Lyonya and I remained as close, like real siblings. We meet regularly and he helps me with everything. He takes care of me.

## Leonid (Lyonya)

My name is Ruderman Leonid Grigoryevich, and I was born on 18 October 1940, in Minsk. I still live in there at Pobediteley Avenue, house 57, flat 11. I am a pensioner. I am married to Ruderman Allie Isaakovna. We have one daughter, whose name is Kauffman Ruderman, and I have two grandchildren.

When the war began, my mother and I lived in Minsk, on Internatsionalnaya Street, house 25, flat 4. My father, Ruderman Grigoriy Hannovich (Grisha), went to join the Red Army. On 19 July 1941, a month after the war started, the street on which my mother and I lived became part of the Minsk Ghetto. We found ourselves prisoners there. My mother died, but had time to save me. She gave me to the Russian family named Krezo. Unfortunately, I was too young to remember my parents. My only memory is of two letters written by mother, and her photograph. I regard Krezo Anna Nikolayevna and Solovyova Nadejda Andreyevna (Nadya) as my own family. These women not only saved my life, but brought me up, gave me an education - and always treated me like their own son and brother. When I grew older, they related the story of my escape from the ghetto: how I came to them, how they hid me in the basement and how they took me to the woods to live with relatives. They read to me the letters my mother had written, giving them to me, along with her photograph. They later made an enlargement of my mother's photograph, and it always hung above my bed.

From the letters and stories, I discovered - that in March 1943, my mother, Ruderman Merson Leah Samuilovna (Liza), in order to save my life, left me with the Krezo family. They gave her their word that they would raise me as their own son. I understand that they risked their lives to save a Jewish boy. They fulfilled my mother's request, and raised me as one of their family. After the end of the war, they began to look for my father, but discovered that he had died on the front line on 26 June 1944. On 29 June 1954, Krezo Anna Nikolayevna became the authorised carer of the orphaned little boy, Ruderman Leonid Grigoryevich. The Krezo family kept my birth name, and preserved my Jewish identity, for which I am very grateful. I will never forget what they did.

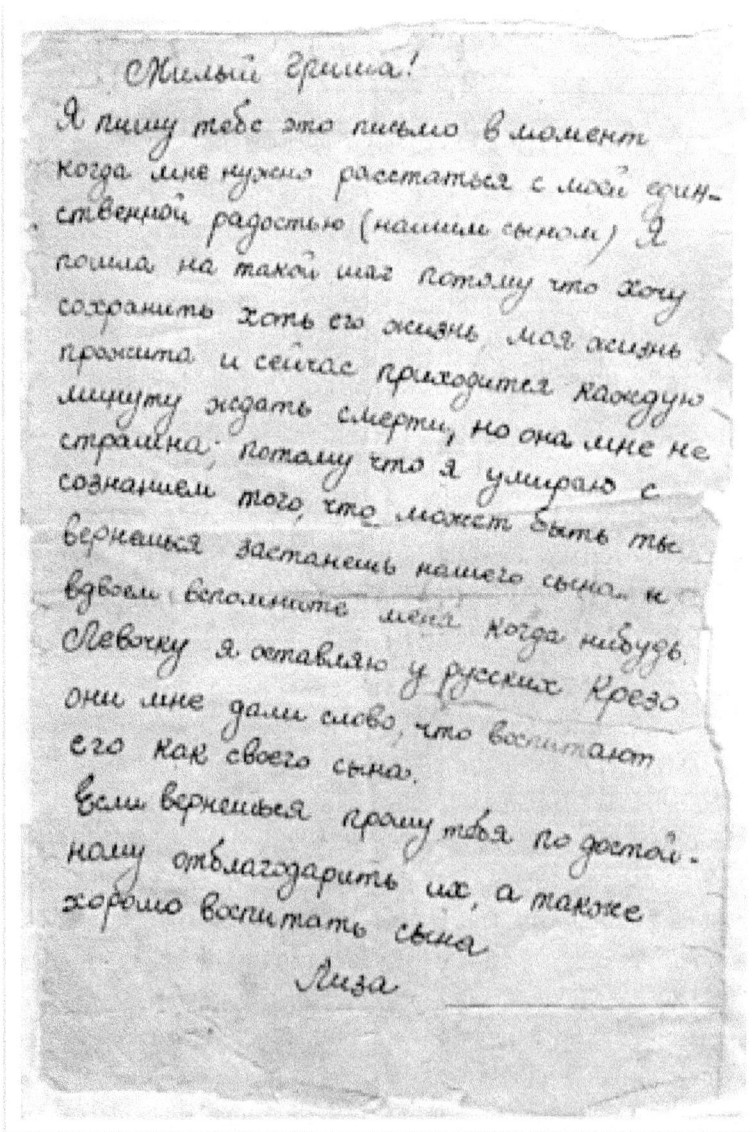

Милый Гриша!

Я пишу тебе это письмо в момент когда мне нужно расстаться с моей единственной радостью (нашим сыном) Я пошла на такой шаг потому что хочу сохранить хоть его жизнь, моя жизнь прожита и сейчас приходится каждую минуту ждать смерти, но она мне не страшна, потому что я умираю с сознанием того, что может быть ты вернешься застанешь нашего сына и вдвоем вспомните меня. Когда нибудь. Левочку я оставляю у русских Крезо они мне дали слово, что воспитают его как своего сына.

Если вернешься прошу тебя по достойному отблагодарить их, а также хорошо воспитать сына

Лиза

**Liza's letter to her husband Gregory (Grisha)**

Darling Grisha,

I write you this letter at the time when I must separate from my only happiness, our son. I took this step because I want to save his life at least. My life is lived, and now every minute is spend waiting for death. Death is not frightening to me, because I am dying with the knowledge that maybe you will return. Maybe you will meet our son, and together you will remember me. I have left Lyonya with the Russian family, Krezo. They have promised me that they will raise him as their own. If you return, I ask you to show them enormous gratitude, and also to raise our son well.

Liza

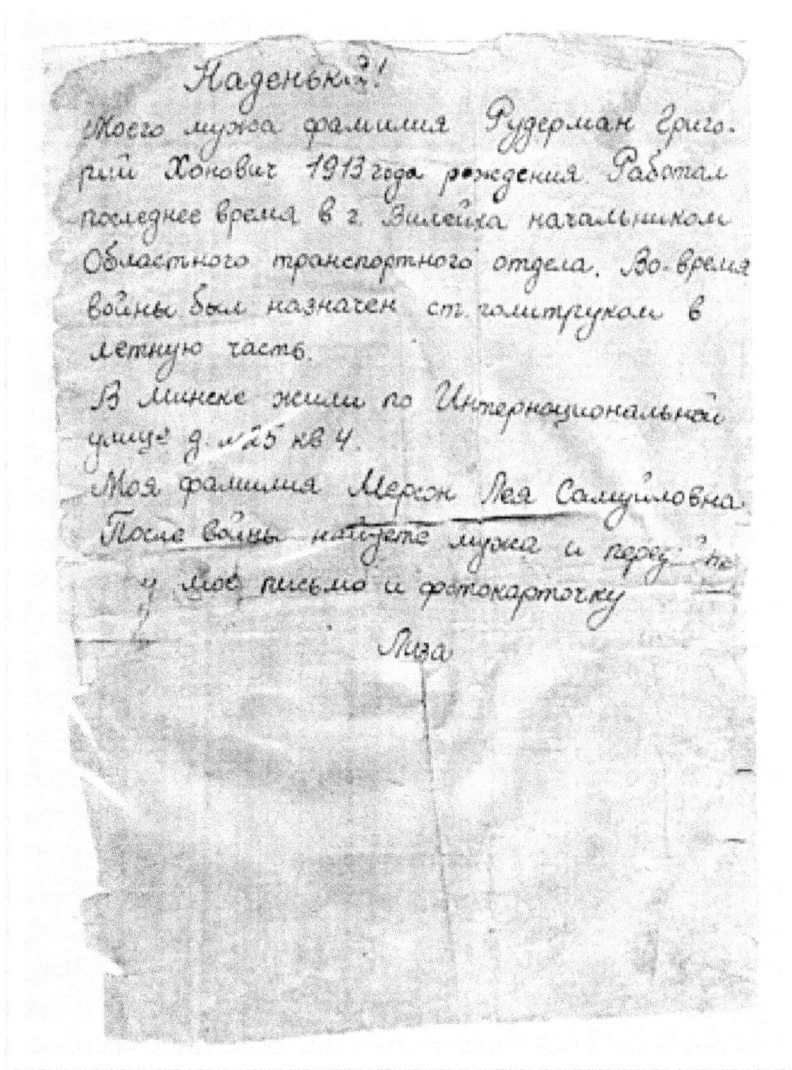

**Liza's Letter to Nadya**

Nadya,

My full name is Ruderman Merson Leah Samuilovna. My husband's full name is Ruderman Gregoriy Hanovich, and he was born in 1913. He worked most recently in the town of Vileyka as a manager in the Regional Transport Department. At the time of the war, he was given the position of Senior Political Commissar in the Air Force. We lived in Minsk, on Internatsionalnaya Street, house number 25, flat 4. After the war, please find my husband and give him my letter and photograph.

Liza

# My Memories

**Boris Srebnik**

**Boris Srebnik**

I am writing this on 23 October. On this day in 1943, the population of the Minsk Ghetto was completely destroyed. My family and relatives were killed, together with many thousands of Jewish people of all ages. In memory of them, and in honour of those who bear the names of their dead relatives, I want to tell at least part of what it is that keeps my memory of that terrible time alive. Those memories start in June 1941, at the start of the Great Patriotic War, when the Germans started to bomb Minsk. We stood on the porch of our wooden house on the outskirts of the city and watched that terrible spectacle.

All of the events which I describe here are fixed firmly in my memory with photographic accuracy, down to weather conditions and the colour of the trees... However, I am unable to tell you how old I was at that time, as I do not know my date of birth. Those relatives who might have known are now dead, and the pre-war documents in the Minsk archive did not survive. It was not until 1949, that I was finally able to confirm the year of my birth. It was then that I paid a visit to the registrar, and it was he who calculated that I must have been born in 1934, because I hadn't yet started to attend school in the years preceding the war. He concluded that I must therefore have been just seven years old at the beginning of the Great Patriotic War.

My actual birthday was a random decision made when I was living in an orphanage, some time after the war had ended. My cousin found me there and took me to live with her, and we gathered some recently demobilised friends together. One of them began making notes and listing our dates of birth. It was a kind of game: he went down the list and we each gave our date of birth and told some funny story. When my turn came, I was really sad and upset that I didn't know my actual birthday, so I just said the first thing that came into my head: 29 December! So this now became my birthday, and it is what subsequently appeared in all of my official documents!

As I recall, my father worked in a radio station near the village of Tsna near Minsk. It was near Bolotnaya Station. In the early days of the war, my father would take us to work with him, and during the bombing we hid in the trenches which had been specially dug in the grounds of the radio station. One day, all the members of staff, together with their families, were loaded onto trucks and taken to the Moscow highway in the direction of Moscow. As I understand it, we were trying to break through to the east, However, on the way, we were cut off by enemy troops. The families got out of the vehicles and went into the woods, while only the men, all of them employees of the radio station, were left on the trucks. This area was full of German troops and we knew that their chances of escape were slim.

**Boris Srebnik (right) 1945**

I spent the night in the forest with my mum Riva and the other family members. I recall burying my father's spare military uniform (a shirt and trousers) in the ground. Judging by the fact that we could see a large radio mast near the road, I am guessing that we were probably somewhere in the Kolodishchi district of Minsk. The next morning my mother and I met some people who were on their way to Minsk on foot, and they told us that the city had already been surrounded by the Nazis.

I never saw my father again. I never discovered what happened to him, or how he died. Not even a photograph remains. After the war, I wrote to the military archives in order to obtain any possible news about him, but I always received the same answer: his name did not appear in the lists of dead and wounded. To this day, I do not even know his Hebrew name. At home, he was just called Velvl. I did not remember the name of his father - my grandfather, whom I had never seen. Much later, on 17 December 1949, when I was in the Voroshilov district registry office in Minsk trying to obtain my birth certificate, I wrote that I was born 'in the second half of 1934.' I also had to write the first name and surname of my father, so I said that he was Vladimir Illich (like Lenin). In those years, for obvious reasons, I did not want to be known as 'Velvlovich' (the son of Velvl). So I now became Boris Vladimirovich (son of Vladimir).

**Boris Srebnik, a member of Opera Studio, of the Minsk *Dvorets Profsoyuzov*, 1963**

It turns out that it is not only my first name that contains a kind of story, but also my surname. After the war, 'restructuring' began, so I applied for the documents which were then being made available to survivors of the ghetto to prove that I was a survivor of the ghetto. However, my documents could not be found in the Minsk archive. I then requested a document confirming that, as a boy, I had been based in the 5th Partisan Unit, in the area of Porechye village. (This was where I had arrived at the end of 1943, following the liquidation of the Minsk ghetto). The answer from the archive was that there was no record of me in this partisan unit. It was not until many years later, in the spring of 2011, that a fellow survivor, Maya Krapina, called me from Minsk. She was a former prisoner of the ghetto, and had been with me in the partisans. She told me that a Belarusian historian had tracked down a relevant document. It stated that, after the liberation of Minsk, myself and three other partisan children had been sent to the Minsk orphanage. And I was finally able to see for myself that I had not been identified as Srebnik B.V., but as Srebnikov B.V. That is why I had been informed that my name did not appear in the archive's lists.

So, to return to my boyhood story, mother and I returned to Minsk, and to our house in the area of Bolotnaya Station. The Fascists were there already and so the anxious days of waiting to know our fate and that of other Jewish families now began.

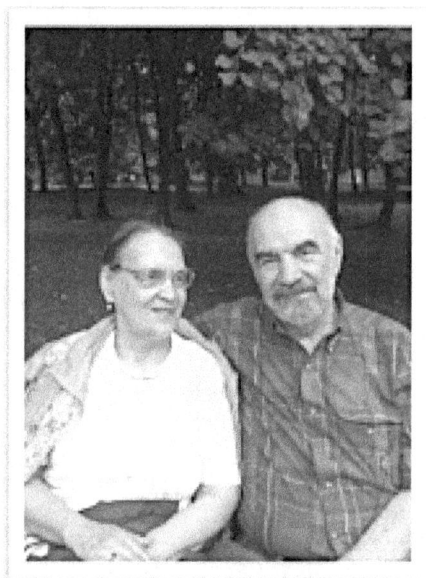

**Boris Srebnik with his wife Ludmila**

It was during the second half of July 1941, that the order was issued by the German commandant that a special area within the city of Minsk had been allocated to house only Jews. All Jewish residents of the city of Minsk were to move to this Jewish district within a specified short period of time, and it quickly became the most crowded place in the city.

That was the start of my life in the Minsk Ghetto. According to the order, the Jewish population was compelled to wear a yellow patch. We called it *lata* [see glossary]. Jews were obliged to sew the patch onto the chest and back of their outer garments. Failure to comply with this order of the field commandant would result in arrest and severe punishment. What were we to do but obey? Mum was with me, her sisters, their children and my grandfather Isaac (my mother's father). We were only allowed to take simple household goods with us into the ghetto – bedding, clothes, and a few farm implements. We now took up residence in Sukhaya Street, in a wooden house near to the Jewish cemetery. So the history the largest occupied ghetto (Minsk Ghetto) of World War II began. Not only were all the Jews of the city assembled there, but very soon more Jews were herded in from nearby towns, and there were others brought from Germany. According to documents made available much later, in this small area fenced-in by barbed wire and near to the Jewish cemetery, more than 80,000 Jews from Minsk, around

10,000 from nearby places and over 30,000 those brought in from Germany were gathered together and destroyed.

Entering and leaving the ghetto, and contact with those living in the Russian area, was not permitted. In spite of this, however, food and other items were smuggled in secretly, under threat of punishment or even death. For example, locals would regularly approach the other side of the barbed wire offering us flour and potatoes. So the days passed, full of surprises and dangers, each of which could become the last.

On 6 November 1941, on the eve of the anniversary of the October Revolution, a rumour began to circulate that there would be a pogrom. I remember that, on that night, my mother's older sister Lisa said that she had dreamed of meat; this popular belief was always considered a bad omen. On that same night, my mother decided that a pogrom would probably most affect the people living close to the cemetery. We therefore decided to move away from the cemetery for one night only, and we went to stay with friends on Khlebnaya Street. So much for so-called 'Jewish luck'!

The rioters did not go to the cemetery at all, but instead turned their attention to that area of the ghetto which included Khlebnaya Street, where we were hiding. For the rest of my life, I will remember the gloomy morning of 7 November 1941. It was frosty and had snowed a little. There was a sharp knock on the door of the house where we had spent the night. An order was barked at us, so we left the house and went out onto the street. We were pushed with the butts of rifles, and driven into the yard of the nearby bakery, where many people had already been herded. Then we were pushed out into the street and lined up in a column of twos. The queue was about fifty meters long. These people were moved onto some covered lorries which had been brought in earlier, and then the line grew longer as more people were brought out from the yard of the bakery. Each lorry was tightly packed and then away it went. A rumour was circulating among the people standing in the queue. They were saying that everyone getting into these vehicles would be shot. As it turned out, no one who was taken away in one of those vehicles ever returned to the ghetto.

There was another rumour going about that some people were being released from the line by the Germans and their collaborators. These collaborators, who were Lithuanians, Latvians or even Ukrainians, were dressed in yellow-green outfits and were indeed pulling some people back out of the vehicles. The rumour spread quickly that those being released from the group were people whose men were from families specially selected to work in the professional camp on Shirokaya Street. They were not to be taken away. It is now well known that, after the establishment of the ghetto, the Germans had selected some Jewish men with specialist skills to be placed together in a special camp near Komarovka.

On this terrible day, as my mother and I got closer to the front of the queue, I remember that I was crying and asking if I could sit in the vehicle. I really wanted to ride in there with her! But my mother pushed me away from her and frantically screamed that her husband was exempt (even though it was not true), and requested to be released. Although they beat her with rifle butts, she was fearless and she desperately dragged me to the back of the group. Finally, when it became dark, the thugs ceased loading people into the trucks, and pushed the ghetto inhabitants back into the yard of the bakery. 'Get up! Sit!' Those terrifying commands and shots fired into the air would go on for a long time. Finally, when it got dark, those of us who remained in the bakery yard were released, and we were able finally to return to our house by the cemetery on Sukhaya Street.

**In the Synagogue at Poklonnaya Gora on the Day of Commemoration for those who died in the Minsk Ghetto**

After some time in the ghetto, the first of several raids occurred. It was during the second half of November 1941. They were capturing male adolescents, many of whom never returned. My cousin Yasha was 14 or 15 years old at the time. He had just gone to bed when the Germans rushed into the house. We told them that he was ill, that he had a temperature... but they did not listen to us. He was just lifted up and taken away. We never saw him again.

The day after this round-up is one I remember very well.  My mother decided to crawl under the barbed wire fence of the ghetto and go to the so-called 'Russian district' of the city [see glossary].  She planned to visit our previous neighbours, who were still living on the street where we too had lived before going into the ghetto. She wanted to ask them to take me out of the ghetto and move me to somewhere in the countryside to their relatives. At that time, I was quite blond and did not look particularly Jewish. She was trying to save me from death - but she did not return to the ghetto, and I never saw her again. Where and how she died, I do not know. After the war, I heard from the neighbours of our house where we lived before the war, that she was turned in and by some policeman who was now living in our old house and must have recognized her in the street. Apart from her image, which has remained in my memory, I have nothing left of her. As in the case of my father, I do not even have a photograph.

Soon after this terrible day, an order was issued that the ghetto inhabitants were to give up everything valuable to the German authorities, including warm clothes. Some of these were items which we would have been able to exchange through the barbed wire. They were things which, at least for a while, could save us from starvation. So my grandfather Isaac, who was living with us, took up a corner of the floor boards and dug a small pit. We then concealed our remaining clothes in that space under the floor, together with other things that could be taken from us. Such a hiding place was called a *malina*. We pushed a pile of rags and single bed over this hole. There were half a dozen people who slept in this room, most of them on the floor.

However, by the end of 1941, everything we had concealed in the *malina* was gone in exchange for food. At this time there was a boy living with us. He was a few years older than me and I never knew his real name.  We just called him 'Mayka'. He was of Ukrainian origin and he lived in the house with his grandmother.  Every morning, Mayka would creep under the wire in order to get to the Russian district. Once there, he would go from house to house begging for food, and now he invited me to go with him.

We would crawl under the barbed wire on Kollektornaya Street and then went in the direction of Surazhsky market or behind the concrete railway bridge, and down Kamiennaya Street, Chkalova or other streets in the area near the commercial railway station. The station was now a metal dump. In the evening, we would return to the ghetto by joining the crowd of Jews who were driven daily by the Germans to work at the dump. We usually hid in the back of the truck at the feet of adults. Sometimes the German guards carried out checks and when we were discovered, we were just thrown out of the truck by the scruff of the neck.

Mayka and I did not have high expectations. The residents either had very little themselves, or they were simply afraid to help Jewish people in any way. Mostly, we would search through the rubbish. We had one big success, which I will remember for the rest of my life. It was winter, and we found a whole frozen potato among some peelings, which we later boiled and ate. To this day, I still remember its appearance and taste. It reminded me of 'potato cake'. Some of the things that we found we would take back to Mayka's old grandmother in the ghetto. There were times when the local boys from the Russian district ran over to report us to the police officer, suggesting that he 'tell the little Jews to go home'. That is when we had to run.

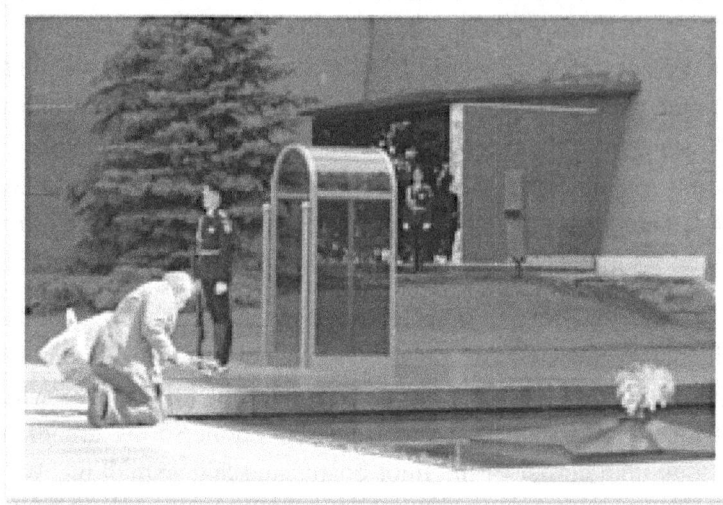

**Laying of flowers at the tomb of the Unknown Soldier near the Kremlin Wall on 9<sup>th</sup> May**

Meanwhile, in the ghetto, there were frequent nighttime raids. Often, after those terrible attacks, the corpses of victims would be transported in carts to the cemetery. Then, in the morning, the bodies would be dumped into big open pits which had been dug in advance. The bodies were sometimes burnt, and then covered with a thin layer of earth. However, they were not completely buried until such time as the pit was filled to the brim. Since our house was located next to the cemetery, I witnessed all of this. The sight of it is deeply etched on my memory.

In the autumn of 1941, a large number of German Jews had been brought into the Minsk ghetto. We called them the 'Hamburg' Jews [see glossary]. The 'Hamburg' area was surrounded with barbed wire - a ghetto within the ghetto. I once stole a potato from our house and handed it across the wire to the German Jews and, in return, they gave me a caramel in a wrapper called a 'Bon-Bon'. I still to this day remember this caramel, its colour and even the wrapper. But the Hamburg Jews were soon to die. Like so many of our own adults, they were all murdered.

Periodically, during the night, looters from the Russian district came through the cemetery and into the ghetto. They broke into the houses, saying that they would kill anyone who did not give them valuable things, and demanding gold. I recall that they once wounded a neighbour, threatening to pour kerosene over the house and set it on fire. After that, we hung a piece of metal on the rails outside the house and then tied the metal to a wire. When looters broke into the house, we would pull the wire in order to create some noise and send a signal to the German night patrol.

I recall one evening when two German soldiers had deliberately positioned themselves in our house for the night (people said they were Czech). When looters broke into our house, the soldiers appeared suddenly, detained one of them and took him away. I remember feeling quite sorry for this marauder. I have no idea what they did with him.

Sometimes, especially at night, riots occurred which were called 'mini-pogroms'. On these occasions not only were Jews attacked, but sometimes they were even burned alive inside their wooden houses. The residents of our house, together with the people living in a nearby house, secretly dug a hole under the barn which stood next to our home. At night we would hide in there. The secret trap door in the shed had tobacco sprinkled over it. They said that, if the Germans came around with dogs, the smell of the tobacco would prevent the dogs from detecting the scent of people. I remember that one night, during such a 'mini-pogrom', a child (maybe a baby) burst into tears and those who were in there 'shushed' her sharply. I still remember the sound of that 'shushing' to this day. I did not know then how this child was eventually calmed down and can only imagine....

One of the most terrible massacres took place in early March 1942. It started in the afternoon. All of the things that we had been hiding in the hole under the floor had, by now, run out; so my grandfather Isaac now hid everyone in this empty pit: me, my aunt Liza and the neighbour who lived in our room. We huddled very close to each other in this small underground space. My grandfather scattered rags on the floorboards and pushed the bed over it. He himself hid in an empty cupboard in the hallway. From our hiding place, I heard the rioters burst into the room with a roar. They didn't find anyone, but on the way out they found my grandfather. He had asthma and had probably alerted them by clearing his throat. We heard the sound of them dragging him out into the yard, and then we heard two dry clicks. Thus ended the life of my grandfather Isaac, who had sacrificed himself in order to save the rest of us on this dreadful day of death.

There then followed a day without food or water. We were afraid to get out of our hiding place because we did not know whether the massacre was over, or if the Germans were coming back... Finally, we were still under the floor, when we heard a voice. It was Olya, my cousin and the daughter of Aunt Liza. When she hadn't found any of her relatives inside the house, she had begun to sob and cry loudly. We heard the terrible sound from under the floor, but were still afraid to go out. This was not even sobbing; it was a heart-breaking inhuman sound. It was a long time before we summoned the courage to finally start tapping on the board covering our pit.

It turned out that Olya had been saved from death because she had been in forced labour outside the ghetto. Labourers were usually taken away to work in the morning and brought back to the ghetto in the evening. However, the German supervisor of the sewing studio in which

Olya's group worked, had known about the impending massacre, and so had not sent the workers back into the ghetto at the end of the day. Instead, he allowed them to spend the night in the studio. I do not know if he did it for humanitarian reasons or because he was unwilling to lose his workers who were, by now, fully trained. I really do want to believe that he did it in good faith. Either way, I thank him for the fact that, even in this mayhem, he managed to save Olya, and those others with her, from certain death.  Olya (Olga Ozder) later escaped from the ghetto, and was a member of Partisan Troop No. 106 until the end of the war.

I experienced every single pogrom that took place in the ghetto, and each time I somehow survived. *To this day, I still feel that those of us who did manage to remain alive must continue to tell our stories in memory of those others who failed to escape.*

For almost two years, I went with Mayka to beg from houses in the Russian area of Minsk. Sometimes, we even stole food at Surazh market or the trading train station. I never went out alone, unlike Mayka, who sometimes went out and brought food back for me.  One rainy autumn morning in 1943, however, his torn shoes just fell to pieces, and he could no longer go out to beg. I really did not want to go alone, but I could not bring myself to tell him of my fear. So, for the first time, I went under the wire alone. It was leaving the ghetto on that day that saved me. It was 21 October, the day of the last pogrom, when everyone still remaining in the ghetto would finally be killed, including Mayka, to whom I owe my own life.

While I was in the city, I was not aware that there had been a pogrom, and I decided to return as usual with the Jews who worked at the metal dump. However, when I arrived at the dump in the evening, there were no Jews and none of the usual trucks. Instead, I found myself looking up at a huge redheaded German.  I recognised him as the soldier who had repeatedly thrown me out of the truck when I was found hiding among the legs of the adults. I started to run into the landfill in order to reach the entrance located on the opposite side of the dump. The German ran after me… but very slowly. He knew what I did not: on the other side of the landfill, a new high wooden fence had been constructed. When I finally reached it, I realised that I would not be able to climb over. I remember still, how I was overcome with hopelessness and fear. However, at the last moment, I noticed, a narrow gap at the bottom of the fence, where one board was shorter than all the rest. This small hole was big enough for a dog or a cat to get through. It was quite an effort for me to wriggle through. However, once I was on the other side, the soldier could no longer pursue me, and for the second time on this terrible day, I escaped death.

Having got away from the German, I now started back to the ghetto but, before I got there, I saw a crowd at the corner of Myasnikova and Kollektornaya Streets. The people were standing far back from the wire fence of the ghetto, and I recognised some of them as residents from the nearby Russian area. They were saying that all the Jews who had been inside had been killed.

**Boris Srebnik (left) with university students and veterans**

I quickly left this place and ended up spending a rainy night and morning wandering round the city. By the end of the day I came to the west side of the bridge and sat on the wooden steps of a newspaper kiosk wondering what to do. I even began considering returning to the ghetto. Of course, as I realise now, this would have been a tragic mistake. Finally, an older boy came up to me with a little girl, his sister. I recognised him and knew his name from the ghetto as Yoska. He asked me what I was going to do, and I told him that I really could not decide. He said that he knew the way to the partisans, and offered to take me to them. Of course, I immediately agreed.

That evening we slept on the metal dustbin at the railroad station where, only a day earlier, I had been running away from the German. Before I settled down for the night among the mountains of scrap metal lying around, I went to inspect the gap in the fence. It seemed impossible to me that I could have squeezed through that small space, even if I had been forcibly shoved. To this day, I still wonder how I managed to slip through such a small hole. In fact, years later, when studying psychology at the University, I learned that, when under extreme pressure, a person can do the most incredible things. Obviously, that was just such a moment!

We spent three days at the railroad station, during which time a group of nine other boys had also gathered there. They had all escaped from the ghetto. There was also one girl, the youngest of us, Yoska's sister. We all hid in a big empty iron container for three nights. It had a side hatch through which we could come and go, and in the daytime we would go out to discover what was happening in the ghetto. We begged for food from people arriving at the station, and I remember that we managed to save some of the rectangular German bread. We hoped that it would be enough to feed us for a short time on the way to the partisans. At first, we did not want to believe that the ghetto had been destroyed completely. However, after three days, when we were quite certain that there was no one left there any longer, we set out in search of the partisans.

It was a foggy morning, so we walked in pairs, within sight of each other. Yoska went first with his sister, and I was in the last pair as the youngest one. To get to the partisans, we walked for three days. It was a journey of about 90 kilometres. This was a very thorny path, especially at the beginning when we were actually stopped and questioned by Germans before being released. The worst moments were when we met local people, especially teenagers. They were hostile and targeted us, even with our shabby clothes and shoes. So we tried to keep to quieter rural areas. Finally, at the end of the second day, Yoska who had previous experience of leading groups from the ghetto to the partisans, announced that we were about to enter a partisan zone. However, just at that moment, we were stopped by some young men in police uniforms. We concocted a story that we were travelling from such and such a village, but they said that they knew that we were Jews, and that they would shoot us.

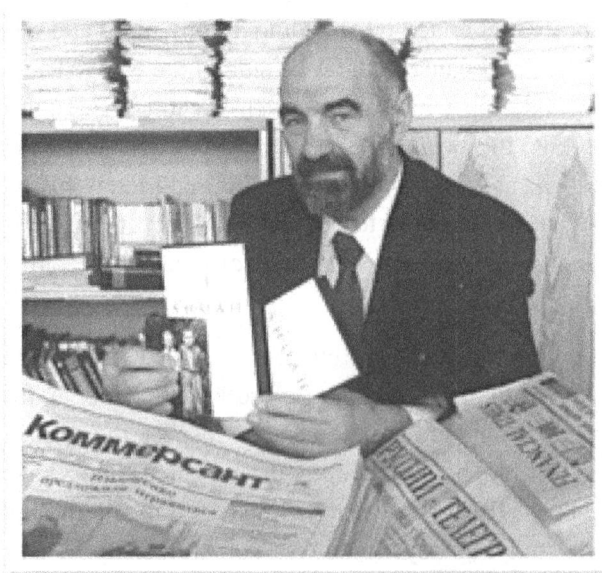

**From the German magazine, Stern. March 1998.**

We were made to face the bushes and they started clicking their triggers. None of us asked to be spared and nobody cried. I remember feeling a terrible bitterness – I still see it all in my dreams – why did we have to suffer such hardship for so many days, only to die for nothing, just when it had seemed that we would reach safety. Suddenly one of our captors said, 'Guys, we were joking. We are an advanced partisan unit.' No-one believed them. It was only after they literally turned us around with our backs against the bushes, and asked if we had any bread because they had herring, did we start to believe that they were really partisans. They were wearing police uniforms as a cover, because they were based at a point where the German and partisan zones met.

The remainder of our journey took just one day more, so it was the following evening when we finally arrived at the location of the 5th detachment of the 2nd Minsk Kutuzov Partisan Brigade, in the village of Porechye in the Puhovichsky district. For the rest of my life I will remember the moment when, as night fell, Lapidus, the detachment commander, took from my hands a half-eaten cabbage which I had found on the road several days previously. He threw it away and told someone to give me some bread. Following that, he baked potatoes in the fire and we ate them together with milk. Oh, that was a delicious meal! I remember the taste to this day.

Initially, the partisans put us all in one house and assigned a young woman as the leader. I think her name was Galya. Then she disappeared and we were split up. Some of us stayed in the homes of villagers in Porechye, and others lived close by in settlements located near the area of troop deployment. The Germans did not appear in those places until the beginning of summer 1944, close to the period when the Red Army began the liberation of Byelorussia. We lived there from the end of October 1943 to July 1944. We will always be grateful to all the villagers who gave us shelter. They somehow fed us as best they could. They kept us from starvation.

Finally, as the Red Army advanced, the Germans, as they departed, decided to get rid of the partisans. At first the partisans withdrew from the villages into the forests and swamps, while we, the children, who were there in the detachment zone, did our best to follow them into the forests to hide. The German blockade lasted for ten days, and when we finally returned to the village of Porechye, we discovered that almost all of our boys had been recovered from the forests. Only one boy did not return. It was Yoska... the same Yoska, who had saved us from death in Minsk after the destruction of the ghetto. He was the one who had led us to the partisan detachment, but now he was gone. I have always remembered him and have never forgotten that I owe him my life. Whenever I have spoken about the ghetto and how I managed to escape, I have always registered my sadness at the deaths of Mayka and Yoska, who could have been the closest people to me in my life.

On 21 October 1993, an event took place to commemorate the 50th anniversary of the destruction of the Minsk Ghetto. On that day, survivors of the former ghetto, together with members of the government of the Republic of Belarus, gathered in Minsk. We stood at the obelisk near the pit on Fruktovaya Street, in one of the many places where thousands of Jews lie buried who had been shot in the ghetto [see 'Yama' in the glossary]. I was approached by my friend Felix Lipsky, the former president of the Belarusian Union of Former Jewish Prisoners of Ghettoes and Concentration Camps. He told me that there were some in the audience who had been with the partisans in Porechye. He pointed out a small woman. I approached her and asked whether it was true that she had been in the Porechye unit and she confirmed that she had indeed been there. However, neither of us remembered the other. Then she asked if I recalled any of those who were there with me. I said that ten of us had been brought there together by Yoska, who had been accompanied by his little sister. She told me that she was this little girl. I tried to express my sincere condolences to her for the sad death of her brother, who had so bravely rescued us, only to die during the partisan siege in the early summer of 1944. She stopped me, gesturing toward some people standing nearby, saying, 'How is he dead? Here he is!' It turns out that Yoska had been captured after the siege, and, after many twists and turns of fate, he had ended up in Riga after the war.

This meeting made me happier than I had been for many decades. It brought tears to my eyes. Yoska's name is now Joseph Levin and he lives far away abroad. Good health to you, my dear one. If there is a God, he will surely repay you for what you did for me - and not just for me. Thank you! The little girl, his sister, is now Maya Krapina. After living in the children's home, she spent some time as an acrobat in the circus. She now lives in Minsk [see Maya Krapina's story].

In 2008, while in Israel at a meeting with former prisoners of the ghettoes, I ran into Levy Pasherstnik who is now an Israeli citizen. We had both lived in the same area of the Minsk ghetto, and then, after its destruction, we were together again in Porechye. I was very glad to meet him again, 65 years after the end of the war.

**At the time of writing his story Boris Srebnik added the following: -**

*Boris Srebnik is Professor of 'Financial Markets and Financial Engineering' at the Financial University under the Government of the Russian Federation, Honoured Worker of Higher Education, Ph.D., senior researcher, Professor, member of the New York Science Academy, and member of the Methodological Council of the Financial University under the Government of the Russian Federation. He teaches the following subjects:*

- *Stocks and bond markets.*

- *Professional activity in the bond market.*

- *Finance and financial institutions.*

*He is the author of textbooks and teaching aids for schools: 'Economics of Trade', 'Marketing', 'Bonds Market', 'Financial markets', and co-author of textbooks and manuals: 'National Economy Planning', 'Organisation of Commodity Circulation Planning', 'Theory and Practice Crisis Management ',' Foundations of Entrepreneurship', 'The Management of Organisations: The modular program for managers', 'Management of State Property', 'Professional Activities in the Securities Market', as well as guidelines for market research and management of economic activities.*

*He worked as director in the development of scientific methods studying and demanding forecasting, as well as implementing a forecast for trade markets capacity using the same methods.*

*He trained at the Institute of European Bank Associations (Germany), the International Centre for Management Training 'CROWN AGENTS' (United Kingdom) and on the Frankfurt Stock Exchange.*

*He participated in international programs ('TACIS' etc.) and taught as a visiting professor at universities in the USA and Israel.*

# Sixty Years Later
### David Taubkin

*In memory of my mother and sister*

As I write this, I am flying to Belarus at the invitation of the Belarusian Association of Jews of the former Minsk Ghetto. I am a member of an official Israeli delegation which will participate in the ceremonies commemorating the 60th anniversary of the liberation of Minsk, and of the whole of the Republic, from Nazi invaders. Minsk was not only the city of my carefree and joyful childhood, but also the place where I experienced the deepest personal grief during the German occupation.

## War

Before the war, my family lived at 15, Voroshilov Street in Lyahovka, an area in the southeast of Minsk. The house was in the 'closed' part of the courtyard, surrounded by gardens, acacia shrubs and huge old maples. On one side of the courtyard were allotments with greenhouses, and on the other side there were military barracks.

12 April 1941 was my ninth birthday. I had been a late but welcome child, but I suffered from poor health. My family was very loving and, as the youngest, they pampered me. My father, Aron Davidovich Taubkin, was a physician. He graduated from the medical faculty of the University of Kazan and then served in the Russian army during the imperialist war. He was a medical officer with the rank of captain. After the revolution, he returned to Minsk, where he continued to work in the medical institutions of the city. My mother, Rosalia Mikhailovna (née Levidova), met my father in Kazan where she lived. She was studying at the faculty of history and philology at Kazan University. After the revolution, she came to Minsk to be with my father. By this time, she had begun to teach Russian history at the university. However, being a woman of principle, she did not accept the new Soviet interpretation of history and so began to teach a course on Russian literature. When that also became impossible because of the proletarian ideology of the syllabus, she moved on to teach German at the Minsk Institute of National Economy.

Mum was kind, gentle and extremely scrupulous. Her character had a lot in common with that of the girls in Turgenev's novels. As subsequent events demonstrated, when the time came to act, she turned out to be a deeply conscientious and courageous person. I also had a wonderful sister. Her name was Lida, and she was ten years older than me. She took care of me and taught me by example. My nanny Lenya (Leonarda Ferdinandovna Divaltovskaya) also lived with us, and was considered to be a member of our family. She was very kind to me and always forgave my childish pranks, of which there were many.

Lida and I studied at the prestigious School Number Four, from which Lida graduated in June 1941. However, I was only able to complete the first grade of that school. We were planning to go away as a family for the summer, leaving for Moscow on Saturday 21 June 1941. However, our departure was delayed for a week because the school was to hold a graduation ceremony, which Lida and our parents were to attend. The graduation evening duly took place. It was both a joyful and solemn occasion, and Lida was presented with her final certificate with honours. However, this delay was to change our destiny.

On the very next day, 22 June, the war began. Nothing had forewarned us of this alarming event. Everyone had believed the Soviet propaganda concerning the power and might of the Red Army, and we thought that the enemy would be defeated within a few days. At first, the city seemed calm. The only things that were moving around at high speed were military vehicles. However, from the porch of our house, we could see the triangles of East German aircraft flying at high altitude. Anti-aircraft guns occasionally shot at them, but the shells burst far below them. On the same day, Dad was summoned to the military enlistment office where he was given orders to attend for duty at a military hospital in Borisov the following day.

Then, on the morning of 24 June, an air-raid was announced, and the residents of the neighbouring houses had to go to the nearest 'bomb shelter'. This shelter was simply the basement of one of the ordinary wooden houses. We went to the shelter, and then our Dad arrived. He was already in uniform, with two insignia patches indicating his rank. He said goodbye to us and went by car to the hospital. Just an hour after his departure, the most terrible bombing of the city began. The whistle and roar of falling bombs shook the walls and it lasted for a very long time. When it suddenly stopped, we were finally allowed to leave the basement.

The bomb had not hit our house, but right next to our porch there was a gaping crater where it had landed. We went inside and my mother immediately picked up a bag and started to put valuables into it, including documents, money and the book *Paganini* by Vinogradov. Lida made up a bag of food, and packed it with a prayer book into a bag of shoes. I picked up a teddy bear. With this light load, we left our house and started to walk in the direction of the Mogilev highway. Although it was evening, it seemed quite light. That was when we realised that the city was on fire. The glow of flames and smoke accompanied us almost until morning. By now, crowds of refugees were moving along the highway. From time to time people threw away their belongings which had simply become too much to carry. We spent the rest of the night in a peasant hut and then, in the morning, we received the news that the Germans had invaded. So now, all of us refugees were told to return to our homes. We walked along the roadside back to Minsk as trucks rushed past us full of German soldiers. Instead of the normal steady flow of cars, the traffic now consisted mainly of armoured work details. German military power was moving to the east.

Back at the house, we heard from our neighbours that Dad was trying to find us. Early that day, 25 June, he had returned to the city by car from the hospital in Borisov, but he had been unable to find us and had to go back. We missed him by just a few hours...

A few days later we were visited by Pesya Goldberg with her son Vova (Vladimir), who was three years older than me. His Dad, an army doctor, served in a military unit near Minsk, and the family was often at our house. Two weeks before the war, they had moved near to Brest. Aunt Pesya told us that when the war started, she and her son had managed to avoid the advancing German army and get back to Minsk. Mum asked Pesya and Vova to come and live with us. Then they received news that Vova's father had been captured and was in the Masjukovshina camp [see glossary]. Aunt Pesya and Vova went to the camp and found him. They told us that they had been able to pass him cigarettes and some food. It was some time later that we heard that the Jews had eventually been separated from the other prisoners, and that Goldberg had died there of starvation.

## The Ghetto

Meanwhile, things were becoming difficult for us and looting began. For example, I remember that there was a distillery on our street and local residents would raid it, carrying away buckets of alcohol scooped out of the factory vats. They also robbed stores of provisions and textiles. However, our mother banned us from participating in all of this looting.

Then, just three weeks after the arrival of the Germans, the Commandant announced the order to establish a ghetto in Minsk to which all the Jews were to be relocated. Resettlement had to be completed within five days. We were all subject to mandatory registration and, after the closing date, Jews seen outside the ghetto would be arrested. We were allowed to take some property with us. The Jewish council, the *Judenrat,* and the Jewish security force was put in charge of the relocation. These two groups were responsible for maintaining order. The *Judenrat* was headed by Ilya Mushkin, his composition was decided by the German authorities. I remember this unfortunate man Mushkin, who had grey, flowing hair. He lived in the ghetto not far from us. He was entrusted with the huge responsibility of organising daily life in the ghetto. Later the Germans shot him, and they also executed the chief of the ghetto guard service Zyama Serebryansky. Almost simultaneously with the decree for the establishment of the ghetto, the order was given for the mandatory wearing of Jewish identification by anyone over the age of 10 years. This took the form of two circular patches of yellow, which were to be worn attached to our outer garments, both front and back, or a white armband which the ghetto residents referred to as 'armor' [see glossary]. Jews were also forbidden to walk on the pavements, to take part in entertainment such as theatres, cinemas, libraries and museums, or to attend school.

After the order concerning the formation of the ghetto, we received expressions of sympathy from our Russian neighbours and offers of help began to arrive at our house.

Klementiy Lisowsky arrived first. His son Kim and I were friends. Lisowsky was an elderly and careful person. He said to my mother, 'Don't go into the ghetto, I'll help you to hide.' Mother thanked him, but said she could not violate the order of the German commandant. She could not risk either the lives of her own family, or of members of the Lisowski family. No-one at that time, at the very beginning of the occupation, could have imagined that it would result in the near total destruction of the Jews. Some friends arrived from the city, bringing food. Our mother gave some of our valuables to several of these people. I remember that she gave some carriage clocks to Madame Siegel, an Estonian lady. After the war, she returned those clocks, and today they are in my house. Almost all of the remaining things, including some furniture and a piano, were left behind because they were not popular, and were not going to be easily exchanged by us for food. Our nanny Lenya remained in our old flat to look after the property. Once we were in the ghetto our new neighbours asked, 'Didn't you have any valuables in your old house which you could have brought with you in order to exchange them for food?' But the only valuable thing we had brought was a sewing machine, which we did eventually manage to exchange for a rotten bag of flour. We possessed few clothes or good shoes, so we had nothing that would have been profitable to sell. My family had never been materialistic. They had other less tangible interests such as the education of children, study and work.

When she first learned about the resettlement, Mum had gone to petition for new housing within the territory of the ghetto and she had also enquired about taking household goods. The authorities allowed us to carry only the necessary utensils. I remember that we took wood, because we would have to spend the winter behind the barbed wire. Following the wagon with our few possessions, we had to walk in the road as Jews were now forbidden to walk on the pavement, and we finally arrived at our new home on Obutkovaya Street.

Inside the ghetto, large numbers of people would be housed in just one large room. In our room, for example, lived the owner of the apartment with his three-year-old son, a woman with a fourteen-year-old son, and another family consisting of a grandmother, her son and his wife and their eighteen-year old daughter. Thus, thirteen people had to fit into this one living area. In the daytime, people would leave the house. So now Mum got a job as a translator in the *Judenrat*. In the evening we all settled down for the night, each in his or her own bed. Nearby was a kitchen with a Russian stove where the people from our room, as well as the other inhabitants of the house, could reheat food. In our family, the food was organised by Aunt Pesya. At first, rye flour was used to bake delicious bread, and there were potatoes fried in fish oil that my mother was able to obtain outside the ghetto. However, the diet soon became much more meagre.

Meanwhile, the news was becoming increasingly alarming. We heard rumours about executions of Jews in the town. Precise data was not available, as the Germans concealed their crimes and spread rumours about the 'resettlement' of Jews, saying that they had been moved to work in another locality. At first, the guarding of the ghetto was not very effective, mainly because there was no solid fence around it – just the barbed wire. Sometimes Lenya came and brought some items which she had exchanged for things in the apartment, but she was afraid to come into the ghetto. I remember how she trembled with fear and was always anxious to get away.

One day in October, shots rang out in the street. Armed Ukrainians burst into the houses and began to drive the residents out of their homes, forcing them towards the four-storey school - the tallest building in the ghetto. It was not possible to escape, as armed German guards were standing around everywhere. In the school yard, thousands of people were gathered in front of the building, and there were machine guns aimed at the crowd. Climbing onto the porch, a German officer announced in Russian that those who had gold or money must hand it over. Doing this would save them from being subjected to punishment. We had Soviet paper money, so Aunt Pesya took me and Vova by the hand and, together with Lida, we approached the school porch. We gave the money to the Germans by putting it into a suitcase which was lying open. It was already full of gold wedding rings, the gold rims of glasses, and dozens of gold chains. We were detained there until the evening, and then the guards were removed and we were all allowed to disperse.

However, on our return home, we discovered that it was impossible to gain access. The whole area had been re-allocated to accommodate new arrivals. These were Jews newly arrived from Germany. So now we moved to a new location in Green Lane, a road which began at the 'Pit' and ran along the Tatar Gardens at the border of the ghetto. The so-called Russian section, outside the ghetto area, began at our yard. Now, even more people were housed together in the same room. There was an elderly couple, their adult daughter, a son of 14 years, and our own family, which had now increased because Marya Borisovna Taubkina, the wife of my father's brother Isaac, had joined us. Isaac had recently died in the ghetto. All of my family, Marya Borisovna, Aunt Pesya, Vova, Lida, my mother and I, slept across two beds placed side by side. If during the night someone turned over, everyone else also had to turn over.

Now we were eating significantly poorer food. A piece of bread and some soup containing a few dumplings made of rye flour was the whole of lunch and dinner. Breakfast was a just piece of bread and a drink of tea made with grass. The main supplier of food was my mother. As an employee of the *Judenrat,* she received 400 grams of bread a day and she occasionally went into the Russian area in order to exchange things for produce. Mum did not look like a Jew, but her excursions were fraught with enormous risk. Once a policeman detained her and she had to pay him off by removing her engagement ring from her finger and giving it to him. That day she came home dejected at what had happened, but she bravely continued to go out of the ghetto. The family had to be fed. Once Aunt Pesya took a sleigh and, taking me with her, slipped under the wire fence. We went to the warehouse of the city council on Kirov Street. Here, using a warrant issued by a Russian friend, we managed to get a bag of frozen potatoes. Unharmed, we returned to the ghetto. We were eating frozen potatoes for a long time after that!

The tragic events of 7 November 1941 caught most of the inhabitants of the ghetto off-guard. We had learned from the *Judenrat* that preparations were being made for a pogrom. Some people had already created a *malina* or hiding place. A *malina* might be located in a basement, or in a concealed or disguised space in a room or attic. However, at first, no-one knew exactly how many people would actually fit into such a space. On the evening of 6 November, Lida took Vova and me out of the ghetto to the Russian side of Nemiga Street to stay with mother's pre-war co-worker Kandibo. Lida left us there and returned to the ghetto. We spent the night in Kandibo's apartment and early the next morning, she led us to our old house on Voroshilov Street where Lena was living. Moving along the Russian side of the street in the direction of Respublikanskaya Street, we saw groups of SS standing in all the doorways. On the opposite side of the street, the Ukrainians (the henchmen of the Nazis) and police were expelling Jews from their homes, while mercilessly beating them with whips. I saw a woman standing with a baby in her arms, while a Ukrainian lashed her shoulder with a strap. She was trying to protect the child with her hands. No one stopped us, and we soon arrived at our old house. We ate some food, but were then afraid to leave the house. When it became dark, Vova took me to a nearby flower farm through the hole in the fence. Lenya worked in a greenhouse there, and she made a bed for Vova and me on the boxes of seedlings.

I was awakened suddenly by the glare of a flashlight. Two policemen were standing there. 'Who are you?' they asked. Without hesitation, I said that I was the son of Leonarda Ferdinandovna Divaltovskaya and that Vova was her nephew. Then they questioned us for a long time about our fathers, so we whispered some information to them. The policemen interrogated Lenya separately, and she also said that we were the son and nephew of Divaltovskoy. The police spent a long time searching for adults who might be hiding in the greenhouse. Of course they found no-one, but by the time they finally left, it was daybreak. We later discovered that this kind of raid had been carried out in all of the nearby houses that night. Apparently, the Germans had been warned about the presence in the area of hidden partisans. However, police searching for partisans that night, only found Vova and me!

When it became light, Lenya, with trembling hands, led us out into the street, and we returned to the ghetto. Our neighbours were all there. On this occasion the German *aktion* had taken place near Respublikanskaya Street, and our neighbourhood had not been touched. We later learned that all of the Jews in that other area had been herded together, apparently into a marching work detail. They were then taken to Tuchinka suburb, where they were shot.

We found it hard to believe the news that was reaching us from the front through the official Byelorussian and German newspapers. It was impossible to imagine that German troops were already close to Moscow and Leningrad. We were hearing a few rumours about partisan activities, but we in the ghetto felt no real connection with the partisans at this time. Occasionally, the city was bombed by the Soviet air force, and this caused some excitement. We were not afraid of 'our own' bombs. Meanwhile, we children continued with our lives as best we could. We went about the ghetto quite calmly, especially in our own area. For example, on our street there was a quarry where, before the war, clay and sand had been excavated. At the top of the quarry was the border of the ghetto, and the quarry itself was part of the ghetto. When winter arrived, and it snowed, we children started skiing and sledging in the quarry. Russian children would also come and slide down with us. One day, some of them took away my ski, which I was very disappointed about.

The house was cold, and we were constantly hungry. However, I read a lot. I remember books entitled *Captain at Fifteen* and *Children of Captain Grant,* both by Jules Verne, and another called *Luda Vlasovskaya.* These were books that my mother had grabbed out of our old house as we left. It was nice, if only temporarily, to be able to forget the harsh reality of life in the ghetto. Vova thumbed through textbooks for the fifth grade and tried to solve maths examples. I remember one day in winter, when Vova and I went into the yard close to the wire fence, we saw a lady who was calling to us from the Russian side. It appeared that her chicken had wandered onto our side and she wanted us to 'shoo' it back to her. We did, and she gave us two chicken eggs as a reward. There was great joy in the house that day!

However, such relative calm was broken on the morning of 2 March 1942, when I heard shots close to our house. In the kitchen, we had access to our *malina.* There was an area of flooring which could be raised, revealing a space through which it was possible to get into the cellar. There was enough space for two or three dozen people to hide down there. However, in order to use this hiding place, it was necessary for someone to stay up top in order to close the hole and cover it with the dirty mat, so that dogs would not be able to detect the scent of people hiding below. Several people went down, while Mum remained. She was the one who had proof that she worked in the *Judenrat,* while many other inhabitants of the house were members of the underground [see glossary]. Mum dropped the board over the hole and covered it with the wet mat. Above our heads, we heard scuffling noises, gunshots, screams and the cries of those unfortunate people who had failed, or did not wish, to hide. All this seemed to go on endlessly... I was in the dark huddled and trembling in the farthest corner. I was sure that the Germans were about to discover us and throw in grenades, or even let the dog in. That was what they usually did when they found a hiding place, and we all knew it. It seemed like an eternity until the board began to rise and light penetrated into the cellar. Up above was mother. I climbed out and clung to her crying.

The following morning, I went out onto the street. By the porch lay an old man. I remember his funny name, Zheltok, but we had always called him Yolk. He had been shot in the head. On the street there were many other bodies, and almost all the residents of the neighbouring houses had disappeared. German documents were found much later, which revealed that the *Judenrat* had secretly been ordered to select and assemble 5,000 Jews from the ghetto to be 'dispatched' by the Germans. On the appointed morning, 2 March 1942, the ghetto was surrounded by the Germans, but no Jews had been assembled by the *Judenrat*. Therefore, new commands were issued on the spot, and physical force was applied. Thousands of people were rounded up and shot. Others were gathered together in a long work detail which was directed to the Minsk goods station. Here they were loaded into the wagons of a long train which was then sent to Koydanovo station, 30 km southwest of Minsk. Once there, the Jews were unloaded from the wagons under guard by Lithuanians. They were taken to already dug trenches... and 3412 Jews were executed there.

In Minsk, the day was sunny and we saw bloodstains on the bright, white snow. The bodies of those killed were lying there, just dumped in the quarry. Today, in that exact place in the centre of Minsk, there is now a memorial called *Yama,* 'The Pit'. This monument was the first in the Soviet Union to be erected to the memory of dead Jews. It was constructed in 1948 with money raised by Jewish survivors from Minsk. On the monument there is an inscription in Yiddish and Russian, which reads: 'here lie the Jews who perished at the hands of... the German Nazi criminals.' Readers should note that it states 'The Jews' and not simply 'Soviet Citizens'.

After that pogrom, life in the ghetto just continued. Vova was sometimes able to get into the Russian area and exchange things for millet cereal, and once he even came back with a piece of butter. Meanwhile, my birthday was approaching.  April 12 was a day which we had had previously celebrated lavishly.  Now, as we gathered around the table, Lida recalled that, just a year ago, we had been sitting at a table full of cakes baked by Lenya. Dad had been there with us and it was such a happy time. Now, Mum took a loaf of bread which she had put by for this day, she poured sweet tea for everyone, and then we celebrated my first and only birthday inside the ghetto.

Spring had arrived, and it became all the more apparent that the Germans were planning to completely destroy the Minsk Ghetto. Every day, the work details marched out through the gate under escort and, in the evening, they returned to the ghetto as usual. However, despite this routine, the ghetto residents realised that this way of existence was temporary. The next pogrom was merely a matter of time.

### Leaving the ghetto: The Russian Children's Hospital

This was when mum told me about a plan: I was going to be moving into the Russian area outside the ghetto. I was to be placed in a children's hospital where I would be considered a Byelorussian and would have a new surname. I did not want to be parted from my mother, but I agreed on one condition: that I would stay in the hospital for just a short time. I understood that I would be well cared for and fed, but then I would come back. Mum had turned for help to a pre-war friend Elena Nikolaeva, who was the head physician at Children's Hospital 9 on Internationalnaya Street. Elena was considered to be one of the best doctors in Minsk. Her eldest daughter Natasha had been in the same class as Lida at school and they had been close friends before the war. Elena agreed to help us, even though she knew how much of a risk it would be. Hiding a Jewish child would put her in mortal danger.

At the end of June 1942, Lida and I left the ghetto. The process of getting across to the Aryan side was fraught with danger. It was always necessary to choose the time and place of transfer carefully. For example, it was not good to move too early in the morning, because the streets were likely to be less populated and you were very visible. On the other hand, at times when there were a lot of people around, you were more likely to be seen getting under the wire. Once out, it was best to move away from the ghetto boundaries quickly and to merge with the locals. Going back, it was always easier. We had learned that, if a guard noticed us as we approached the ghetto, we should go to the first possible house and ask to be allowed to stay there until the guard or policeman had gone.

However, on this occasion, Lida and I encountered no problems and we reached the children's hospital safely. I was placed on a ward where a medical card was issued in the name of Victor Savitsky, a Byelorussian name. Fictitious information about my parents had already been invented. Elena explained that I needed to remember the story that I was of Byelorussian origin and, under no circumstance, should I admit that I was a Jew. However, I had a serious problem – I was unable to pronounce the Russian 'r' sound, as this didn't exist it my native Yiddish. Before the war, this had simply caused a smile, but now it might have betrayed me as a Jew. So I took a lot of care in avoiding words containing the letter 'r'. I practised whenever I was alone and, as a result, I eventually trained myself. It took a long time, but, by the beginning of 1944, I had eliminated the problem.

Lida was not allowed to stay at the Children's Hospital and had to return to the ghetto. She was 19 years old, and could no longer pass as a child. Vova Goldberg was also sent back because he had been circumcised shortly after birth through the ritual of *brit milah* [Hebrew: ritual circumcision], and so his Jewish origin could have been discovered. He returned to the ghetto. On 28 July 1942 Vova was returning to the ghetto with his work detail, but they were unaware that an *aktion* was taking place. The entire work detail met their fate. Vova tried to run, but was killed.

I stayed at the hospital alone. I was there for more than a month. There were children of all ages and some, like me, were clearly not sick. In my opinion, many were Jews. Once a girl came onto the ward with whom I had been at school. We had been in the same class, and I remembered her last name - Mayorova. When she saw me, she said: 'I know you – you were an 'A' student at school.' This could have been a really dangerous moment. Sometimes, I was taken to the infectious isolation ward for inspection and verification, so we had to be careful at all times. However, at the hospital, neither I nor the other fugitives were ever betrayed. I think that this may have been due to Elena and her authority among the staff.

### In the children's home on Shirokaya Street

In late July, I was approached by a health worker at the hospital and told that I was going to have to leave. The hospital was to be converted into a children's home. My parents had not come for me so, as it was no longer possible to keep me in the hospital, I would be moved elsewhere. The health worker accompanied me to Shirokaya Street, and I was placed in Children's Home Number 4 under my new name, Victor Savitzky.

The children's home environment was unlike that of the hospital. This place was home to several small 'cubs' and here they had to fend for themselves. After a few battles, I settled down and took my place as a member of the children's 'pack'. The food was very poor, so we regularly went into town to obtain food. I 'hunted' at the passenger station, and sometimes sold newspapers to German soldiers in exchange for anything edible. My ear needed to be keen and my eyes wide open. We scurried about trains, and were sometimes caught by the German gendarmerie and brutally beaten. Once, my friend Vilya Nikitin (Livshits) and I were walking along the platform, when I suddenly noticed that the rest of the kids were scattering all over the place. Vilya and I also started to run in the direction of the square in front of the railway. Suddenly we became aware of pursuers behind us and realised that one of the gendarmes had let his Alsatian dog off the leash. It quickly caught up with me and grabbed me by the elbow. Vilya continued to run, so the dog let go of me and ran after him, and now it was my turn to run for dear life. In this way, we would bait the dog and then run away, until the gendarmes finally called the dog off and stopped chasing us.

One day in early autumn, passing near to the station, I saw a group of Jews who were dismantling some ruined buildings. Among them I saw Lida. We hugged, and she asked how I had managed to stay alive. However, when I began to ask about my mother, she started to cry. I did not say anything, but I think that I understood my mother's fate. I gave Lida all the food that I had earned at the station just as the head of the brigade arrived and said it was time for her work party to go back to the ghetto. We said goodbye and I never saw Lida again.

After a few months at the orphanage, I was suddenly returned to the children's hospital. I was not sick, so I suspect that my transfer may have been arranged by Elena Nikolaeva. She may have been aware that a Commission would soon be visiting the orphanage, and that this might have put me under threat of exposure. Elena Ivanovna Nikolaeva hid many Jewish children and was constantly under threat of arrest. She also smuggled medicine to the partisan detachment. One day when she was on her way into the partisan zone, the police detained her and she was sent to the Gestapo. After several months, without achieving any kind of confession from her, she was sent to forced labour in Germany. She was ultimately released after the war by the Red Army, and was able to return to Minsk, where she continued her work at the medical school.

After the war, Dad and I met with Elena and thanked her warmly for saving me. She died in 1994, but her memory shines on brightly in my heart.

## The children's home at Krasivaya street

A month later, I was transferred from the hospital to Children's Home No.7 which was located in at Krasivaya street. It was managed by another kind soul - Vera Leonardovna Sparning. The kindly yet disciplined approach in this orphanage differed sharply from the cruel and sinister atmosphere that prevailed in many other children's homes. Although the home was fenced in, you could get out through a gate into the street, and if you thought that you might be out for a long time, you had to warn the staff. They fed us quite well, and Vera Leonardovna used every opportunity to supplement our diet. For example, she managed to reach an agreement with the administration of the local dairy plant, whereby the orphanage had access to leftover milk, which we would fetch from the plant in heavy cans.

Our orphanage was looked after by the Evangelical Protestant Church and, in addition to prayers, we would read both the Old and New Testaments. Some of the parishioners brought us food to supplement our rations. At the orphanage there were various moneymaking enterprises in existence. For example, there was a shoe repair shop. All the revenue from that particular venture went into a common pot. We also had the opportunity to earn food by selling newspapers and clean the boots of German soldiers at the railway station, where many troop trains stopped. All the money we obtained, we brought back to the children's home and shared with our friends. Some of this revenue was passed on to the girls, as they were forbidden by Vera Leonardovna to leave the orphanage. Many of us collected money to buy winter shoes and extra food for the winter, a time when the cold weather made it more difficult to earn money. By Spring 1944, I had managed to save two thousand occupation marks. I had intended to buy boots with this money but, thank God, things worked out so that I didn't need them.

In the children's home there were a number of Jewish children. Some were recognisably different from the others, but Vera Leonardovna pursued a policy of 'we have no Jews here' and strictly punished any sign of 'children's anti-Semitism.' When an official audit was expected, the purpose of which was to identify Jewish children, she tried to hide those children with typical Semitic features by tucking them into bed and saying that they were sick. Thus, in this orphanage of 120 children in total, there were more than thirty Jewish children waiting with the others for the arrival of the Soviet Army. Among the rescued were Elena Antonova, Anatoly Dikushin, Lidya Korotkina (Avkhimovich), Emma Dulkin (Silvestrova), Marat Halperin (Kalinovsky), Nella Gerbovitskaya, Vilya and Emma Livshits (Nikitin), Sonya Furman, Larisa Frankel, Rosa Greenberg (Chekalova), Bella Vladimirovna, Rosa Davidova, Inna Grabovetskaya, Garik Blekh, Ida Borshcheva (Lipovich), Ella and Mirra Mikhchin, Galya Zlatkina and Sonya Zlatkina, Inna and Ira Remenchuk, Maryema Galimova and me - David Taubkin (Savitsky). There may have been others.

It should be noted that the heads of children's homes took a great risk in hiding Jewish children. The official position regarding such children was contained in a directive which stated: 'All the Jewish children who, for one reason or another, have been accepted into your orphanage should, on your personal responsibility, be isolated and then transferred to a hospital in the ghetto.' That would, of course, have meant sending them to certain death. More than thirty Jewish children were saved at orphanage No.7 in Minsk. It was a unique case, and tribute is due to Vera Leonardovna. Those children owe their lives to her heroic activities. She was of Latvian nationality and a woman of the highest moral standards, strong-willed, and with remarkable organisational skills. She worked all her life in children's institutions. When the Germans first arrived in Minsk, she had organised a search for orphans regardless of their nationality, and gave them shelter. The orphanage grew out of the kindergarten, of which she had charge during the war.

After the war, I often met with Vera Leonardovna. She was a welcome guest in our home and, after I moved to Moscow, we corresponded with her until her death in 1984. The memory of this remarkable woman will forever be engraved in the hearts of the children who were rescued and saved by her. At the Jerusalem Memorial Institute Yad Vashem, Vera Leonardovna was posthumously awarded the honorary title of 'Righteous among the Nations of the World'. Her name is engraved on the Wall of Honour 'as a sign of deep gratitude for the assistance given to the Jewish people during the Second World War.'

After their release, the Jewish children adopted their original names and, for the most part, did not wait for the appearance of parents and relatives who might have been killed in the Minsk Ghetto. They had to organise themselves without any kind of support because, after the restoration of the Soviet regime in Belarus, children could only remain in an orphanage up to the age of fourteen. At that point they were left to their own devices and were generally forced to take on all the hardships of post-war life as beggars. This was exactly what happened to me, until I was reunited with my father who returned from the army immediately after the liberation of Minsk.

I believe that many Jewish children survived, not only due to luck and the help of kind and selfless people, but because of an incredible *will* to survive. They showed extraordinary personal initiative. Maybe this was brought on by the extreme circumstances in which they found themselves, and the hard lessons which they learned. For example, while we were at the orphanage, we children knew of everything that was happening in the ghetto: we were even aware that prisoners were being taken to Trostenets for execution. Although the Germans carried out such executions in secret, the locals, including the children, knew the details and places of such mass murders only too well. On a lighter note, I recall that Vera Leonardovna was very insistent that we did not engage in theft. However, one morning I went with a friend to a potato field where we dug up tubers and carried full bags of young potatoes back to the orphanage. We took them to the kitchen to cook them, but found Vera Leonardovna waiting for us and we were severely scolded. Her reprimands worked and I learned my lesson well – I never stole anything after that!

After the final pogrom in October 1943, members of the Russian population were resettled in the area of the devastated ghetto but, even then, there were some Jews remaining in the city.

In Spring 1944, we learned from refugees that Smolensk had been taken by the Soviet Army. However, news of the offensive stopped after that. Then, at the beginning of June, there were reports that the Allies had landed in Normandy and were moving eastwards. Even so, the news was confusing and disturbing because we knew that the Germans would retreat and maybe they would even take people back with them to Germany. There was a continuous atmosphere of fear.

### Release

In late spring, I told Vera Leonardovna that I was leaving the orphanage to spend a few days with my aunt on Lodochnaya Street. This was where my pre-war nurse Lenya now lived. She had been forced to move house when a policeman's family had been relocated to our old home. I found out about all of this during the winter, when I had become concerned that Lenya had stopped visiting me in the orphanage for several weeks. When I finally went to the old address and spoke to the police, they told me that Divaltovskaya had moved.

So that is how I came to be standing, early one summer morning, on the banks of the river Svisloch. For several days now I had been staying nearby on Lodochnaya Street with Lenya. Here, by the river, I was not known by anyone. I had been happy to leave the orphanage because I feared that, during their retreat, the Germans might send the orphanage children to Germany and I very much wanted to stay in Minsk. I knew nothing of my mother's death at that point, and was still hoping that I might see her again. I also dreamed about meeting Dad. I really believed that he was still in the army and that he might eventually come back to our house.

I was looking towards the bridge which was located about half a kilometre from where I was standing, and I noticed a truck. It was carrying Germans and going west towards the train station. I was a little surprised at this because rail travel had not been possible for several days. (I was quite sure about that as I had only recently returned from the railroad station to the orphanage with German newspapers that I had been unable to sell… because there had been no one there to buy them!). As I watched, the movement of German transport on the bridge stopped. There was silence, apart from the occasional distant thunder of explosions. Most local people could not see or hear any of this because they were hiding in attics and basements, or in hiding places dug in their yards and gardens. Then, suddenly, into the silence there burst a terrible roar. Down Garbarnaya Street, only a few metres from where I was standing, tanks started to appear. They were green with red stars on the turrets. At first, I rushed headlong toward this tank convoy. From the doors of the nearby houses, people were hurrying out to do the same. The first tank turret opened, and a military helmet appeared, followed by an overall uniform. Then there was a cry in the crowd,' It's a trap!'

Three years earlier, we had said farewell to the Red Army who had distinctive marks on their lapels. Was it possible that, three years later, this army had returned, but with different stripes on their uniforms? There was total confusion. People started to run in all directions. A soldier in the turret of a tank looked very like a member of the Russian Liberation Army, the so-called 'Vlasovtsy' [see glossary]. But when I turned and looked more closely I saw that one of the tanks was displaying a red flag. Very soon people started to turn back. These must be our tanks! Very soon more vehicles appeared and we could recognise the armoured work detail. By now, I was standing by the roadside, sobbing.

A man in uniform with a weapon asked: 'Why are you crying? The Germans will not return! Can I give you something?' And, looking at him through my tears, all I could think of to say in reply was: 'Give me Soviet newspapers.' During all the months of living in the ghetto, we had often imagined the arrival of our liberators. We dreamt that they would rescue us and take revenge on the Germans and the police for the deaths so many innocent people. Now at last, here in our own yard on Lodochnaya Street, were Soviet tanks and a convoy of military vehicles. For the next three days, even more vehicles continued to arrive, while the Soviet soldiers and officers retired inside the houses, and huddled together to sleep. Then, as suddenly as they had arrived, the vehicles and troops withdrew from the city towards the west. Now German planes arrived and heavy bombing began in the areas where the military equipment had been.

We hid in a shelter in a nearby garden and this dugout saved us. Although a bomb fell very close by, the damage and the debris did not penetrate to where we were concealed. Finally, Lenya and I returned to the house. Almost everything had been reduced to rubble. Only some furniture had remained intact, although the mirrors in the wardrobes were shattered. Maybe the *policemen* had deliberately tried to damage everything that they were unable to carry away before they and the Germans escaped. Neighbours began to arrive bringing food, and for the first time in a long while, I was able to quietly fall asleep on my own bed.

The next day a man and a woman arrived. They were wearing defence uniforms. The man announced that his name was Dr. Rahmanchik and that he had once lived in this area. He was looking for the family doctor called Taubkin, who had lived at this address before the war. He was also searching for his own family. (We later discovered that his entire family had been killed). As soon as he discovered that I was the son of Aron Davidovich Taubkin, Dr. Rahmanchik told us that he had worked with my Dad in Narkomzdrav (The People's Commissariat of Public Health of BSSR). He said that my father, the chief inspector of hospitals in Byelorussia, had told him that he would be returning home in a few days. Dr. Rahmanchik suggested that I went with him to the First Soviet Hospital, where Red Army medical personnel had recently arrived. I met several doctors and nurses there. They were anxious to ask me if I knew anything about the fate of relatives, who had remained behind during the occupation. I told them that I did not know anything about their individual relatives, but warned them that almost all the Jews had been killed. I was given a bag of groceries (canned food, bread, concentrates) and taken back home. I had not seen wealth such as this for many years!

A few days later, my friend Kim Lisovsky ran into the yard of the house with a cry of joy 'Your Dad is coming!' He and I fell into each other's arms and wept. When he asked about my mother and Lida, I said that maybe they were alive. I told him that I taught myself to pronounce Russian 'r' sounds. This was a big achievement, and it had helped me to survive. My father was dressed in his blue breeches, the military tunic, the army belt and boots. These were the clothes he had been wearing on the morning of 24 June 1941, when he came to say goodbye to us.

After a while, Dad was able to make enquiries about the fate of my mother and Lida. It turned out that mum had been arrested outside the ghetto and for some time was kept in the Minsk jail on Volodarskogo Street, where she was interrogated by one of her former students. Then she was taken to Trostenets where she died. Lida was helped to get a Russian passport in the name of Marya Pavlovets in order to reach the partisans, but she also died during the Nazi blockade of the partisan zone. However, Dad was protecting me and it was some time before he finally revealed to me the terrible details of all that he had discovered about the sad fate of our most loved ones.

# What I remember
## Vladimir Trachtenberg

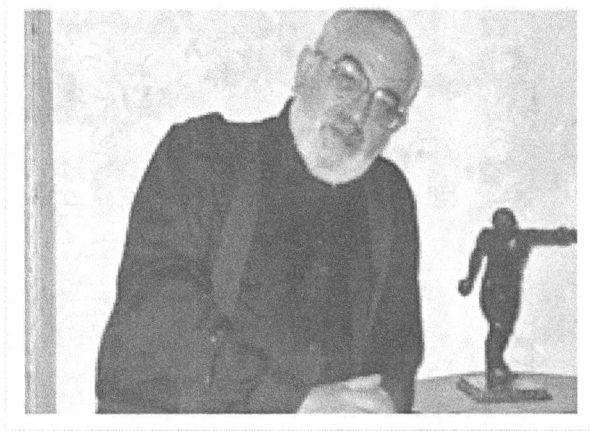

**Vladimir Trachtenberg**

My name is Vladimir Trachtenberg and I was born on 21 August 1938 in the city of Mogilev. My father Lazar Trachtenberg was born in 1913 and my mother Liza Moroz in 1915. They were both typesetters by profession. They met and were married in Mogilev.

After the reunification of Western Belarus [see glossary] in 1939 father was transferred to a new place of work in a small, newly incorporated town called Stolbtsy in the Minsk region, where he became the local director of the printing house. However, when the war began, he immediately decided to move us all to Khlebnaya Street in Minsk, since that was where his mother, sisters and brothers were living with their families. By the time we reached the city, however, it turned out that his family had already been evacuated. Nevertheless, we stayed in Minsk and my father volunteered for the front. Very soon after his departure, the ghetto was established and as my mother and I already lived on Khlebnaya Street, we found ourselves inside the ghetto from the very beginning. I was still a very young child and although I do not remember specific dates, I do have some vivid and powerful memories of that time.

The border of the ghetto was actually located along Khlebnaya Street and I recall that just across the road from our house there was a bakery which was outside the ghetto boundary. Our home, like most of those in the ghetto, was a one-storey wooden hut while, by contrast, the bakery was the only large building in the area. It was guarded by Lithuanians. My mother told me later that these Lithuanian guards would sometimes take shots at people inside the ghetto, including her. I have heard there are still trees in that area with bullets lodged in the trunks.

Khlebnaya Street was only about 250 metres long. Today it no longer exists. There are only high-rise buildings in that area now. Of the pre-war streets, there remain only the trees and a small alley.  My mother was a young woman, only 26 years old. I was not yet three, and I didn't really understand much of what was happening.

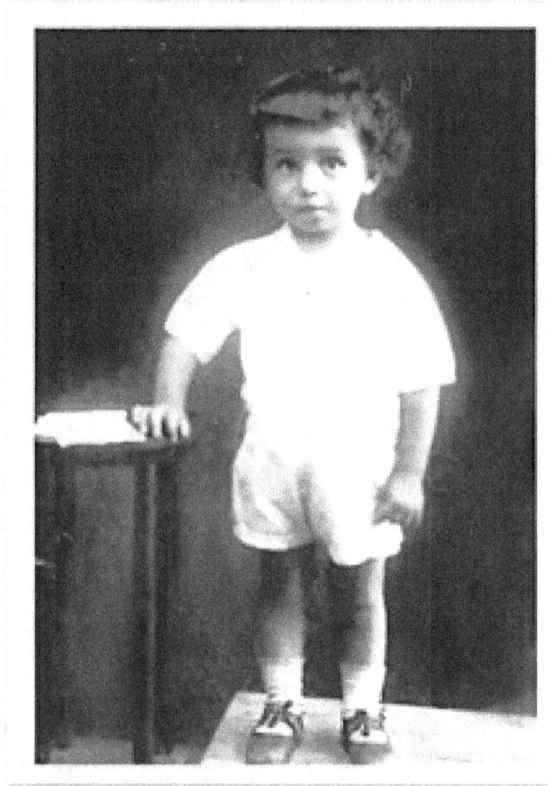

**Vladimir (Volodya) Trachtenberg, 1940**

During our first few months in the ghetto the Germans were just establishing their regime and things were relatively calm. Mum was taken to work regularly and there were a lot of people living in our house. I cannot say for sure, but I think there were around ten or twelve. It certainly seemed crowded. When we all slept on the floor, there was almost no free space left. Of the people who lived with us at that time, I remember only the two boys Abrasha Livshits and Boris Kopilevich, and their mothers. I have been told that some of those people are in America now and others are in Israel, but I do not remember the other adults.

However, I can still see clearly in my mind's eye the wall of barbed wire which encircled the ghetto. At that time, my Mum was on very friendly terms with Liza Livshits, Abrasha's mother. I remember that I played outside with him in the summer months. He was about a year older than me, and we wandered around as far as the ghetto borders allowed.  I recollect how, one day, we got under the fence and went beyond the ghetto limits, not far from the Jewish Cemetery.  We did it because someone had dared us to risk it on the promise of food. We crawled out secretly and came back the same way. When our mums found out they punished us and warned: 'For God's sake, do not go near that fence again. You could be shot!'

People have asked me if I remember seeing Germans for the first time, but I just recall people in black uniforms. I remember one in particular who had a large vicious dog. Later, as I grew a little older, we seemed to see Germans more and more often.  Later, when I lived with the partisans, I remember them bringing captured Germans back to where we lived. These Germans were dressed in grey overcoats, unlike those that I had seen for the first time in the ghetto.

Very soon after we arrived the weather worsened. The temperature dropped and we wore winter clothes. People were cold and afraid. I know now that this must have been around the time when rumours were circulating about a possible pogrom. I recall times when my mother would pick me up and carry me in her arms to my granny's house, which was also on Khlebnaya Street. There was a really big basement in that house in which we were able to hide. Other people also hid in there with us. I still remember the total darkness down there.  A cellar or basement like that, where you could hide away, was called a *malina*.

There was some kind of wooden construction down in that basement, but I cannot say for sure what it was. I recall one time when Mum made me hide behind it. She told me, 'It is really important that, whatever happens, you stay here. You must sit still and remain very quiet.' Of course, since I was only three years old, I eventually started to cry. It was then that my Mum whispered some words in my ear, which I have remembered to this day: 'Stay quiet, or the Germans will kill you!' After that, I was silent.

Soon after she had uttered those words, there was a sudden bright burst of flame, followed by a terrific crash and a loud crack. Now, most of the people in the *malina* began to scream. My mother held me tight, and we remained sitting very quietly in the same place. Then someone tried to climb out of the cellar, and others were still screaming. The noise was terrifying – so much crying and shouting! Mum held me tightly and we just sat together while she kept repeating: 'We won't go. Just sit still and try to be quiet.' Then the crash occurred again. It was much later that Mum told me that the explosions had been caused by two grenades which had been thrown into the *malina* one after the other. It was so hard to sit still like that. For one thing, there was just not enough air to breath. However, we just had to stay in that basement until people finally arrived and started to pull us all out. Then the rest just followed. When at last we emerged into the light of day, we could see for ourselves that a part of the house had been completely demolished. We crossed the street and saw people lying on the ground all around us. I kept asking my Mum, 'What happened to those people? Why are they sleeping here in the cold?' I remember my Mum replying that they would be asleep for a long time. 'Don't look at them, just walk on.'

**Ex-juvenile prisoner of the Minsk Ghetto, Abram (Abrasha) Livshits -**

**friend of Vladimir Trachtenberg**

So now, we moved into another small wooden house on nearby Tankovaya Street. I remember that house well, because I had an accident there. One day, I spilt something that was boiling on the stove. I knocked the pan over and the hot contents spilled all over me, badly burning my chest. It was quite a serious injury and coming, as it did, after the trauma of the cellar and the explosions, it made me feel very weak and ill for some time afterwards. To make things even worse, very soon after this accident, there was an infestation of lice - one of many back then - and there was no water in which to wash!

Then there was another incident, which I remember as if it happened yesterday. Mum had decided to take me to work with her. However, just as she was putting me onto the transport, the German driver appeared and told all of the children to get out of the lorry. I was clutching a small paper cone containing a potato. At that moment, all I wanted to do was eat the potato because I was so very hungry. I suddenly decided to eat it there and then, despite the circumstances and the fact that Mum had told me to make it last for the whole day. My only thought was to consume that potato and stem my hunger. Then suddenly, an older boy ran up and grabbed my little cone. What is more, the lorry now drove off, and I was left hungry and alone in the ghetto! I was just a small tot and knew nobody, so I tried to find my way back home alone. Eventually, someone picked me up and took care of me until my mother came back late in the evening. They may even have fed me.

Some people remained kind despite everything. There were those who shared their food or provided places to hide. Some even sheltered children in their homes, like Frieda Reizman's mother, Auntie Dora, who was just such a person [see Frieda Reizman's story].

**Ex-prisoners of the Minsk Ghetto,**

**Vladimir Trachtenberg (Belarus) and Liza Vertkina (USA)**

She gathered children around her and somehow found a piece of bread for everyone. There were, of course, others who would take away your last mouthful of food. However, since everybody was desperate to survive, maybe we should not reproach them for that.

During our first months in the ghetto, my Mum worked at a firm which she called '*Krieg*', which is German for 'war'. At first, she just said that her job involved loading clothes, planks, benches, stones and so on. It was only later that she told me that she had been working for the Gestapo. They had commandeered the buildings of the University of Medicine. Her duties sometimes even involved the disposal of corpses. Her most continuous period of work was at the railway removing wreckage from the lines after bombings. Yes, that is the kind of work she did. No academic degrees were required for this hard and dirty physical labour. Meanwhile, I stayed alone in the ghetto where I often cleaned the streets, carried litter, and raked leaves.

Many children did this. Sometimes, we were even given morsels of food for carrying out such tasks.

I remember another incident, which occurred on a day when Mum had been able to take me to work with her. At the end of the day, the German in charge prevented our group from returning to the ghetto. Many years later, I discovered that a big pogrom had been planned for that day. It seems that the German had deliberately kept us from returning to the ghetto in order to protect us from almost certain death. Of course, I was unaware of all that at the time. Yet, I do recollect that he had a loaf of bread with him, which he cut into slices. He covered them with honey, and distributed them to all of the children. The taste of that bread is still vivid in my memory. When we eventually returned to the ghetto, we saw that many of the houses had been completely destroyed. Inside others, we could see traces of blood, and around us lay adults and children who would never stand up again. People were removing them in wheelbarrows and carts. My Mum tried to prevent me from seeing all of that, but those brief glimpses will remain forever in my memory.

What else do I remember? The fact is that I was always hungry. I do not recall what we ate, or what is was that enabled us to survive. I just remember that gnawing feeling of hunger. Then there were the gas vans. Mum often warned me that, as soon as I saw vehicles, no matter where, I had to run and hide at once. Those vans were called *dushegubka* [Russian: stranglers of souls]. People were forced inside the van, and then exhaust gas would be piped into the airtight compartment until everyone suffocated.

**Vladimir Trachtenberg with his wife Anna Ivanovna Zhevnyak-Trachtenberg**

My mother used to tell me that, if I somehow found myself in such a van, the first thing I should do was to take off my jacket, shirt, or any other articles of clothing and (please forgive me, but she used to say exactly this) to pee onto them. The garment should then be held near the mouth and used as a filter through which to breathe. Maybe then, she said, I would stay alive. However, I was one of the lucky ones. I never once entered such a van. I do recall that we children were forever discussing with each other where to hide, or who could hold their breath the longest in order to appear dead. All this was in case Germans came into the house to take someone away.

**Vladimir Trachtenberg with his wife Anna. The yard of the Mark Chagall Museum in Vitebsk 13th August 2011**

I was in the ghetto from the first day to the last. We stayed alive only because we were lucky. For everyone who survived, at least five others perished. Finally, someone suggested to our mothers that they should take us to work with them whenever possible, so that we would be outside on the day that the ghetto was to be liquidated. Once again we were saved by that high ranking German who had kept us from the pogrom previously. He warned us that this was to be the last day of the ghetto, the day when the very last pogrom would take place. After that, the ghetto would be no more. 'Run! Run as far away as you can. The ghetto is finished. Tomorrow, I will have to hand you over to the Gestapo.'

I remember that day. Towards evening, our three families (my Mum and I, Liza Livshits with her son Abrasha, and Liza Kapilevich with her son Boris) fled in darkness from our workplaces and hid in an old shed. There we spent the next 24 hours – one day and one night. Then the shed owner warned us that the Germans were organizing an inspection and, if we were found, we would immediately be shot. So we all climbed onto the roof of a freight train and off we went. When we had travelled some distance from Minsk, the train suddenly slowed down and we jumped off. Mum told me later that that an inspection had started on the train, and that is why we had to run away.

Now we continued for a long time on foot until we finally reached a village. My mother asked if there were partisans in the area. We were told to wait near a small country estate – I recall that there was a water mill there. We waited for a long time until partisans did eventually arrive and started asking which of us had come from Minsk. Then we went along with them into the forest. I particularly remember this journey during which we encountered Polish partisans and Polish soldiers. They rode red horses and had dogs which seemed huge as wolves. The men wore uniforms with quadrangular hats. Those hats have stuck in my memory for all these years. As for our group, we finally joined Zorin's partisan detachment [see glossary]. It was a typical family partisan detachment made up mainly of old men, women and children who did not fight.

**Vladimir Trachtenberg with his wife Anna, daughter Yulia and son-in-law Mikhail.**

Life was very harsh. We constantly had to hide. I was with my mother all of the time, staying alongside her every moment of the day. If she went somewhere, then I went with her. If she went to the kitchen to peel potatoes – I would be there, also peeling potatoes. At least, there was always the chance of getting a potato to eat! Whatever the task, I went with her. We lived in big earth houses which seemed to be full of people all of the time. There were probably thirty or forty people in each house. Structures that looked like long wooden shelves ran along both sides of the room, and that is where we slept.

However, we did not spend long in that detachment. My mother was a highly qualified typographer and so she was quickly allocated a job in a secret partisan printing office. During the winter of 1943, she was taken to the Baranovichsky Partisan District Centre (a territorial division within a region). Before the war, Mum had worked together with Girsh Smolyar [see glossary]. He already knew her as a professional typographer. When he heard that she was attached to Zorin's unit, Smolyar talked to commander Vladimir Zenonovich Tzaryuk and suggested taking my mother to the partisan printing office. The publications produced there included newspapers and journals. Some of them are now exhibited in the Great Patriotic War Museum in Minsk.

Here is a little anecdote from that time, when Stepchenko was commander of the partisan headquarters: One day, he and the editorial staff were all sitting together, checking copy for the newspaper *Golas Selyansha* [Byclorussian: *Voice of the Farmer*], which had been typed by my Mum. This was routine. Whenever the newspaper was ready, a sample copy was made up and edited, providing one final opportunity to correct mistakes. So all the editorial staff would sit at the table, with the rough copy of the newspaper tied-up with threads. I was little at that time and had crawled under the table. I tied all the people to the table with one long, loose thread and sat there very quietly. When they finally came to the conclusion that all was well with the newspaper, they stood up and the table tipped over. Of course, the sheets and the typed print flew apart and they had to start again from the very beginning. Now, three big angry men chased me, a little boy, until I found myself in Commander Tzaryuk's arms. He had 'rescued' me from the anger of those three. It was years later that this story was recounted to me by Yanka Bryl, a Byelorussian writer who was also in the detachment. He asked me, "Do you remember this story?" and I replied that I had forgotten it. It remains one of the few funny stories from that time. However, when we were in that partisan detachment, it was certainly easier to live than before. For a time, life did not seem so terrible.

We had a big white horse in the camp, a beautiful animal which we children really liked to feed because it would take the food directly from our hands. However, one snowy day in winter, there was heavy bombing of the camp by the Germans. When it started, I ran out of the earth house and saw the horse fall. Its legs twitched convulsively and then it stopped moving. My mother later found me lying injured in the snow, beside the horse. She lifted me up and carried me to the doctor. I had shrapnel in my back and leg, and there was a small piece of metal in my thumb, which has remained there to this day. I had an operation to remove the shrapnel. Thank God, it had not penetrated deeply.

**Vladimir's grandchildren**

All the partisan detachments were now under serious threat from the Germans. They were out to annihilate us all. That is when Tzaryuk gave the order that all children and those who were injured should be evacuated immediately. Only those able to fight should remain. So this is how we, the injured and children, came to be transported on planes, beyond the front line to Gomel, and delivered to an orphanage. My Mum came there later to find me.

The end of the war occurred while I was in Stolbtsy. There, after the liberation, after everybody had emerged from the 'cauldron', my mother started working again in a printing office. One night, we suddenly heard shots and you could see luminous rockets and spotlights across the sky. I was really frightened and crawled under my bed to hide, but my Mum said, 'It is alright! Come out of there! The war is ended! This is victory day!' It was incredible how people rejoiced and laughed. This was finally the end of the war! I remember that moment so clearly. I should mention here just one traumatic effect of the war, which remained with me for many years: I was afraid of crows. I really thought that they were planes in flight!

In 1945, I went into the first form of school. Around the same time, my father left military service, having been injured many times. He was in one of the first groups to return, but he was now disabled. That is when our ordinary Soviet lives began. My younger sister Sophia was born in Stolbtsy and we then moved to Minsk. I finally left school many years later, and ultimately graduated from the University of Medicine. Nowadays I work as a doctor. My wife is a doctor, my daughter is also a doctor, and my son-in-law is a doctor too. I have a little grandson who is already able to run! We all live in Minsk.

Father died in 1981 and was buried in Minsk. My mother and my sister went to Israel in 1990. In 2002 Mum died and was buried in Ariel. My sister and her family still live in Israel. Believe me when I say that my dislike of Germany stayed with me for a long time. Such was our upbringing. We were taught to see a Fascist in every German. But, as you grow older, your perception of the world changes, especially when you work as a doctor and witness people's suffering. For the last twenty years (at the time of writing this), I have been a pacifist. I dislike war in any form. I cannot understand why people kill each other, and I believe that I never will.

Today, there is no question of asking for forgiveness or of forgiving. No! Our task is to prevent another war. Those of us who were touched by that War, those of us who were in the Minsk Ghetto or any other death camp, will not remain alive for much longer. But perhaps it is important that the memory remains - albeit without bitterness. If any of us carry spite, hatred or bitterness deep inside us, then these emotions should remain with *us*, and we should not pass them on to our children. I really believe that, against all the odds, there will be peace on earth and people will love each other.

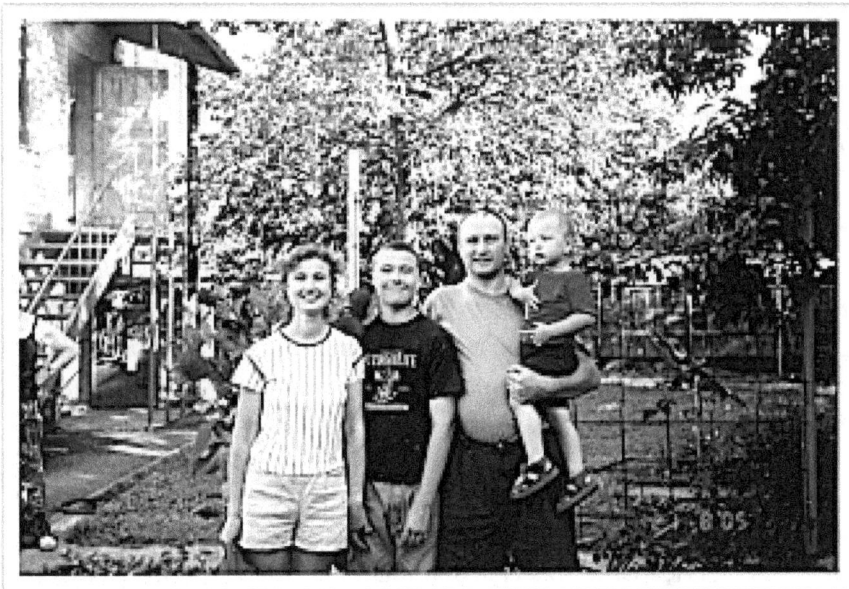

**Vladimir's daughter Yulia with her husband Mikhail, and their children**

# Transportation to the Other World
## Mikhail Treister

**Mikhail Treister**

*The SS concentration camp at Shirokaya Street in Minsk existed from 5 July 1941 till 30 June 1944. Shirokaya Street used to be situated where Masherova Avenue is now. (It was previously called Varvasheni Street). The camp was located in the former cavalry barracks, in the very place where there is now a military hospital. From August 1943 four gas vans circulated regularly between that camp and the annihilation camp Maly Trostenets. On the way there, people died from the gas coming from the exhaust pipe. The bodies were burnt in Trostenets. From August 1943 until June 1944, twenty thousand people in total were annihilated in the camp at Shirokaya Street. Most of them were prisoners from the Minsk Ghetto.*

Four heavy open lorries appeared unexpectedly and filled the large yard of the 'factory', as the VVS Air Force Service Base was called at that time [for VVS, see glossary]. On the front ramp of each vehicle, there were four soldiers in unusual greyish uniforms and grey steel helmets with the white inscription ROA. This was the Russian Liberation Army or Vlasovtsy [see glossary]. Machine guns dangled from their bellies. These were serious men! They stood very still, as if they were in a line of duty at the Mausoleum. It was clear that they had come for us. It seemed that our turn had come.

Experience had already taught me that extreme situations require rapid reactions and swift decision taking. I therefore understood at once that we needed to escape quickly, and that we must move immediately, while those guards were still standing to one side. Outwardly calm, I strolled out of the workshop, pretending to have a job to do and barely resisting my urgent desire to run away. I went slowly to the corner of the yard, towards the familiar pillbox (DOT) over which I had climbed more than once on my way to my old pre-war street Rozochka. The most important thing was to get to that DOT, and then I would think again about my next step. I covered fifty metres and began to remove my *lata* [see glossary], when I suddenly heard Grossmaister Rohse's strident voice:

'*Mikhail, wohin?*' [German: Michael, where are you going?].

He pointed a finger at the workshop. His face never seemed so disgusting to me as it did at that moment. I had no choice – I turned back.

Meanwhile, an order was issued that, within fifteen minutes, all Jewish men from the workshops were to get into the vehicles. It was clear what would happen if anyone were to disobey. There was only ever one punishment meted out, and that was to be shot where you stood.

So I now started to edge towards the tailgate of the furthest lorry. Only when I was actually sitting in the vehicle, did I realise that I had made a good decision: it would be easier to jump from this position. I then calculated that if the lorry turned right from former Sovetskaya Street – then it would be going in the direction of Trostenets. In that case, I would have to jump. Of course, there was not much chance of my succeeding in this, but it would be better to get a bullet while escaping, than to be later forced to lie in a trench and be shot. On the other hand, turning left would mean that we were going in the direction of Shirokaya Street, where people were not generally shot on the spot. From there, they would generally be transported on, to the 'other world'. It was well known that the Shirokaya Street camp was a collection point from which prisoners were sent to various other destinations. So while they might still be heading to their annihilation in Trostenets, it was also possible that they could be going further away to concentration camps in Germany or other European countries. At least, if I went to Shirokaya Street, some options might become possible. Most importantly, the journey would last for some time, providing more potential opportunities for escape.

We turned left. I was not exactly happy, but I felt a little better. Fate had spared me the necessity of taking an immediate and difficult decision. When we arrived at the camp at Shirokaya Street we were confronted by a mountainous fence with barbed wire above. There were control towers with spotlights and machine guns at the corners, and huge gates. Dante's words came to mind: 'Abandon hope, all ye who enter here'. Once through the gates we saw a huge asphalt drill field, and beyond that were the former cavalry stables. On the left, there was a shed with piles of bricks. Somewhere on the right, was located a large work zone with workshops, a kitchen and the barracks where the prisoners lived. I was sure that, in comparison with candidates for annihilation like us, those prisoners were aristocrats! At that moment, I believed that the likelihood of their being shot was not nearly as great as ours. However, it turned out that by July 1944, all of them had been killed.

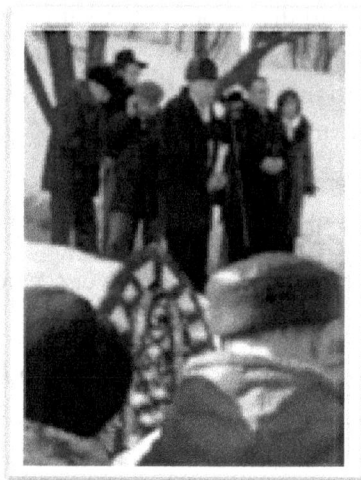

**Commemoration at the 'Yama' complex**

The days spent in the camp passed as in a nightmare. On arrival, our heads were shaved bald with sheep-shearing equipment. By the afternoon, what seemed like a few thousand of us were standing, sitting or lying on the asphalt having our first meal in Shirokaya. From then on, the same tin of rotten thin broth was served to us just once a day. The long queue to the cauldron stretched to the back of the work zone. We were forced to move almost at a run, and many who did not manage to put their can into the container in time, just had to pass by the cauldron without having even that one meagre meal.

At night, people were forced into the huts. Machine guns were set in front of the huts and dogs would be released. There were only enough plank beds for one third of us. The others could only stand, waiting for their turn to sleep for a few hours. However, some of us managed to sleep standing: in such overcrowded accommodation, it was difficult to fall down! On one occasion, it was discovered that a piece of bread had been stolen from another group, the 'Hamburg' prisoners [see glossary]. It was then announced that if such a theft occurred again, the guilty person would not be sought out, but every tenth person among us would simply be shot. There were no more thefts after that.

Sometimes in the daytime, when the crowd filled the drill field, some local noisy agitation or scuffle would occur. Then the commandant, a tall, thin snake-faced German, took his gun and without even aiming, he would release a whole stripper-clip into the crowd. The prisoners would stagger back towards the stables, with the killed and injured remaining on the asphalt. The injured were then shot, and the corpses removed. Everything would then calm down.  With such random killings, and the constant deaths occurring from malnutrition, there was a kind of selection going on. Some of us formed a little group and that helped us to survive in that hell, but there was terrible anxiety and tension. We were constantly waiting to be killed or taken away. We wondered whether we only remained alive because the trenches in Trostenets had not yet been prepared for us?

## Epstein's list

And then suddenly, the most powerful man in the ghetto, Naum Epstein, arrived in the camp accompanied by four Jewish policemen. At that time, he was the director of the labour registry office. Within minutes, it became known via the 'camp telegraph' that there were thirty-six particularly valuable specialists and experts among us, who should not have been sent to Shirokaya Street at all. Their expertise was required by German manufacturing companies, and their reassignment had been approved by the commissioner-general. These were thirty-six people without whom, it would seem, the Germans could not manage, even temporarily. They would come from among us, despite the harsh schedule of the 'final solution'! It was easy to guess what *my* chances would be of getting into that select group!

Imagine the scene: Epstein was standing with his policemen by a little table in the middle of this vast drill field. He held the list in his hands. The crowd of prisoners was pushing and shoving, attempting to force their way closer in order to hear what was being said. Camp guards pressed them back with their rifle butts and dogs. Between the crowd and the table, walked the camp commandant with a machine gun in one hand and a bamboo stick in the other. Finally, things became quieter and then it was silent… something absolutely unnatural for such a large number of people. Even the dogs stopped barking, as if they felt the solemnity of the moment. This felt like an instant of ringing silence between life and death. Now names were called, each followed by an almost instantaneous cry of: 'Present!' followed by a murmur from the crowd of 'Lucky man!' as the chosen worker pushed forward towards the table.

Another name was called: 'Naum Rozin!'

Above the drill field, there was a seemingly endless silence. It may only have lasted a second or two, but long enough for Naum himself to have shouted back if he was alive. But there was silence. Then, before that eternity expired, someone's gruff voice sounded: 'Present!' It turned out to be my voice! As if in a dream, I forced my way to the table. Epstein, knowing me, and maybe the Naum Rozin in question, looked surprised but said nothing. So I joined the group of the 'fortunate', feeling a total misfit among that chosen elite.

The group was eventually complete and we were split up into work details of pairs. The commandant now did the final inspection. When he set eyes on me, a scrawny sixteen-year-old, who was supposed to be a 'particularly valuable specialist', without saying a word, he began to beat me with the bamboo stick around my shorn head. Then he pointed to the crowd with his stick. Epstein looked on silently. My scalp was battered, and blood was running into my eyes. Forcing my way through the crowd to a tap, I started to wash off the blood. I then reached into my pocket and pulled out my ragged head-covering (it was not worthy of the name 'hat') and stretched it onto my head. Then I noticed that the commandant had moved away to the furthest corner of the drill field to sort something out in the crowd, and I made one final attempt.

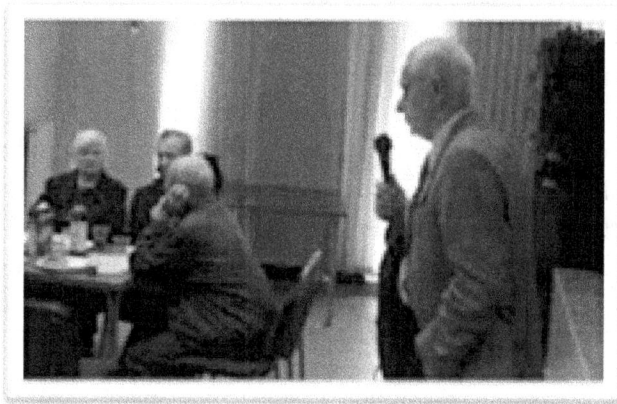

**Evening of 23 February 2011 - Congratulating the veterans**

I forced my way back to the group of experts. They were standing behind the brick pile, about to leave. I saw Epstein's anxious look, and realised, with some surprise, that he had some kind of sympathy with me. I also knew that another beating from the commandant would be my last. But it was too late to think. I just went all out for it. I stood at the end of the queue. The commandant, judging by the sounds of his gun, was imposing his usual discipline somewhere on the right wing of the drill field. He was absorbed and not paying attention to us. I cast a last glance at familiar faces in the crowd, and accompanied the group out of that nether world. So that is how it happened that Naum Rozin, who didn't survive to that day and whom I never even knew and Naum Epstein, gave me the gift of life. Those I left behind survived for only two months more - until October 1943 – while, by a twist of fate, my life was to continue for many long years until this day. When I meet them in the other world, I will bow low.

And so I did not 'flee' the camp, but just walked away – even though any kind of escape from the SS camp on Shirokaya Street was supposed to be impossible.

### Back in the ghetto

However, more unexpected events were to follow. The group was being returned to the ghetto and, as we neared the entrance, we were approached by a vehicle carrying some top brass. They drew to a halt, swore at us and promptly started to beat Epstein. It appeared that there had been some mix-up involving the list of 36 specialists: two groups had been approved instead of one. In the confusion, some of the names had been duplicated and appeared on both lists. Since the total number of 36 was not supposed to be exceeded, Epstein was handed a new order, under which all of us who had been liberated were now to be placed overnight in the KPZ, the Preliminary Detention Cell belonging to the ghetto labour registry office. This is where people were usually held who had been captured during raids. Finally, to help resolve the confusion, it was decided that some of us would be released back into the ghetto and the rest taken back to Shirokaya. We would all be replaced by specialists from a completely new list! Accordingly, because Naum Rozin had been on both lists (probably he was very good specialist) and I was assuming his name, I was released back into the ghetto in the morning – and all with Epstein's blessing! To this day, I have never understood Epstein's sympathetic attitude towards me.

So now I simply returned home, trying not to reveal to my family how close I had just come to annihilation. Had my true identity been revealed, I would never have survived. In fact, those terrible days spent in that hell had changed me so much that even my mother did not recognise me when I first appeared. In that short time, things in the ghetto had changed too. For example, one of my neighbours, Rozenblat the police chief had been 'liquidated', while another policeman, Shulman, pretended not to know me.

### Staroye Selo

I waited for a week, trying to decide what to do next, and with whom I might attempt to leave. I decided that I would head for Staroye Selo, a support base for sabotage groups. In other words, Staroye Selo was almost a partisan zone. I needed someone to accompany me, and one possible candidate soon presented herself. In part of our two-storey house on Respublikanskaya Street lived a charming blond sixteen-year-old girl, Vera Rozenberg (Vera Smirnova, who died only a couple of years ago), with whom I had discussed the subject of escape many times. While we were making the necessary arrangements, another Mikhail of the same age joined us. So there were now three of us. We put together some appropriate clothes, and mother prepared some food. For weapons, we had only a bowie knife which I had sharpened like a cobbler's razor. We said goodbye to our remaining relatives and, early one morning, we removed the *lata* [see glossary] from our clothes, crawled under the barbed wire at Opanskogo Street, and started out into the unknown. The road was about 20 kilometres long and relatively quiet. Somewhere about halfway, our companion Mikhail turned back. I will not try to guess the reasons, since 'we are to say nothing but good of the dead'. Vera went with me almost to Staroye Selo itself, but then she also turned back. It turned out that she had just wanted to explore the route in order to be able to guide her relatives out of the ghetto. (However, her future destiny would be terrible: after joining the partisans, she returned to Minsk on a mission, only to be imprisoned and then sent to Auschwitz. She went through all levels of hell but, thank God, she survived!).

Now I was left alone. Those days passed as in a fog. Eventually, when I had eaten all the food that I had brought with me, I began begging at houses. Some people gave me a few scraps of food, but did so reluctantly. One cold night, lying by the dying embers of a fire and dreaming, I stretched out towards the warmth and rolled onto the hot coals. I did not wake up until my jacket had burnt through. A compassionate elderly woman mended the damage to my coat with some patches of white fabric, so now I was beginning to take on the 'heroic' appearance of a hardened army veteran!

### Meeting partisans

Finally, I met up with some partisans from a sabotage group of Ponomarenko's detachment. At first, they suspected me of espionage. They noticed that I had a box of matches in my pocket and that under the matches, I had concealed the tightly folded 'secret sheet of paper' which had been issued to me by the *Judenrat* [see glossary] back in the ghetto. This piece of paper contained my name and place of origin. They praised me for my resourcefulness and suggested that I consider exchanging my excellent boots, (which had been specially sewn by me before I left), for some ragged ones, and that I join the partisans. It was an offer I could not refuse, so I gave up my boots. Later on, when I had helped them to repair their shoes, I got to know these partisans a little better. It even turned out that one of them was Jewish, and eventually we all became more friendly. I was even given a temporary allowance.

Once, I went to the railway with them to act as a lookout while they carried out their sabotage work on the Minsk-Stolbtsy road. They also took me to a major highway, where I was given jobs requiring more expertise. For example, I once had to saw down telegraph poles and set charges, and sometimes there was even shooting involved. When their work in this area was complete, the group finally returned to its base, taking me with them. We covered about eighty kilometres until we reached Nalibokskiy Forest. Here I was finally transferred to Sholem Zorin's Jewish Partisan Detachment [see glossary].

There I was given regular food and was able to wash. When they discovered that I was a cobbler, I was appointed to the workshop run by the craftsman Yankel from Chervenya. That was when my struggle began. I became determined to get myself transferred into a fighting group and to become a guide to the Minsk Ghetto. Everyone was certain that the ghetto was about to be liquidated and my mum and sister Nyuta were still there. That struggle determined the course of my life from then on.

### Forest cobbler

Although I had joined the partisan detachment hoping to fight and perform brave deeds, I now found myself working in a partisan cobbler workshop. The level of efficiency here was far from the order in a German atelier where all the proper materials would be provided and arranged conveniently on shelves. On the contrary, in Yankel's workshop there were old bootlegs, pieces of raw hide and soles made of car tyres just lying around everywhere. What is more, without the proper tools, it required exceptional amounts of force and patience just to cut these soles into the necessary shapes. We even had to make wooden nails out of blocks of birchwood. And then there was Yankel!! He and I hated each other from the very beginning. He hated me because, although I was a capable worker, I did not undertake the work with much enthusiasm. I hated him for his constant efforts to demonstrate his power over me and for being a pathetic stickler for detail.

All around, I was surrounded by a forest filled with armed people and freedom was in the air. By contrast, here in the workshop I was forced to sit hunched over a cobbler's last. In addition to all of this, there was the temptation of a constant smell of fresh bread wafting in from a bakery which was situated in the same earth house and separated from the workshop only by a divider of thin sticks. Who could bear all of this? Not me!

## I become a guide

I was constantly thinking about my relatives in the ghetto and I went repeatedly to the authorities in order to persuade them to send me there as a guide. Finally, I succeeded: I was given the task of going back to the ghetto and returning with a pharmacy technician, a soap maker, and a gun maker. I would also be allowed to bring my relatives, but there was one condition: the total number of the group was not to exceed ten. Large groups were almost always doomed to certain death. In addition, I was tasked with obtaining a car battery, radio components, medicines and if possible, weapons. I was to take the group to Staroye Selo from where they would be led by another guide. Everything seemed clear and feasible - as is often the case *in theory*.

I do not know why, but I have no recollection of my journey from the dense forest to Minsk. Perhaps it is because the journey was straightforward and nothing untoward occurred. It was September 1943.

## Back in the ghetto

The ghetto, now significantly reduced, was in its final weeks or maybe even days. There was little time to lose. I started to search for the required specialists. Although I was supposed to be incognito, various people began visiting me - and not with empty hands. I remember two of my visitors particularly well. The first one arrived with an automatic pistol, a Parabellum in a new holster, together with three cartridge magazines. He brought five people with him. Another gave me a round package, ten centimetres in length, wrapped in a newspaper. There seemed to be an amazing discrepancy between its volume and weight. It turned out to be a parcel of gold coins. I do not remember how many there were. With this package came ten more people.

However, I had to follow the orders I had been given and stay silent about my mission. To all intents and purposes, I was going nowhere.

I even told the same story to my close acquaintances Lusya and Rosa Zuckerman. Fortunately, they survived the war and I was later able to apologise to them for the deception. I hope that, being ex-partisans themselves, they understood that I was executing an order. They knew the risks only too well. Their uncle, a merry fellow called Boris Zuckerman, was caught alive while making reconnaissance as a partisan, and he was tortured by his captors. For a partisan, captivity could mean tortures that are almost indescribable. For example, a red hot pot might be placed over the head of the victim, or the torturers would tie a naked partisan to an anthill, or he might even be torn apart using horses or by being stretched between two birches. Only a gun or a grenade could help avoid such sufferings, but only if the partisan managed to use it on himself or herself first.

### The boiler-house

Finally, I was ready to leave. The group gathered in the boiler-house of the ghetto isolation hospital, where there followed a development that I could not have foreseen. Several unexpected people were there already, huddled together. They had miraculously survived after the pogroms and were now homeless. In addition, some others, having heard that our group was forming, had joined them. Among all of these people, I saw the son of my workshop colleague Sholom Kaplan with a familiar young woman called Klara and her daughter. I would have to take them with me. In brief, 25-30 people were gathered there. On the one hand, I realised that the chances of leaving the city with this group were probably non-existent. However, on the other hand, I knew that I could not leave without them. Our departure time arrived and I did the only thing I could: I ordered them all to wrap their shoes in any piece of cloth so that we could go through the city in the night as noiselessly as possible. At precisely two o'clock, we cut the wire at Opanskogo Street and left the ghetto to face our fate.

### Surviving till dawn

Somehow, we managed to get out of the city, which eventually petered out somewhere behind Kalvariya cemetery. To this day, I still feel that even to get that far was a miracle. However, difficulties soon occurred when we found ourselves in a huge potato field located in the centre of a triangle of roads. We were approaching one of the roads when an explosion occurred ahead of us. We quickly lay down in the grass and, thank God, it was long enough to give us protection. Meanwhile, on all three sides, vehicles were appearing. We could hear sirens blaring and the guttural shouting of instructions. I did not know what had happened, but it is easy to imagine the fearful state we were in. To be discovered there at dawn would mean certain death. After a while, things quietened down a little and we began to creep forward very slowly.

We finally came to one of the roads and crossed it. This was not the route that we had originally chosen, but another quieter one where there was almost no movement.  However, that change of direction had thrown us off our course for Staroye Selo and it became clear that we would not be able to reach our destination that night. Dawn caught up with us and we were forced to hide.

## Tragedy

We rested in bushes for a while, and then a discussion began. I was in favour of scouting out the road in the daytime and continuing to move at night. The adults objected, preferring to move in the daytime. While we were arguing, a young shepherd appeared who had discovered our hiding place. With the aid of a bribe, we persuaded him to promise that he would not to tell anyone about us. But we all understood what that promise meant, so the adults won the argument. Three youngsters scouted out the road and we then split into three groups, each one led by one of the scouts. We decided to move off in the direction of our destination at intervals of twenty minutes. My group would be the last to leave.

The first group set off, then the second, and finally it was my turn to go. I took the lead and the rest of my group followed me at a distance of about fifty metres. The terrain was difficult: a hill, a narrow pathway, a steep dip in the road, and finally another hill towards a wooded mountain. Somewhere beyond that was the Rakovskoye highway.

As I was approaching the narrow pathway, I suddenly heard a kind of dry crackling noise in the dip ahead. It did not frighten me but I was puzzled. I waved back to my people and signaled to them to lie down. I then started to creep towards the sound. I looked down and saw a scene that is still vivid in my memory. In the low terrain ahead, to the left of the path, there was a feeding trough, and near to that trough some Germans were shooting at the second group at point blank range. Further up ahead, some police thugs were firing rifles at the first group which was fleeing up the wooded mountain slope and running for cover into the forest. I saw some people fall. Later, when we met up, we were forced to the conclusion that the second group had been completely destroyed. Of the first group, only half remained.

I returned to my people and ordered them to descend to the bushes. Only when we arrived there, did I tell them what had happened. By some miracle, the Germans were now nowhere to be seen. Apparently, they had decided that nobody was left alive. You can only imagine how distraught we were as we waited for night to fall.

## Finale

To this day, I cannot decide who had been right in our argument. If the shepherd betrayed us, then the adults were right: we had to leave immediately. If not, mine would have been the right decision because, in that case, we could have saved the whole group by staying in the bushes till dark. But history knows no 'ifs and buts'.  What happened, happened. I cannot judge whether it was my fault, especially as the main supporters of the daytime crossing died and there was nobody left to discuss it with. It took two more nights of travelling on out-of-the-way roads to reach Staroye Selo, but we finally arrived there safely. Our reduced group consisted of the pharmacy technician Smolyansky, his daughter Klara, her child, Sholom Kaplan, my mum, my sister Nyuta, me and two or three others whose names I no longer remember.

We were taken to Nalibokskiy Forest, which was the relocation place of detachment 106. Our guide was a little girl named Katya. The group had already covered about 80 kilometres and by now, their feet were covered with blood. At the end of the journey, some of us were forced to cut off our boots, but we all arrived safely without further losses.

## The Place of Tragedy

After the war, I could not find that tragic place. However, in 1960 during a ski-walk, I was climbing the wooded mountain Monastyrskaya, which has now been dug for open-pit mining. Suddenly I recognised the bushes, that pathway and that smooth forested way up from south to north. The bushes were situated not far from the present day crossroads between Sharangovicha and Goretskogo Streets. Nowadays, the Volkswagon Dealership which stands just opposite the factory called NPO Tsentr marks the approximate place where our people had died.

Recently, in the Museum in Minsk known as 'The Historical Workshop', one of the scientists claimed that, in September 1943, a number of 'Hamburg' Jews [see glossary] were being taken to work in the zone of Mountain Monastyrskaya and were shot for their attempt to escape. That is not true. No so-called 'Hamburg' Jewish people ran anywhere from the ghetto. They had no place to run to. It is most likely that the rumours relate to the story of our group. At least, the place and the time coincide. I often drive on this roadway and each time I recall the final act of that distant tragedy.

And so we finally reached the partisan detachment. A lot has already been written about Detachment 106, and I hope that even more will follow. It was created in the spring of 1943 by the order of Vasily Chernyshev, commander of the Baranovichsky partisan unit. The Commander of the 106 Detachment was Sholem Zorin, the Commissioner was Haim Feigelman, and Chief- of-Staff was Anatoly Vertgeim [see Zorin's Brigade in the glossary]. At the time of liberation, the unit consisted of about 600 people, among whom there were approximately 140 in the fighting group. Also in the detachment was a cobbler, a tailor, a weapons workshop, a mill, a bakery, a smoke house, a *banya* (sauna) and an excellent medical unit dealing with everything from surgery to gynaecology. They served not only Detachment 106, but also the other detachments and brigades of the Ivenetskaya zone.

In our detachment, there were approximately 150 orphaned children. Many of them studied at a partisan school, where they wrote on birch bark with coal. The detachment structure was as follows: fighting and household squads, a preparatory troop and finally, field and construction brigades. The field brigade reaped the harvest in the fields belonging to villages which had been burned, while the construction brigade equipped the camp with all living necessities. There was also a herd of cows which had been seized from police thugs.

Apart from fighting operations, the detachment's task was also to care for children and the elderly who had miraculously survived the ghetto. These tasks were not easy to fulfil in the harsh conditions which existed in the forest, but the Zorin people accomplished them brilliantly. Finally, on 9 July 1944, the detachment linked up with some Red Army units.

### My First Rifle

So now, despite my eagerness to fight, I found myself once again working in the cobbler's workshop. An important condition of joining a partisan fighting group was the possession of a weapon, so I now decided that I would have to provide one for myself. I found an old gun barrel somewhere and, over the course of a few nights, I polished it until it was shining like a mirror. I exchanged my German Stamper watch for a bolt, and worked on it until it was in perfect condition. I also had to find a club and a gun-stock, but that was another story. - In the detachment, there was an agreeable chap by the name of Isaac Grinberg who did the joinery. He was just one or two years older than me. We agreed a deal whereby I would make him a pair of good boots out of 'devil-knows-what' materials, and he would carve a club and a gun-stock for the rifle. On completion, everyone said that they were much better than the manufactured ones! Finally, I acquired one and a half dozen '*maslyata*'(bullets). At last I was 'armed and very dangerous.'

### Man's Destiny

Incidentally, Isaac Grinberg's destiny is interesting. After the liberation, we lost touch and I was sure he had died in the war. But a few years ago, he unexpectedly came to Minsk from St. Petersburg along with a group of ex-prisoners, and we met. It turned out that Isaac the joiner had become a 2nd rank captain. He had created and commanded a VMS (Military Naval Force) training centre for many years, where, among other things, submariners were taught how to leave a submarine during an emergency. We recalled our earlier *gesheft* [Yiddish: business arrangements] and spoke of his amazing girlfriend Rita. Isaac and Rita had been the cutest couple in the detachment!

### Again under guard

But let's come back to Yankel and the end of our personal conflict.

'I will not be working tomorrow', I said, after an exhausting work day and yet another confrontation with the craftsman.

'We'll see about that', he replied harshly.

Accordingly, on the following morning, I settled down under a sheepskin jacket. I intended to catch up on my sleep after a long night spent chatting with Yulik Dvoretsky. He was in the course of telling me the plots of all the novels by Dumas which he had read before the war; on that particular occasion it was *The Black Tulip*. Suddenly, the door opened. A bolt clanked and a rough voice barked the orders: 'Get dressed! Get out! Hands behind! Forward, march!' Yankel, inserted a bullet into his cartridge and took me under guard through the whole camp to the workshop, provoking much hilarity among passers-by.

## Liberation

However, I never did get properly established in Yankel's workshop. My case finally came to the attention of the commander, and with my handmade rifle, I was accepted at last into the preparatory troop. Now I was given drill training and carried out patrol duty. I was taught the necessary skills for creeping along the ground, how to harness a horse and to economize on bullets. Of course, the training was not a 'bowl of cherries', but at least I was far away from Yankel and from working with half-soles in the cobbler's workshop. I do realise that Yankel was an honest worker, and it was not his fault that I had been allergic to the profession of cobbler since my time in the ghetto.

## Obsession

During the war, and later in the mountains, where I spent many years, there have been situations where my life hung in the balance – and not only mine. However, there is one particular moment, the memory of which still makes my hair stand on end and my throat go dry. It is a story that I do not often tell, probably because it seems too incredible. However, it is the whole truth from beginning to end. It happened on 6 July 1944 after the last battle, in which six of our people died and three others, including the commander, were seriously injured. In that final battle, after becoming aware that our sides were not equal, our people started to fall back, and finally fled. We all started to run, but within ten minutes I had swerved away from the others and then I completely lost my bearings. As I was standing there wondering where to go, I became aware of shooting nearby. This was not a salvo or serial fire, but single and frequent shots. I concluded that our people had returned and were continuing the battle. I started to move towards the shots, as they were the only indication of where the fighting was taking place.

The sounds were reducing in volume as I went towards the edge of the forest. The bright sunlight was in my eyes and, in that blinded state, I saw some shaded silhouettes about one hundred metres away. I thought that I recognized my people and waved to them out of joy. Suddenly, one of them aimed his rifle at me and fired. The bullet zinged nearby. The whole situation started to become unreal. Maybe they had not recognized me. I cried out, 'I am one of yours! One of yours!!!'

Then I saw that they were about to shoot at me again, so I threw myself to the ground and landed on a sandy mound. Two more shots were fired and sprays of sand filled my eyes. The bullets lay only half a metre from my head. I wondered if it were possible that they had not recognized me yet? I looked up and saw that they were gesturing towards me, ordering me to stand up, to throw up my hands, to come towards them. I stood up, raised my hands and went, realizing that something was wrong. I broke into a cold sweat.

I took a few steps and emerged into the shade. Oh God, now I understood it all – Germans! In front, were the two people who I had mistaken for ours. They were wearing the badges of field gendarmerie and behind them there were about six others, with more coming from the forest. They were all laughing and cackling. I could already hear some voices speaking broken Russian, but with a German accent: 'Partisan, come here!' Only fifty metres separated us. I would have given anything for a grenade at that moment... I could already see their grinning faces. Those closest to me even lowered their automatic rifles. I was going towards them as a rabbit goes to a boa constrictor.

I thought it was a pity that they had not shot me in the forehead, but I knew that they preferred to capture me alive. I took a decision. Without taking my eyes off them, I nodded to signal that I was surrendering. However, as if I was just staggering, I shifted my direction slightly towards the forest. Between me and the forest edge, there were maybe three metres, while to the shooters maybe thirty or forty. They reacted, raised their automatic rifles... and then the moment of truth.

I leapt aside, towards the forest and then through it. Behind me I could hear the cracking sound of shots. Trees were being cut to shreds by the bullets, branches and splinters kept hitting me in the face. I do not know for how long I ran, but eventually I fell to the ground, sure that I was dead. However, apart from a few minor wounds, some abrasions and scratches, nothing! I would live! After about an hour and a half, I went out onto the road and finally caught up with a cart carrying our wounded commander. Now, back among my people, the threat of death no longer seemed so imminent.

## My Partisan Universities

I will honestly confess that I carried out no heroic deeds as a Partisan. However, I learned a lot. For instance, I now knew how to fell trees, build shelters and earth houses, and ride a horse – at a gallop and without a saddle. I even knew how to land after a fall - on all fours, like a cat! What is more, during my stay in the detachment, I joined the Komsomol. This meant that I would later be able to become Secretary of the Komsomol organisation in the faculty at the polytechnic. Unfortunately, in 1948 I would be excluded from that position as a dissident.

It was in the detachment that I began to understand the nature of humanity and after the war, I began to think about this a lot. It was in the dugout shelter which we proudly called 'The Red Corner', that I first learned to dance. My teachers were the girls who danced with me to music which we produced ourselves by just humming or singing. We called it music 'from under the tongue'.

During my time among the partisans, I broke the record for confinement in the guardhouse, and I freely admit that I deserved it. However, there in the forest, for the first time in my life, I saw a Jewish man praying and another keeping kashrut [Hebrew: Jewish dietary laws] in unimaginable conditions, and all of that made me reflect deeply on many things. I made true friends there, and many of them still remain my friends to this day. It was with the partisans that I came to understand that, even though human life is invaluable, there are some things which are of even greater worth and significance.

# Sheets Wet with Tears
## Nelly Shenker

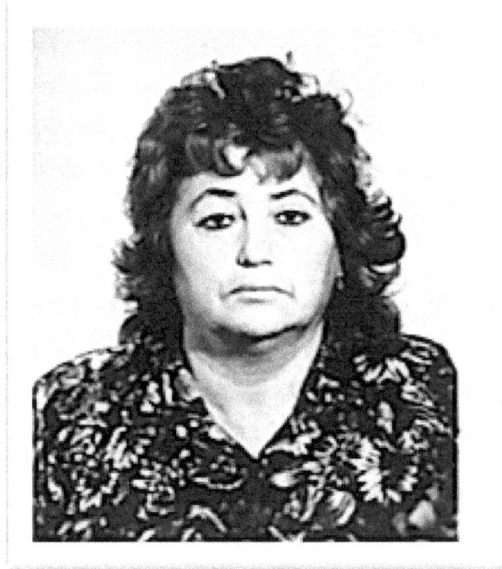

**Nelly Shenker**

I was born in Minsk and lived on the street that is now called Bogdanovicha. When the war broke out and the Germans started to bomb Minsk, a bomb landed on our house. We managed to escape and went to Opanskogo Street where my granny and other relatives lived, but they had all left the house. It was empty.

The German army then invaded the city, and I recall seeing our war prisoners walking barefoot in the street without belts. I also remember, as if it were today, the time when a small child suddenly escaped from a line of prisoners, only to be recaptured and murdered by a German soldier. The child was just torn apart so that the blood flowed everywhere. It was sheer horror. I was crying and screaming so much that my mother grabbed me and put her hand over my mouth.

It was soon after that incident that our street was fenced off with barbed wire, and our family, together with all of our Jewish neighbours, was forced to move to Tankovaya Street. It was terribly overcrowded there. There were so many people in each room that it was impossible to sleep. There was no firewood and the place was dirty. We were so hungry all the time and constantly afraid that a grenade might be thrown into the house during the night.

I have fragmented memories of the first pogrom. It was 7 November 1941. Mum had gone to work with a work detail, and I was playing in the house with my cousin and two other children – twins. There were some adults in the house hiding in the secret hiding place, the *malina*, but they seemed to think that the Germans would not be interested in harming us children, so we were left to play. I know now that this pogrom lasted for three days. I remember that, at some point, police thugs came into the house and began beating us children and driving us outside. My brother went out even though I begged him not to go, but they left me inside, saying that they would be back. I hid behind the door, and dug myself into a pile of clothes, but then I heard a shot outside. I was terrified and began knocking on the *malina,* where the adults were still hiding. It seemed such a long time before they finally opened up and told me to look outside to see where the other children were. I opened the door and saw my brother lying on the floor of the porch with blood still coming from his nose. He was dead.

The area was deserted and strangely silent. I went out and walked towards Yubileinaya Place until, turning a corner, I saw police and a great number of people lying on the ground. They had been murdered. It was a scene of pure horror. I was terrified and ran back to the house. I started knocking again at the *malina* begging them to open and let me in. I called out to them, telling them what had happened, but they did not open until I threatened to go and call the Germans and expose them. Only then did they let me into their hiding place. Once inside, I burst into tears and complained that I was thirsty and needed a drink. At this, one woman tried to stifle me with a pillow until another woman removed it from my face and silenced me by saying that, if I asked again for food or drink, they would suffocate me to death.

Finally, after that pogrom, my mum and sister returned to the ghetto with their work detail. From then on, I just recall being hungry all the time. In fact, I cannot recall eating anything but grass for a long time after that. My mum still had to go to work every day, and several times I tried to run away from the house in order to go and find her. I hid whenever I saw Germans, but often they just caught and beat me. This happened a lot. Even now there are scars on my legs. One wound in particular marks the place where a piece of flesh was ripped out. The hole remains to this day.

Then there was the day when my mum did finally take me to work with her. Unfortunately, we were spotted and both beaten mercilessly until I was so weak that I couldn't stand. Then we were told to dig a hole big enough to contain us both. We had no choice but to start digging. Luckily for us, the soldier was called away and we ran off. That was the end of my mum's work with that work detail.

Then, there was another pogrom.  It took place on 20 November 1941, in the area of Tuchinka in Minsk. There was a camp there to which thousands of Jews from the Minsk Ghetto were taken and killed. My granny and an aunt with her three children were working there as members of a very big work detail. All of them were shot that day, except for one of the children called Taits. He managed to run off and survived.

That was when my mother decided to escape. She asked her sister and niece to help her by lifting the wire. At first her niece resisted. 'I don't want you to die,' she said. But mum was determined to go. 'If we stay here, very soon none of us will remain alive. It is better to die while trying to escape. Lift the wire!' Her niece replied 'God help you!' and lifted the wire. We started to run. At first the Germans fired their weapons over our heads. However, several other people now started to follow us and that was when they started to aim their shots straight at us. They also set their dogs on our tracks. A few people escaped but most were shot. My mum and I, and her sister Asya, ran away.

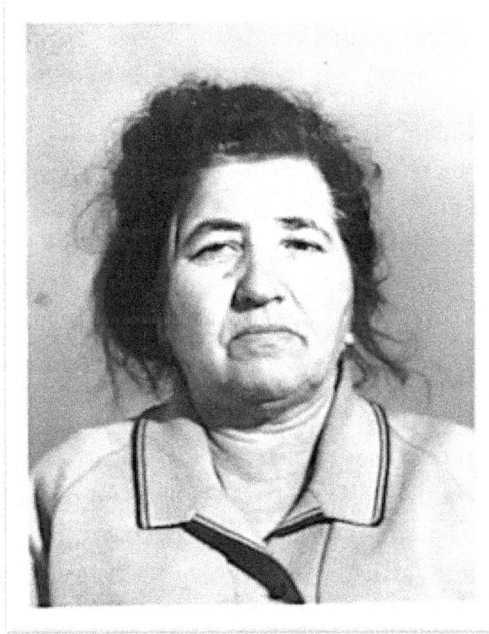

**Mum - Genya Losifovna Tsypkina**

Another episode. It happened at Respublikanskaya Street when mum and I were returning to the ghetto with her work detail. I remember the wooden houses all around. I saw that there were Germans in the street who were seizing children. I was so scared that I asked mum to hide me in the cloth bag she was carrying. However, before she could even think about it, they started to pull me away from her. 'Mummy, don't leave me', I screamed. I clutched at her, but they pulled me away. I was still hanging on to her bag. The house in Respublikanskaya to which I and the other children were taken no longer exists, but I remember it well. There were some other children already gathered there, and eventually we were all driven to the prison at Volodarskaya Street. I did not cry and I did not talk. I was convinced that I was to be killed and I just waited for that to happen.

I do not know how many children there were but now, so many years later, I estimate that there may have been around thirty, some of them the children of policemen. However, I do remember the ward that we were taken to. It had a cement floor and there was a huge barrel standing in the centre of the room. Here the children had to stand on each other's backs when they needed to relieve themselves. Nobody would have cared if one of us had fallen into that barrel of shit, and drowned.

After several weeks in that prison, policemen in the ghetto started to collect gold to bribe the warden. When they gave gold to the warden some of us were selected to be returned to the police-station. However, we were warned that if we saw our parents or anyone else we recognised, we were not to run to them or cry out. When we arrived at the police station we were released. I saw mum from a distance, but I did not run – in fact, I was so feeble that I could hardly walk. Mum had previously been told that some children would be returned, but she had not known if I would be among them. The relief for both of us was unimaginable.

Another thing that I remember is the shooting of people from the ghetto at Yama [see glossary]. Mum and I were there at that time and could well have been among those who were shot. However, my mum jumped into the pit with me and we hid among the dead bodies. During the night vehicles trampled over the dead bodies to lower the level in the pit, but not everywhere. Finally, in the morning, when we crept out from under the dead bodies, exhausted and bleeding, we expected to find the area guarded by Germans, but there was nobody around, so we finally crept away. We found our way to a water fountain in order to wash off the blood. It was so very cold.

After this pogrom, mum and I set off to look for her sister and niece. When we arrived at Stolpetsky backstreet everything was quiet. There was no-one near the wire fence, but the ghetto chief saw us. He came across and asked us what we were doing there. Mum, who spoke German very well, replied that she had been begging for a piece of bread for her little girl. She promised to move away now and go back to Shirokaya Street. The chief called over to one of his men and told him to give us some bread. We were to eat it and go back to Shirokaya immediately. However, once he left, we continued our search. I don't recall how long it took us, but we eventually found mum's relatives and a few others, including that boy Taits who I mentioned earlier in this story who had survived in Tuchinka the previous year.

In all, I spent three years in the ghetto and then eight months in the partisan detachment. What I have written here is just a fragment of my childhood memories. I could write so much more, but I am feeble and my health is just not strong enough. These little sheets are already wet with tears.

**Nelly with her mother**

# Across the Years
## Riva Sherman (Raisa Hesenevich)

**Riva Sherman**

My family led such difficult lives full of deprivations and hardships. In 1910 our father, Sherman Girsh Leizerovich, went to America, leaving his penniless wife and two tiny daughters, Dora and Dvosya, in the village of Yurevichi. Hunger and poverty had driven him there in order to earn some extra cash. It was quite some time before money started to arrive from America, and it was not until 1913 that he finally returned.

My mum was poor and illiterate. She was a very kind woman who spent all of her time caring for her big family and constantly worrying that she would not be able to satisfy their appetites. There were eventually eight children: in addition to Dora and Dvosya, there were Genya and me (Riva), both born in 1914, Leva in 1917, Semen 1921, Mikhail 1924 and Ilya 1929. Mum possessed only one dress, a print which had been neatly patched and mended in many places, but she always looked neat and tidy. She also repaired the children's worn-out clothes which she washed, darned and mended at night. Whenever dad would yell at a naughty child she would always compensate for any punishment with caresses. How I loved those tender hands when they held me, or when they combed my hair. I recall how hungry we were all of the time, and I can still remember the smells of food from those days.

My paternal grandfather died before I knew him, but I remember my grandmother really well. She was a very bossy woman, but a good housewife. I recall how, when the White Poles came to Yurevichi, grandma got me to climb into bed and told them that I was suffering from typhus.

My father was a professional tailor and an amazing person. He spoke Yiddish and also mastered the Russian language all on his own. I remember that he was keen on Jewish songs. He constantly tried to find new ways to alleviate the strains of poverty. He earned extra money by seeking work in nearby villages, and people just paid him whatever they could afford. When he did these trips he would take his older daughters with him. We, the young ones, would wait impatiently for him to return with his earnings. We knew that he would be bringing food for us to eat.

I recall one anxious autumn night when the Bulak-Balachovicz gang [see glossary] broke into our house and starting slashing at our father with sabres, while we children were hiding in a nearby shed. It was a miracle that he survived. At this time, I was seven years old, but I could not go to school as I had no shoes and hardly any clothes. My older sister Dora went to a Jewish school and it was only by watching and copying her that I learned to read and write the Hebrew letters. When she moved to a Russian school, I used the same method to master the Russian alphabet and learn arithmetic.

**Riva's mother, Asya Mayerovna Sherman**

**(killed in the Minsk Ghetto 1941)**

**Sister Genya Sherman with her son Iosif, June 1938.**
**Both killed in the Minsk Ghetto 7 November 1941.**

I reached the age of 9 without going to school at all. I remember well how I would sit and watch the other children returning home each day. However, one day, the schoolteacher Nevyadomsky came to our house to order some trousers from my father. Dad asked him for permission to use any remaining cloth to make a pair of felt boots for me, saying that these remnants would be sufficient payment for his work. That was when an arrangement was finally made for me to be accepted into the first grade. I was so happy. Shortly after I started at the school, I had to take a test. As a result, I was moved to the second grade and then to the third. That is when I began to realise that my learning at home had been lacking. I had to work really hard to reach the standard required for the third grade.

Eventually, I left Yurevichi with my father and mother, and we joined my older sister who was in Minsk. That is where I attended the Polytechnic and met fellow student Suleiman Safarovich Hasenevich, who was to become my husband. In 1937 my son Lenya was born, and in 1939 I gave birth to a daughter, Eleanora. When the war broke out, I was working as a construction engineer in the Beldrev Trust. Eventually my husband received a notice from the military commissariat and, on 24 June 1941, he was sent to the front. That was when I moved in with my parents at 34, Kolhoznaya Street. However, it was not long before this house burned down in a fire and we were left destitute with no shelter or food.

**Riva's children - Lenya and Ella (Eleanora) Hasenevich**

When they had started to bomb Minsk, I rushed to the kindergarten to collect my son. However, when I arrived there, with planes flying overhead, I found no-one there. I was eventually told that the children had all been taken away. My daughter, who was just two years old, was at a nursery in the countryside, so I walked many kilometres, scouring the area, before I found my Ellochka (Eleanora). Those little children of between two and four years old had run away and were just wandering around on foot. I searched among them and, at first, could not see my daughter. I finally recognised her thanks to the one little boot that she was still wearing.

**Riva Hasenevich (Sherman) and her husband Suleiman Hasenevich with children Eleonora and Leonid, 1958**

Since the Germans had invaded the city, we were now homeless and I was forced to beg on the streets for several days. It was then that the Jews were compelled to move into the ghetto, and so I went there with my Ellochka, my Mum, my sister Ghenya and her children. My heart could not bear the inhuman conditions in which we now found ourselves. Every day, I and other ghetto dwellers would go to work shifting and removing debris, while my daughter stayed at home with her grandmother. On 7 November 1941 there was a pogrom and many people were killed, including my mother, my sister and her children. At the time, I was with my daughter at the other end of the ghetto. When that happened, all I wanted was revenge for my family. I often wonder how I survived all of that!

**Riva Sherman with son Leonid (left), daughter Eleonora (back),
son-in-law Eduard (back right), daughter-in-law Ludmila (right).**

Eventually, at the end of December 1942, kind Byelorussian friends helped Ellochka and me to escape from the ghetto. We were transported to the partisans known as the Voronyansky 'National Vengers' Brigade, in Pleshchenitsky region. I had to carry out assignments for the brigade, and I was forced to leave my daughter with strangers. We spent over a year in this way.

May and June 1943 was the worst time. We survived, but at such a high cost. This was when we had to go to Lake Palik and I took Ellochka with me. After a few days, a blockade meant that we had to change course and we were forced across very difficult terrain. We were constantly stumbling and, on one occasion, Ellochka tripped over me and fell into the boggy ground. It was terrifying. This was how we slowly moved forward… for two months! I swore to myself that, if we survived, I would get us thousands of miles away from that place. At one point my four-year-old child said to me: 'I know why you don't fall into the bog when there is shooting. You want our heads to get blown off!' However, it would have been impossible to lie down in that terrain. If I had done so, I would not have been able to get up onto my feet again. Neither did I want to lose the rifle, which I was carrying on my back. However, I would not let anyone else carry my daughter. I did not trust anyone else with her. What if we were separated, or shooting started and I was killed? What if my child were to get lost? It was impossible…

**Daughter Eleanora Suleymanovna Banakh (right)**
**with her spouse Eduard and daughter Natasha May 1967**

When the blockade finally ended, I was very ill and covered in boils. We had to wait for a plane from Bolshaya Zemla [see glossary]. We were told that, when the plane finally arrived, seriously ill people, including my Ellochka, would be air-lifted to safety. I still remember the exact moment when I had to send her away. A Douglas airplane arrived and the injured reached out for my Ella. They all remembered her from when she had sung a song for them in the hospital. (The song was called, 'How to Make It Possible to Survive till Marriage.')

The pilot asked:

'Who are you with little girl?'

'With my mum. She is over there.'

'Call your mum to fly with you.'

'No, she cannot fly away. She must stay and defeat the fascists.'

I looked at her little face and I convulsed into spasms. Would I ever see her again?

**Suleiman and Riva Hasenevich with their children and grandchildren**

So now I will tell the story of how I was reunited with my son. After the liberation, I was told that he may still be alive and that I should to go to the house where my husband's parents had lived. When I went there, my knees were weak with anticipation! Some of the older women in the detachment had warned me: 'If you see him, don't confess at once that you are his mother. Can you imagine what he might have experienced?' I had to wait for a girl to arrive who lived nearby. She told me that Lenya was indeed alive! I couldn't move: I could hardly believe her words. She explained that Lenya had been living with my husband's parents, but when they both died from typhus, a woman who lived in the neighbourhood had taken Lenya in. I was then taken to the neighbour's yard. I recall that I was dressed in a German soldier's blouse, a black mended skirt and some old boots. The neighbour recognised me, but said nothing, and there sat my son barefoot and in threadbare clothes.

'What is your name?' I asked.

'Lenya.'

'And who do you live with?'

'I used to live with my grandparents, but then they died and I buried them. I used to visit them every day and asked them to take me with them to the grave. It was so cold in the house and I had nothing to eat. I was so afraid of sleeping alone…'

'And where are your mum and dad?'

'Dad is at the war and mum was killed by the Fascists. Grandmother told me.'

There were two partisans there with me. They had recently buried their comrades and at this point they began to cry. Now I broke down too.

'Don't you recognise your mum?'

'Mum!' It was such a cry, such hysteria.

We became inseparable. He did not let me go anywhere without him. I had to take him with me where-ever I went, even to work. It was not enough for him just to see me and know that I was near. He had to hold on to me. For instance, when we sat down to dinner, he held me with one hand and ate with the other.

By then, of course, my own mum had died - burned by the Germans. No grave ever existed for her. Nowadays, outside my house, there are lots of flowers; but in one place I have fenced off the flowers with bushes…lilac, hawthorn, a small white rose… in memory of my mother. She needs to have her own piece of earth somewhere.

**Riva (Raisa) Hasenevich (Sherman) with her husband Suleiman Hasenevich**

Eventually, I met my husband again. It turned out that a whole week was not enough for us to tell each other everything that had happened since we had last been together. I found myself telling my story day and night…

NB. This account was taken from the notes of Svetlana Alexievich for her book *The Unwomanly Face of War*. Svetalana Alexievich won the Nobel Prize for Literature 2015 for her 'polyphonic writings, a monument to suffering and courage in our time.'

# Glossary: (of people, places, dates and terms)

*Aktion* see below 'pogrom'.

**Belarus/Byelorussia** Byelorussia became part of the republic of the Soviet Union in 1922 when it was renamed as the Byelorussian Soviet Socialist Republic or Byelorussian SSR. On 27 July 1990, the parliament of the republic proclaimed the sovereignty of Belarus. On 25 August 1991 it was renamed Belarus.

**The Bielski Brigade** was a partisan combat group formed in the spring of 1942 and initially based in the forests around Novogruduk (Навагрудак) and later in Lida in German-occupied Poland (now western Belarus). The group spent more than two years living in the forest. The Bielskis were four Jewish brothers who established the organisation. The group's commander was the oldest brother, Tuvia. Under the group's protection, 1,236 Jews survived the war, making it one of many remarkable rescue missions of the Holocaust.

**Bolshaya Zemlya** means 'Big Land'. It is the name of part of the remote Arctic territory located off the northern coast of Russia. During WW2 this part of the Soviet Union was not invaded or occupied by the Nazis. The term 'Bolshaya Zemlya' thus came to refer to any unoccupied region or home front. It was a safe haven.

**Bruskina, Maria (Masha)** (1924 –1941) was a Jewish member of the Minsk resistance during World War II. She volunteered as a nurse working with wounded members of the Red Army. She helped many of them to escape by smuggling civilian clothes and false papers. Betrayed to the Germans by a patient, she was arrested on 14 October 1941. In a public hanging, an example was made of Bruskina, along with two other members of the resistance: 16-year-old Volodia Shcherbatsevich and World War 1 veteran Kiril Trus. Before the hanging, Bruskina was paraded through the streets with a placard around her neck, which read: 'We are partisans and we shot at German troops.' The hanging took place in public on Sunday 26 October 1941, in front of Minsk Kristall, a yeast brewery. The bodies were cut down three days later and buried.

Until 2009, her name was not acknowledged on the memorial plaque at the execution place and she was officially referred to only as 'the unknown girl'. In 2009 the plaque was replaced. The inscription now reads: 'Here on 26 October 1941 the Fascists executed the Soviet Patriots K. I. Truss, V. I. Sherbateyvich and M. B. Bruskina.'

**Bułak-Bałachowicz, Stanisław** (1883-1940) was a general and military commander in the Russian Imperial Army and a veteran of World War I, the Russian Civil War, the Polish-Bolshevik War and the Invasion of Poland at the start of World War II.

In the early 1920s, around the time described in Riva Sherman's story, he was commanding a troop composed mostly of Byelorussian volunteers. His forces crossed into Russian-held Byelorussia and started an offensive towards Gomel. He was hoping for a Byelorussian all-national uprising against Bolshevik Russia. After some initial success the force withdrew. It is well documented that Jews suffered greatly at the hands of the hooligan gangs commanded by General Bułak-Bałachowicz during pogroms in Yurevichi in 1920. Today, although highly regarded by some historians, he has been described by others as an adventurer.

**Bialystok** became part of Byelorussia in 1939. At the start of World War II, when Poland was invaded by Nazi Germany and the Soviet Union, the city came under Soviet control as a result of the Molotov-Ribbentrop Pact. It was incorporated into the Byelorussian SSR from 1939 to 1941. After the Nazi attack on the Soviet Union in 1941, Bialystok was occupied by the German Army on 27 June 1941, during the Battle of Bialystok–Minsk. The city then became the capital of Bezirk Bialystok, a separate region in German-occupied Poland, until 27 July 1944 when it was liberated by the Red Army. On 20 September 1944 Bialystok transferred back to Poland.

*Cheder* [Hebrew: room] refers to a school or part-time class for Jewish children, in which Hebrew and religious knowledge were taught. In pre-war Byelorussia such lessons would generally have taken place in the home of the teacher, and would have been attended by boys only.

**Gebelev, Mikhail** (1905- 1942) was an anti-Nazi resistance leader in the Minsk Ghetto. He liaised between the communist resistance movement outside of the ghetto and the ghetto fighters led by Hersh Smolar.

**Hamburg Jews** After the two pogroms of 7 and 20 November 1941, trainloads of Jews from Central Europe, many from Hamburg, arrived in Minsk. Many were shot upon arrival and the rest, numbering several thousands, were brought into the Minsk Ghetto, where a special area (a separate 'ghetto within a ghetto') had been 'cleared' and then fenced with barbed wire in order to house them. Contact between these people and the general ghetto population was forbidden.

*Judenrat* [German: Jewish Council] was a council of Jews appointed by the Germans to be responsible for the internal administration of the ghetto.

*Komsomol* Комсомол, a syllabic abbreviation of the Russian: *kommunisticheskiy soyuz molodyozhi*. This organisation was the Union of Communist Youth (1918-1991). Members were aged 14-28 and membership was nominally voluntary. The *Komsomol* played an important part in teaching the values of the Communist Party of the Soviet Union to youngsters. Active members received privileges and preferences in promotion.

**Krasnoye** is a village located approximately 16 km south-east of Molodechno (about 57 km from Minsk). A Jewish Ghetto existed there from 1941-1944; it occupied a small area in the centre of the village. In 1942, Jews from Bukovina and Bessarabia were brought there. In March 1944 survivors of this ghetto were liberated.

**Kube, Wilhelm** (1887-1943) was Generalkommissar for Byelorussia in the occupying government of the Soviet Union. His headquarters were in Minsk, He was assassinated in his Minsk apartment on September 22, 1943.

*Lata or Laty* [Yiddish: patch] refers to the circular pieces of yellow fabric, which Jews in the Minsk Ghetto were ordered to wear. The order applied to everyone over the age of ten. The patches were to be 10cm in diameter and attached to the outer garments, on both the left side of the chest, and on the back. They referred to the patches in Yiddish, as *lata* or *laty*. (In Yiddish transliteration as standardised by Yivo, the Institute for Jewish Research, the word is spelled '*late*', but we have employed '*lata*' or '*laty*' here to avoid confusion with pronunciation).

In some photographs, Jews in the Minsk Ghetto can also be seen wearing the yellow star, or armbands displaying the Star of David. These would probably have been worn by Jews who had been transported to Minsk from other areas in Europe (see Hamburg Jews).

*Malina Малина* [Byelorussian: raspberry] was the Minsk Ghetto code word for 'hiding-place'. It has been suggested that the word 'raspberry' was chosen to describe a place of concealment in the ghetto because, in this region, raspberry bushes were traditionally well covered during the sub-zero temperatures of winter in order to protect them from frost. For the people of the ghetto, as for the plants, concealment was a matter of survival.

**Masyukovshina (Masjukovshina) Concentration Camp** was near to Minsk. Established in July 1941, it was the first concentration camp for prisoners of war. It covered about 16 hectares. During the three years of the war, more than 70 thousand people died or were killed there.

**NKVD** refers to the People's Commissariat of Internal Affairs – The Communist Secret Police.

**Order of the Red Star** This was a military decoration of the Soviet Union, awarded for a major contribution to the defense of the USSR in war and in peacetime and for ensuring public safety.

**Pogrom** (in German *Aktion*). The word originates from the Russian. A pogrom is an organised massacre. In the Minsk ghetto, while random killings were taking place constantly, there were a series of pogroms as follows:

> **7 Nov 1941** - first pogrom

> **20 Nov 1941** - second pogrom

**2-3 March 1942** - third pogrom held at the time of Purim (a celebration of Jewish deliverance as told in the Book of Esther). This pogrom included the massacre at Yama (see Yama below).

**April - May 1942** - a series of small organised actions

**28-31 July 1942** - fourth pogrom – this was the largest pogrom. It lasted for four days. All of the non-working population of the ghetto was destroyed. Estimates of the numbers killed range from 18,000 to 30,000 with around 12,000 remaining live in the ghetto.

**21 Oct 1943** - fifth pogrom and final liquidation of the ghetto. There are no precise figures for those remaining alive, but estimates are less than 100.

**Porechye** was a village in the Minsk region. In late 1943 it became a destination for Jewish children escaping the Minsk ghetto with assistance from the partisans. The lives of many of the children were saved by village families and individuals who accommodated and cared for them at that time. A monument in honour of those courageous people was unveiled there in 2000.

**Pukhovichy** was the location where 1,260 Jews were shot by the Nazis on 22 September 1941, and their bodies buried in two large pits.

**Russian District** This was the area of Minsk, located outside the barbed wire perimeter of the Minsk Ghetto.

**SD** Full title: *Sicherheitsdienst des Reichsführers.* An organisation which was, in effect, the intelligence agency of the SS, the Nazi Secret Police.

**Smolar, Hersh (Smolyar, Girsh/Grisha)** (1905-1993), a Polish and Soviet Yiddish writer and editor. He was a leading member of underground resistance in the Minsk ghetto and became commissar of a partisan group operating in Byelorussian forests. His wartime memoirs, *Fun Minsker geto* [Yiddish: From the Minsk Ghetto], were published in 1946.

*Stürmbannfürer* was a Nazi SS military rank equivalent to battalion commander

**Tuchinka** was an execution area outside of Minsk. On 7 November 1941 (the date of the first pogrom in the Minsk Ghetto) thousands of Jews, probably numbering between 12,000 and 17,000 in total, were marched from the ghetto to Tuchinka and shot. On 20 November, a second pogrom took place when a further 5000 to 10000 Jews from the ghetto were also massacred at Tuchinka.

**Trostenets** was a World War II Nazi German death camp and burial site located near the village of Maly Trostenets on the outskirts of Minsk. It operated between July 1942 and October 1943, by which time virtually all Jews remaining in Minsk had been murdered. While Jews were brought to Trostenets from across Austria, Germany and the Czech Republic, the primary purpose of the camp was the killing by firing squad and mobile gas chambers of Jewish prisoners of the Minsk Ghetto and the surrounding area. A memorial site opened at Maly Trostenets in 2015.

**Underground** In October 1941, groups of Jewish communists inside the Minsk Ghetto formed an underground organisation with the aim of transferring people from the ghetto to partisan groups in the forests. [See above, Hirsh Smolar].

**Vlasovtsy** The Russian Liberation Army, also known as ROA or the Vlasov army (Власовская армия, *Vlasovskaya armiya*). The force consisted of a group of predominantly Russian collaborators who were opposed to communism. They initially fought under German command in WWII. The army was led by former Andrey Vlasov, a defected Red Army General. Members of the army were often referred to as Vlasovtsy (Власовцы). On 14 November 1944, however, it became known as the Armed Forces of the Committee for the Liberation of the Peoples of Russia, and no longer formed part of the German Army.

After the war the Soviet government labelled all ROA soldiers (Vlasovtsy) as traitors. Those who were repatriated were tried and sentenced to detention in prison camps. Vlasov and several other leaders of the ROA were tried and hanged in Moscow on August 1, 1946.

**VVS** In Russian: Voyenno-Vozdushnye Sily (Военно-воздушные силы). This was the official designation of one of the air forces of the Soviet Union.

**Western Belarus** was part of the Second Polish Republic during the inter-war years. After World War II the area was ceded to the Soviet Union by the Allied Powers.

**Work Detail** Most able-bodied adult Jews from the Minsk Ghetto were assigned to groups with whom they would work regularly outside of the Ghetto, in the Russian District. In these stories, this kind of group is generally referred to as a 'Work Detail'. The groups would be marched out of the Ghetto each morning under armed guard and transported to various work-places in or around Minsk. Some workers were employed to carry out menial tasks such as the clearing of rubble on building sites. There were also a number of 'specialist' groups, from needlewomen to factory workers and skilled technicians. The workers sometimes received limited food rations which some took home at the end of the day to share with their starving families inside the ghetto.

**Yama** The word in Byelorussian means 'the pit', and refers to an area inside the Minsk Ghetto which had originally been a quarry bordering on Ratomskaya Street. It has now given its name to a monument which marks the location of the largest punitive action to have been conducted in the Ghetto: In early 1942 the Jewish council of the Ghetto was ordered by the German authorities to gather together 5000 Jews for deportation. When news of the order spread, many of the ghetto inhabitants went into hiding. On 2 March it became obvious that the quota of 5000 people had not been fulfilled. German security forces consisting of Byelorussians, Lithuanians, and Ukrainians then entered the ghetto and began randomly taking people. Many were shot trying to hide or escape. More than 5000 people were taken to the large pit on Ratomskaya Street and shot.

The memorial, which now marks this location consists of an obelisk, which was created in 1947, and a bronze sculpture created in in 2000, entitled 'The Last Way'. It represents a group of people, walking down steps to their doom in the pit. The sculpture was created by Leonid Levin (1936-2014), Belarusian architect and Chairman of the Union of Belarusian Jewish Public Associations and Communities between 1991-2014, together with Israeli sculptor Elsa Pollak and Belarusian sculptor Alexander Finski. On the obelisk, in Russian and Yiddish, appear the words 'The bright memory of five times the light of thousands of Jews who perished at the hands of sworn enemies of humanity - German-fascist monsters'.

**Zorin's Brigade** was a Byelorussian partisan unit, led by Simcha (Sholem) Zorin. In June 1941 Zorin had escaped from the Minsk Ghetto and fled to the forests to join the partisans operating in the Staroye Selo region, about 19 miles southwest of Minsk. Toward the end of 1942, it was becoming apparent that the Red Army would ultimately prevail, but that the Germans would destroy the Minsk Ghetto before retreating. In early 1943, in the Staroselskiy Forest close to Minsk, Zorin obtained permission from partisan leaders to form a new unit which would not only offer protection to the growing number of refugees coming out of the Minsk Ghetto, but also actively bring out more people. The unit was called the 106th. It consisted of an armed unit of partisan fighters, and also welcomed children, the elderly and the infirm. It ultimately totalled around 800 Jews. After the liquidation of the Minsk Ghetto, the brigade moved to the Nalibokskiy Forest where it survived to the end of the war. In 1956, a monument was erected in the Nalibokskiy Forest to the memory of the fighters of the 106th Battalion.

## Selection of Documents and Decrees issued by the German Authorities and a Partisan Report

## THE TESTIMONY OF DOCUMENTS

### Regulation of the Field Kommendatura (Commandant's Office)

### on the creation of a ghetto in the Minsk District

Minsk                                                    19 July 1941

1. With the issue of the present regulation, a designated part of the city of Minsk is to be allotted solely for the resettlement of Jewish people.

2. All the Jewish population of the city of Minsk are to move to the Jewish district within 5 days after the issue of the present regulation. If someone from the Jewish people is found beyond the Jewish district after this expiry date, they will be arrested and severely punished.

3. The re-settlers are allowed to take their personal possessions with them. Persons caught trying to export or to steal possessions not belonging to them will be shot on sight.

4. The Jewish district is confined to the following streets: Kolkhozny Lane, Kolkhoznaya Street, the Svisloch River, Nemiga Street, excluding the Orthodox Church, Respublikanskaya Street, Shornaya Street, Kollektornaya Street, Mebelny lane, Perekopskaya Street, Nizovaya Street, the Jewish cemetery, Obuvnaya Street, 2nd Opansky Lane, Zaslavlskaya Street to Kolhozny Lane.

5. After the resettlement is finished, the Jewish residential district is to be enclosed with a stone wall and separated from the rest of the city. The wall is to be built by the residents of the Jewish district. For this purpose, the bricks from non-domestic buildings and buildings to be destroyed are to be used.

6. Jewish people assigned to work teams are forbidden to stay outside of the Jewish district. The work teams are to leave the Jewish district only with a special permission [official document] to the work place designated by the administrative board of Minsk. Those who break the present regulation are to be shot.

7. Jewish people entering and leaving the Jewish district are to move along Opanskogo and Ostrovskogo Streets. Climbing over the wall is forbidden. The German security and the auxiliary police are given permission to shoot offenders.

8. Only Jewish people and military men on duty [in the ghetto on official matters] of German military units and staff members of the administrative board of Minsk are allowed into the Jewish residential district.

9. The Jewish Council is given a loan of 30 000 chervonets [currency of that time] to cover the expenses of the resettlement. The above mentioned sum including interest will be settled within 12 hours after the announcement of this regulation and to be paid to the city pay office of the board [administrative institute] at 28 Karl Marx Street.

10. The Jewish Council is to immediately provide the Housing Department with data on all Jewish properties outside the Jewish district and not yet occupied by the Aryan (non-Jewish) population.

11. The order in the Jewish residential district is to be maintained by special Jewish brigades, a decree of the creation of which [brigades] will be issued in due course.

———————

12. The Jewish Council of Minsk is responsible for the final resettlement of the Jewish population in the allotted district. Any violation of the present regulation is to be met with severe punishment.

*Commandant of the Field Kommendatura (Commandant's Office) of Minsk district*

*NARB [National Archive of the Republic of Belarus], f. [file] 4683, op. [special folder –believed to be one of the highest degree of secrecy] 3, d.[document] 937, l. [sheet] 6-7; f. 359, op. 1, d. 8, l. 1-2; Tragedy of Jewish people in Belarus in the years of the German occupation (1941-1944). Mn., 1995. S. [page] 65-66; 'Nazi gold' from Belarus: Documents and materials. Mn., 1998. S. 19-20.*

**From Communiqué №20 of the Operation Group 'B' on the situation in Minsk**

Minsk                                                    12 July 1941

Minsk is the capital of Byelorussian Soviet Socialist Republic. In 1926 it numbered 131,803 residents, in 1939, 237,772 residents.

Minsk possesses a remarkable industry. The city center has been completely demolished (destroyed) as a result of air raids and fires. The buildings of the University, the Red Army House, the Opera Theatre and the Government House have been partially undamaged.

The outskirts turned out to be less damaged where industrial enterprises are basically located.

The city has been left without electricity and water. The ruling political and government staff members have all fled.

The mood among the population is very depressed since many have been left without a roof over their heads, and the food situation is getting worse all the time. According to the regulation of the Commandant of the Field Kommendatura, in order to provide the security of the logistical communications and to prevent acts of sabotage, all of the male population aged 18-45 has been arrested. The civil prisoners are being placed on trial at the Monument.

According to the last message of the Operation Group 'B', the wooden houses in the western part of the city have been set on fire.

It is evident that the houses have been set on fire by Jewish people since they were to leave them for the returning Byelorussian refugees. The population is ready to start pogroms. The fury of the population has already caused some protest actions against the Jewish people. Some of the Jewish people have been liquidated as punishment for the fire.

[...]

11. The order in the Jewish residential district will be maintained by the Jewish Order Security Service (a special article on which will follow later).

12. The Jewish Council of the Minsk District is fully responsible for the execution of the order regarding the Jewish resettlement. Persons who do not obey this order will be severely punished.

*Field Commandant*

*NARB. F. 4683. Op. 3. D. 948. L. 80-81; MKF, arh[archive] №175, k. 722186-90. Translation from Germ.; Judenfrei! Free from Jewish people: Story of the Minsk Ghetto in Documents. Mn., 1999. S. 27.*

———————

**From an administrative-economic regulation of the Home Front Commander of the group of armies 'Tsentr' on the prohibition of the freedom of movement and trade for the Jewish people**

Minsk                                                    21 August 1941

IX.

To facilitate the strict control over Jewish activities, the following regulations are to be put into practice:

1. Jewish people are forbidden to leave the district of their residence. The exception is Jewish people having written permission from the local Kommendatura delivered as an exception for the benefit of the German Wehrmacht.

2. Jewish people are forbidden to trade (purchase and sell) with the local Aryan population. The prohibition does not apply to the Jewish people who work with the permission of German institutions in cooperation with commercial and industrial enterprises.

3. Violations are to be punished with full severity. [...]

*Home Front Commander of the group of armies 'Tsentr' Infantry General von Schenkendorf*

*NARB, f. 412, op. 1, d. 19, l. 118, 120. Typographic print. Translation form Germ.; Holocaust in Belarus. 1941-1944. Doc. and materials. Mn., 2002. S. 13.*

**From Operation Summary №92 of the Security Police and the SD** [Sicherheitsdienst ReichsführerSS (SD)] **on the execution of an annihilation campaign in the Minsk Ghetto.**

23 September 1941

…Combing out the ghetto in Minsk.

In cooperation with the Security Service Police and with the help of the field gendarmerie, a major campaign has been led in the ghetto. About 2500 Jewish people have been arrested, including women. Of them, 2278 people have been executed over the course of 3 days.

Trouble makers and Jewish activists are principally referred to in this report. Among them, by the way, there was a sizeable number who did not wear the required symbols of distinction on their clothes.

*NARB, f. 4683, op. 3, d. 1065, l. 190; MKF, arh. №175, k. 72379-72380. Translation from Germ.; Judenfrei! Free from Jewish people: Story of the Minsk Ghetto in documents. Mn., 1999. S. 164*

**From an Order of the National Commissioner of Ostland H. Lohse**

Riga                                        September 1941

3. For kikes, the local District Commissioner imposes a special curfew depending on the conditions.

*National archive [Record Office] of Minsk region, f. 623, op. 1, d. 1, l. 146; Tragedy of Jewish people in Belarus in the years of the German occupation (1941-1944). Mn., 1995. S. 67.*

**From an event summary from the USSR provided by the Security Police and the SD №31**

Confidential                                        23 July 1941

Due to the huge number of Jewish people, the foremost and most complex problem is their resettlement in the ghetto. This work is already being carried out. In cooperation with the field and local Kommendaturas, some city areas suitable for these purposes have already been selected.

Economic life has been paralyzed due to the destruction and plundering at the beginning. Some enterprises in Minsk and Borisov are already being commissioned into service. The kolkhoz [collective] production is complicated due to requisitions and thefts that make the food supply of the population suffer. Money does not have any value here yet, so payments are transacted with bread...

A complete agreement and unanimity concerning the treatment towards partisans and former soldiers in civilian clothing have been reached with the Home Front Commander of the group of armies.

Big operations have started with the participation of the Security Police and the SD. They will be executed according to the strict letter of the law.

14.07.1941 the annihilation of 4234 people was reported. By 19.07.1941 the number of the annihilated had increased by 3386 people.

An order has been given about the dissolution of the Communist Party and communist units and organisations. The appropriation of valuable documents, objects of value and so on has been secured. The operation group regularly receives information on successfully completed operations, and so on.

*NARB, f. 510, op. 1, d. 71, l. 56; MKF, arh. №131, k. 721618, 721626-721627. Translation from Germ.; 'Nazi gold' from Belarus: Documents and materials. Mn., 1998. S. 26-27.*

## From Communiqué №31 of the Security Police and the SD on the creation of the Jewish Council (Judenrat)

Minsk                                                                23 July 1941


The solution of the Jewish question during the war time on this territory seems to be impossible to resolve, since the problem of the huge number of Jewish people can only be resolved by means of resettlement. However, in order to create a more or less suitable base for the near future, the Einsatzgruppen 'B' has taken the following measures in the places where it has executed its duties so far.

In every town a temporary Chairman of the Jewish Council has been appointed, who is responsible for the creation of the Jewish Council, up to the number of 3-10 people. The Jewish Council is completely liable for the behavior of the Jewish population. Moreover, it is to immediately begin registering all Jewish people residing in the populated area. Moreover, The Jewish Council is to create labor groups out of Jewish men aged 15-55 who are to work on the clearance of debris in the town and at other works of German institutions and military units. Groups are being created for Jewish women of the same ages.

As the German soldier cannot always unfailingly distinguish Jewish people from non-Jewish local population, in some cases misunderstandings have occurred. A regulation has therefore been issued requiring that with immediate effect, Jewish men and women aged 10 and older wear yellow sewn-on patches on their breasts and backs at all times.

The Jewish Council is to report to the temporary town commissars. Reliable Byelorussians chosen and suggested by Einsatz commands have been appointed to the posts of town commissars.


*NARB, f. 4683, op. 3, d. 943, l. 88-89. Translation from Germ.; Judenfrei! Free from Jewish people: Story of the Minsk Ghetto in documents. Mn., 1999. S. 33.*

## From the Military Actions Diary of the 322d Police Squadron about annihilation operations in the Minsk Ghetto

30 September 1941

… on 30 August 1941 the Squadron without the 8th troop deals with the following military preparations:

At 16:30 a preliminary meeting of the Squadron Commander with Senior Group Leader [Obergruppenführer] Koch from the SD, in the presence of troop commanders, to discuss the question of leading the main operation against the Jewish people on 31 August and on 1 September 1941 in the Minsk Jewish Ghetto has been organised. The deadline for the anti-Jewish operation is 31 August 1941, the start-time at 15:00. To carry out the operation, 2 troops have been allocated.

The Captain of the guard police (Schutzpolizei) Jurke reports on the rotation of the 7th troop.

On 31 August 1941 the 7th and 9th troops execute the operation against the Jewish people.

During that operation, about 70 Jewish people including 64 women are arrested and taken into custody in Minsk.

On 1 September 1941 the 9th troop in cooperation with the SD and NSKK (the National Socialist Motor Corps) participate in the shooting of 914 Jewish people including 64 women in the areas surrounding Minsk. Among them were 700 Jewish men and women arrested yesterday by the 7th and 9th troops during the operation in the Minsk Ghetto. The shooting has been executed without excesses [significant incidents]. Thanks to the well-chosen area and clear instructions, no attempt to escape took place.

The Jewish women were shot because they were discovered to be without Jewish insignia during the execution of the operation in the Minsk Ghetto.

*NARB, f. 4683, op. 3, d. 936, l.43-45; MKF, arh. №454, k. 610-611; Judenfrei! Free from Jewish people: Story of the Minsk Ghetto in documents. Mn., 1999. S. 163*

**Regulation of the Reich Commissioner of Ostland regarding treatment towards Jewish property in the Reichskommissariat Ostland**

Riga                    13 October 1941

1. All movable and immovable property of the Jewish population on the Ostland territory under the command of the Reich Commissioner is subject to confiscation, the Commissioner's ruling and accounting in conformity with the following instructions:

2. Movable and immovable objects along with all belongings, debts, share participations of any kind are defined as property.

3.1. The confiscations are to be executed by the Commissioner of Ostland or via the institutions appointed by him. The confiscation is led with the help of an order regarding particular persons or a general call via an announcement and may be limited to single property objects.

3.2. The items that are not subject to confiscation:

a) a part of household objects necessary for day-to-day life of a person.

b) cash money, bank, savings and valuable documents totaling 100 Deutschmarks.

1. As a result of the confiscation, former owners lose the right to manage the confiscated property.

2. Those who possess the confiscated property or keep it are to manage it hereafter.

Changes relating to managing the property or incomes from it are allowed only within household activities. All actions beyond this limit require the consent of the Reich Commissioner of Ostland, or of the institutions appointed by him.

1. The Commissioner's control may be executed over the property subject to the confiscation if the household activities require it.

2. The introduction of the Commissioner's control is simultaneously considered as a confiscation.

3. The Reich Commissioner of Ostland gives orders concerning the creation and execution of the Commissioner's control.

………

6.1. Confiscated property may be appropriated by the Reich Commissioner of Ostland or by the institutions appointed by him.

6.2. The management of the confiscated property is given to approved institutions.

6.3. The Reich Commissioner of Ostland decides on the regulation of confiscated property by administrative means.

The responsibility is limited by the amount of the market value of the confiscated property.

7. The authorities entrusted with this task [mentioned above] may call the population to register the property subject to the confiscation.

8. The competent institutions may demand information from any person in order to execute their tasks.

9.1. Confinement in prison and a monetary penalty will be applied to those who:

a) hide the objects subject to the confiscation from German civil institutions or from their appointed representatives or who try to sabotage, to disturb, or to impede the confiscation in any way.

b) intentionally or due to gross negligence, do not execute or do not execute completely the allotted task according to the present regulation and the instructions about its execution about the registration of property and its confiscation.

9.2. In serious cases, confinement in prison is applied as punishment. If the guilty acts out of obstinacy or an even more serious case takes place, the death sentence may be imposed.

10. The Reich Commissioner of Ostland issues instructions necessary for the execution of the given regulation.

11. The regulation comes into effect on the day of its publication.

*Reich Commissioner of Ostland Lohse*

*NARB, f. 370, op. 5, d. 2, l. 15. Translation from Germ.; 'Nazi gold' from Belarus: Documents and materials. Mn., 1998. S. 30-31*

**Order №24 of the Commandant of Belarus about the annihilation of Jewish people and the Gypsies**

Minsk                                                                24 November 1941

… Jewish people and the Gypsies:

Orders №9 of 28.9.1941 p. 6.

№11 of 4.10.1941, p. 2.v.

№13 of 10.10.41, p.18.

As is indicated in the orders, Jewish people are to vanish from the surface of the globe as well as the Gypsies who are also to be destroyed.

The execution of operations against the Jewish people on a larger scale is not the task of our Division. The operations are performed by Civil and Police Units according to the order of the Commandant of Belarus if special units are given under his control…

Small groups of Jewish people may be destroyed or transported to the ghetto where they will be subject to the civil control or the SD.

*Baron von Bechtolsheim*

*NARB, f. 378, op. 1, d. 698, l. 32. Translation from Germ.; Judenfrei! Free from Jewish people: Story of the Minsk Ghetto in documents. Mn., 1999. S. 165.*

**From a report of the Chancellery of the Imperial Minister of Foreign Affairs regarding Jewish people**

Berlin                                                    1941

... In the course of the East Campaign, Jewish people showed themselves as diversionists, robbers, spies, terrorists, morally unstable, Communist propagandists, showing passive resistance, spreading defeatist rumors, and sowing disbelief in a successful military advance. It is natural that such behavior, under Soviet control, would result in the disunity of German society, thus it [society] would not be able to function in full force and effect. Some Jewish people managed to pretend to be interpreters and to sneak into German administrative-economic organisations as heads of enterprises working for military needs in order to make use of their positions for hidden hostile activity for their personal advantage.

Such behavior of the Jewish people made it necessary to conduct preliminary clearances...

In total, more than 11 thousand have been liquidated. The detailed data on all annihilated Jewish people in three District Commissariats can be taken from a German book [sic]. Due to the danger of sabotage, most Jewish people had to be isolated in special camps. In big camps, ghettoes were equipped where Jewish people from different places of the district and region were transported...

NARB, f.4683, op. 3, d. 928, l. 45-46. *Translation from Germ.; Judenfrei! Free from Jewish people: Story of the Minsk Ghetto in documents. Mn., 1999. S. 168.*

**From Communiqué №15B of the Security Police Chief and the SD on the annihilation of Jewish people**

16 January 1942

… The clearance is going at full pelt in Belarus. The number of Jewish people given under the civil control of a part of Belarus so far amounts to 139 000 people for the time being.

The operation group 'A' has shot 33, 210 Jewish people since the first day of its activity in Belarus.

*NARB, f. 4683, op.3, d. 913, l. 196, MKF, arh. №175, k. 723979-723981. Translation from Germ.; Judenfrei! Free from Jewish people: Story of the Minsk Ghetto in documents. Mn., 1999. S. 168.*

**From a report of the Commandant of Belarus about the activity of Operation Groups
as of 1 February 1942**

... The number of the Jewish population annihilated by the operation group 'A' in the course of the operation against Jewish people:

Minsk: 41,828 people.

The approximate number of the remaining Jewish people is 128,000 people.

NARB, f. 4683, op. 3, d. 945, l. 35. *Translation from Germ.; Judenfrei! Free from Jewish people: Story of the Minsk Ghetto in documents. Mn., 1999. S. 173.*

**From Communiqué №178 of the Security Police and the SD on the anti-Jewish campaign in Minsk**

Minsk                                                                              9 March 1942

Commander Hoffman ordered a major Aktion against the Russian Jewish people of both sexes from 1st to 3$^{rd}$ March in Minsk and Koidanovo. To keep the planned Aktion secret, the Judenrat was informed that 5000 Jewish people from the ghetto would be 'resettled', and that they were to be selected by the Judenrat and gathered for the resettlement. Every Jewish person was allowed to take luggage up to 5 kilograms in weight with them. The true purpose of the Security Police Chief and the SD was kept a secret. When, on the morning of 1st March 1942, the ghetto was surrounded, not a single Jewish person appeared for the resettlement. The commands allotted to clear part of the ghetto of Jews were put into operation and people were forcibly removed from their houses. Only after that were Jewish people gathered and sent to the Minsk-Tovarnaya Station in a long work detail. Most did not leave their homes willingly and tried to escape the expedition. Force was applied to them, and some of them were shot on sight. After the ghetto clearance, a lot of corpses lay in houses and in the streets, and later they were carried away. At the station, the people were put into wagons which were joined to a long train which was sent to Koidanovo, a place 30 km to the south-west of Minsk, on the Minsk-Baranovichi-Brest-Litovsk railway route.

The next day, on 2 March 1942, all subdivisions of the Security Police and the SD were heading to shoot the passengers on the train. A lot of trenches had been prepared for the campaign near Koidanovo. First, the Jewish people were unloaded from the wagons, then they were split into small groups and under the supervision of Lithuanian guards, were transported to the trenches. During this, force was applied. There they were ordered to take off their coats and outer clothes. It was done to facilitate the shooting. Then Jewish people were ordered to go along the trenches, near which shooters were standing armed with pistols. The shooter group consisted of 10-20 people. Every shooter chose his prey periodically – at the same time he ordered the chosen man to stop or stopped them with his hand. If the prey was in a convenient position, the soldier shot the prey in the back of the head. If after the shot, the person did not fall into the trench, they were pushed into it or thrown in.

The trenches were so wide, long and deep that they could hold at least several hundred corpses.

Groups of Jewish people, situated far from the trenches, could hear shots and could understand that a mass execution had already begun and they were to be executed. Later, when they saw the trenches and corpses lying there, at least to the adults, it became clear what awaited them. Many ran, shouted and cried, but most succumbed to their fate without outcries and lamentations. There was no doctor at the site to certify death. However, attention was paid those who were still moving whereupon they were shot, or if there was any suspicion that someone had not been killed.

On that day they did not manage to shoot all the people. That is why the execution continued on 3 March 1942. In total, not less than 3000 people were killed. How many of them were shot on 2 March and on 3 March was not specified. Nevertheless, it is clear that not less than 1000 people were shot.

According to Communiqué №178 of 9 March 1942, during the campaign led in Minsk-Koidanovo on 2-3 March 1942, 3412 Jewish people were shot.


… The campaign against the Jewish people led on 3.3.1942 in Minsk gave an indication to the city population that in the weeks to follow, bigger campaigns against Jewish people would take place throughout Belarus.


*Federal archive Koblentsa 9ks/62. Justice affairs and Nazi crimes. T. [volume, probably] 19. Current №552. Photocopy. Translation from Germ.; Judenfrei! Free from Jewish people: Story of the Minsk Ghetto in documents. Mn., 1999. S. 175-176.*

### From a report on the activity of the Operation Group 4 'A' provided by the Security Police and the SD for the period from 16 October 1941 to 31 January 1942

Byelorussia

... The question of the decisive and complete liquidation of Jewish people on the territory of Belarus after the arrival of Germans, faces known difficulties. Right here Jewish people make up a percentage of the specialists who are necessary in the region due to the absence of other candidates. Besides, Operation Group 'A' took over the supervision of that territory with the onset of a severe frost which made mass executions difficult.

Another difficulty centers on the fact that Jewish people live scattered throughout the whole territory; taking into account the long distances, the bad condition of the roads, the absence of motor transport and of oil, and insignificant forces of the Security Police and the SD, the carrying out of executions was possible only after maximal mobilizing of all forces. Despite that, 41,000 Jewish people have been shot. The people shot by former Operation Groups are not included in this number...

In spite of the difficulties, the Chief of Police of Belarus has been given instructions to liquidate the Jewish problem as soon as possible. However, for that purpose, it will take about two months, depending on the weather.

The resettlement of the remaining Jewish people in the existing ghettoes and camps of Belarus is coming to an end...

The Nuremberg Trial. Compilation of materials. T. 1. M., 1954, S. 849; *Judenfrei! Free from Jewish people: Story of the Minsk Ghetto in documents. Mn., 1999. S. 172.*

**From the record of the session of the chiefs of the main departments of the General Commissariat of Belarus regarding local and German Jewish people**

Minsk                                                29 January 1942

.... The number of Jewish people cannot be defined although it is very high in the country. The Jewish population in the country is terrorized. For the time being, the complete liquidation of Jewish people is impossible due to frost, since the earth is significantly frozen and digging out holes which could serve then as mass graves for Jewish people is impossible. The total annihilation of the Jewish people is impossible particularly due to the fact that there is a work force among Jewish people [which we rely on].

2 categories of Jewish people are distinguished:

a) Russian Jewish people; b) German Jewish people. Russian Jewish people are of a stubborn nature and work reluctantly. German Jewish people show work diligence and thanks to this it becomes clear that they believe that after the victorious end of the war, they will be returned again to the old empire. Thus, they see this as a struggle for existence. It is important to maintain their belief in returning to Germany and thus, obtain high labor performance.

Finally, spring will see mass executions. Beforehand, Latvians posted for duty in the Auxiliary Police are to carry out trials. The accommodation of the Jewish people in the Minsk Ghetto is bad. In addition to that, speculation flourishes there. Because of the confined living conditions, the surveillance will be complicated in the ghetto.

*GARF [State Archive of the Russian Federation], f. 7021, op. 1, d. 53, l. 164; Judenfrei! Free from Jewish people: Story of the Minsk Ghetto in documents. Mn., 1999. S.171.*

**From attachment №1 to the report on the activity of the Group GFP-723 about the attitude of the local population towards the annihilation campaigns against Jewish people**

Minsk                                        December 1941

...The position of Russians towards Jewish people and the measures being taken towards them [Jewish people] by German occupational authorities is interesting. Ordinary Russians do not know what the race problem is, and it [the problem] is alien to them.

...Russians perceive the mass annihilation of Jewish people as bestiality caused by Germans; however, this bestiality does not bring any loss for them. In different places, incidents occur when mass annihilations give rise to hostile anti-German propaganda, the culmination of which are statements saying that after the Jewish people, the Russians will share the same fate. Any significant success has not been achieved by the instigators. Most of them have been traced and shot.

*Field Police Commissioner and Commander of the Groups Rodbade*

*NARB, f. 4683, op. 3, d. 962, l. 24. Translation from Germ.; Judenfrei! Free from Jewish people: Story of the Minsk Ghetto in documents. Mn., 1999. S. 167.*

### Letter of the Commissioner-General of Belarus W. Kube to the Reich Commissioner of Ostland H. Lohse about the deportation of the Jewish people of Germany to Belarus

Minsk                                                                      16 December 1941 *Top secret*

My dear Heinrich! I ask you personally to give an official instruction about the position of the civil authorities regarding the Jewish people deported from Germany to Belarus. Among those Jewish people there are some who fought at the front [in the war] (during the First World War) and who were conferred with the decoration of the Iron Cross of the First and Second Degree, disabled war veterans who are half or even three-quarter Aryans. So far, only 6000-7000 Jewish people out of the expected 25 000 we were informed about have arrived. I do not know what has happened to the rest of them. During a few official visits to the ghetto I noticed that among them there were Jewish people differing from Russian Jewish people also [particularly] by their neatness. There are some qualified workers capable of doing five times more [things] a day than the Russian Jewish people.

Those Jewish people (the German Jews) will probably die of cold and hunger in the next few weeks. To us, they constitute a dire menace as they catch diseases easily, since they, like us, the Germans, are susceptible to 22 epidemic diseases spread in Belarus.

On my own responsibility, I will not give the SD any instructions concerning the way those people are to be treated, although some Wehrmacht subdivisions and police have already appropriated the property of Jewish people deported from the Reich. Thus, the SD has taken 400 mattresses from them, and also confiscated other things. I am certainly firm in my opinion and willing to contribute to the resolution of the European question but those people, who belong to our culture, differ from the stupid herd of locals. Maybe we can execute Lithuanians and Latvians in massive numbers who are alien to the local population as well. I cannot do that. I ask you to give exact instructions so as I can perform the required action in the most humane manner possible.

*With kind regards, Heil Hitler!*

*Your Wilhelm Kube*

*Annihilation of Jewish people of the USSR in the years of the German occupation (1941-1944). Collection of documents and materials. Jerusalem. 1991. P. 178-179; Judenfrei! Free from Jewish people: A History of a Jewish Ghetto in Documents. Mn., 1999. P. 211*

### Operations Director of the Department of B.C.H.G.M.

### [Byelorussian Central Headquarters of the Partisan Movement]

### Report

Partisan detachment №106 was founded at the end of April 1943 as a national family Jewish detachment.

At that time there was a large-scale annihilation of the Jewish population in the Minsk district. The Fascist invaders sentenced to death all the Jewish population located in the Minsk Ghetto, systematically and according to the plan, daily destroying hundreds and thousands of Jewish people – Soviet citizens.

Young Jewish people along with their Russian and Byelorussian brothers joined partisan detachments in order to exact revenge on the despicable Fascists, and in their footsteps, hundreds of women, children and old men, also escaped into the ranks of partisan detachments and brigades in order to save their own lives.

But the combatant brigades did not have the opportunity to hold such a number of combat-ineffective people: women, children and old men since their presence threatened to weaken their fighting efficiency.

The situation came about such that in the forests and villages of the Minsk region, groups of women and children wandered helplessly. They could not join any of the partisan detachments and would not come back to impending death.

Taking into account that situation, and following the First-of-May Order given by comrade Stalin about saving the lives of the Soviet citizens located on the territory of the invaded areas, the command of the Stalin unit led by comrade Vasilevich and the command of the Budyonny detachment (Ganzenko S.F., Detachment Commander) approved of the initiative of the commander of the cavalry troop of the Budyonny detachment. This allowed and provided Vasilevich with cooperation in the organisation of the national family detachment that was allotted the task of evacuating Soviet citizens out of the ghetto and saving their lives.

The command of the Budyonny Detachment provided Comrade Zorin, the founder of the family detachment, with 18 armed fighters, and that group proceeded to execute their task, having begun evacuating people from the Minsk Ghetto with the help of guides.

By the end of May 1943 the detachment numbered 110 people, including 25 armed fighters.

Due to the fact that the forests of the Derzhinsk region were unsuitable for maintaining such a family camp, the detachment was sent to Nalibokskiy Forest [dense forest] on the decision of comrade Vasilevich, the commander of the Stalin unit. In the Forest, the detachment was split into two groups: the fighting detachment and the family detachment.

The task of the fighting troop was: 1. To evacuate the people out of the ghetto. 2. To guard the family camp. 3. To provide the family group with food.

By 10 July 1943, the fighting troop numbered 45 fighters (the armament consisting of 61 machine guns and the rest represented by rifles) and 270 people from the family camp. A long blockade of Forest

Nalibokskiy began on 13 July 1943, and lasted till 6 August 1943. The military commanders of the troop faced the task of taking the people out of the enemy environment.

Thanks to the efficient working of the reconnaissance unit, the military commanders of the troop managed to take the whole troop out of the environment, having suffered minor casualties (6 people killed).

Since the moment when the blockade finished in June 1944, the fighting troops carried out the aforementioned task.

Provisions operations were carried out in extremely harsh conditions: The Ivenetsky Region given by Comrade Sidorok, Ts. Sh. P. D. [Central Headquarters of the Guerilla Movement] of Baranovichskaya Oblast, for carrying out provisions operations from November 1943, was the place where Polish White Guardsmen (Narkevich's gang) concentrated, and every provisions operation was connected to exchanges of shots and skirmishes between our small poorly armed groups and White Guardsmen and policemen. In those skirmishes, the troop lost 11 fighters.

At the end of May 1944, having obtained comrade Sidorok's permission to organise sabotage groups, due to the rise in armed fighters (93 rifles) by that time, the military commanders began organising sabotage groups that achieved the following results by June 1944:

1. 11.06.44 1 enemy echelon with machines was derailed (1 steam train, 8 platforms with vehicles and armored fighting vehicles and 1 platform with 6 Germans killed).

2. 5.06.44 one vehicle exploded (2 Germans killed and 3 Germans injured).

3. 12.06.44 one vehicle exploded (2 Germans killed)

The bridge on the road Volma-Dzerzhinsk was set on fire.

At the beginning of July 1944, German groups had been smashed, after having broken into Nalibokskiy Forest, systematically attacking the family camp that was situated on a boggy path leading from the forest to Novogruduk. The fighting troop guarded the family camp, repelling the Germans' assaults.

In the battle of 6 July with 150 German automatic riflemen, the troop inflicted losses on the Germans: 9 people killed, 2 injured and 5 people taken alive. In that battle, the troop lost 6 people and 3 people were injured, including troop commander comrade Zorin, who was seriously wounded.

On 9 July 1944, the troop consisting of 137 armed people (the fighting troop) and 421 family unit united with the advanced force units of the Red Army near Kromen.

*Commissioner of p/o №106 Feigelman*

*Wertheim Executive Officer*

2.08.1944

*Six million Jewish people executed by firing squads, stifled in gas chambers.*

*Six million, each and every one of them.*

*This is a memory which opposes oblivion and forgetting.*

*It is a people's call to mutual congeniality, unobtainable without a general prohibition on murder.*

*It is a conviction: THERE IS NO GENOCIDE AGAINST 'SOMEONE',*

*GENOCIDE IS ALWAYS AGAINST ALL.*

*This is what the HOLOCAUST means.*


                *Mikhail Gefter, 'The Echo of the Holocaust'*

# Acknowledgements from the Original Book

**The original book in Russian stated the following:**

The book was published by the Minsk Charitable Public Association GILF within the framework of the project "Club Meetings for the Preservation of Historical memory / My Second Birthday", which won the 2nd Competition of the Humanitarian Support Programme "The Meeting Place is Dialogue" carried out by the International Public Association "Mutual Understanding" with the financial support of the German Federal Foundation "Memory. Responsibility. Future. "

The Chairman of the Executive Board of GILF is Reizman Frieda Vulfovna.

The author and the head of the project "Club Meetings for the Preservation of Historical Memory / My Second Birthday" is Tamara Semyonovna Kurdadze.

**Book compiled by:**

Krapina Maya Isaakovna - member of the Executive Board of GILF.

Kurdadze Tamara Semyonovna - head of the project "Club Meetings for the Preservation of Historical Memory / My second birthday".

Murakhovsky Yakov Moiseevich - member of the Project Coordination Council.

Reizman Frieda Vulfovna - the Deputy Chairman of the Executive Board of GILF Association.

Trachtenberg Vladimir Lazarevich - Deputy Chairman of the Executive Board of GILF Association.

**Editorial Council:**

Reizman Frieda Vulfovna - Chairman of the Executive Board of GILF.

Trachtenberg Vladimir Lazarevich - Deputy Chairman of the Executive Board of GILF.

**Members of the Executive Board:**

Aslezova Elfrida Davydovna, Banah Eleonora Suleymanovna, Golubeva Irina Davydovna, Krapina Maya Isaakovna, Galperina Rimma Abramovna - Chairman of the Revision Commission of GILF, the Coordinating Council of the Project.

We express our gratitude for the help in preparing the collected materials for the publication to the Deputy Chairman of the Union of Belarusian Jewish Public Associations and Communities, to Shulman Arkadiy Lvovich, the Editor-in-Chief of "Mishpoha" Magazine, the Deputy Chairman of the Executive Board of ICF GILF Trachtenberg Vladimir Lazarevich.

We express our gratitude for the help in collecting the memoirs of the former ghettoes and concentration camps:

Krapina Maya Isaakovna, Murakhovsky Yakov Moiseevich, Reizman Frieda Vulfovna.

We express our gratitude for the historical materials provided by the historian - documentarian Chernoglazova Raisa Andreevna.

The publication uses photographs from family archives of the project participants, from the archives of the project "Club Meetings to Preserve Historical Memory / My Second Birthday".

**Only 300 copies of the original Russian book were ever printed for private circulation.**

# INDEX

# We Remember Lest the World Forgets

# We Remember Lest the World Forgets